On the Ethics of Torture

On the Ethics of Torture

UWE STEINHOFF

Published by State University of New York Press, Albany

© 2013 Uwe Steinhoff

For information, contact State University of New York Press, Albany, NY
www.sunypress.edu

Production by Ryan Morris
Marketing by Michael Campochiaro

Library of Congress Cataloging-in-Publication Data

Steinhoff, Uwe.
    On the ethics of torture / Uwe Steinhoff.
        p. cm.
    Includes bibliographical references and index.
    ISBN 978-1-4384-4621-9 (hardcover : alk. paper)
    1. Torture—Moral and ethical aspects.   I. Title.

HV8593.S74 2013
172'.2—dc23   2012017559

10 9 8 7 6 5 4 3 2 1

For my nieces, Jeanette and Gina

Contents

Preface   ix

Acknowledgments   xi

Introduction   1

1   What Is Torture?   7

2   The Moral Justification of Torture   11

     2.1   The Argument from Self-defense   11

         2.1.1   What Is Self-defense?   11

         2.1.2   Proportionality, or: Many Forms of Torture Are Not as Bad as Killing   18

     2.2   The Argument from the Culpability for Creating a Forced-Choice Situation   35

     2.3   The Argument from Necessity   39

     2.4   Reminder: The Justification of Torture Is Compatible with Rights Absolutism   45

     2.5   The Utilitarian Argument   45

3   Defusing the Ticking-Social-Bomb Argument: Against Consequentialist Attempts to Undermine the Right to Self-defensive Torture   53

4   Against the Institutionalization of Torture   61

5   Legalizing Torture?   69

6   Objections   79

    6.1   Attempts to Quickly Dismiss the Argument from
          Self-defense and Other Rights-based Arguments   79

    6.2   The Defenselessness Argument   92

    6.3   But Is It *Really* Self-defense? Whitley Kaufman and Daniel Hill   96

    6.4   David Sussman's Complicity Argument   105

    6.5   Kant's Categorical Imperative: The Three Kantian Formulas   108

    6.6   "Breaking the Will" (and "Dignity," "Subject Status," and
          "Self-legislative Rulership")   112

    6.7   Torture and the Doctrine of Double Effect   134

    6.8   Is the Ticking-Bomb Example Unrealistic?   138

    6.9   "Torture Knows No Limits"   147

7   Is Justifying Torture Bad Even If Torture Is Sometimes Justified?   155
    Conclusions   158

Notes   161

References   181

Index   187

Preface

After having written two articles in which I argued that torture is justifiable in certain narrowly circumscribed circumstances, in particular in certain self-defense situations, I felt no inclination to write anything more on the topic. Then, however, Paul Theodoulou, editor of *Global Dialogue*, asked me whether I would like to write a piece on torture for his journal. I thought, fine, one last piece; all good things come in threes. So I read up on the literature on torture that had appeared since I had last written on it and came across lines like this, brought to paper by an absolutist opponent of torture: "I also found myself increasingly annoyed that—doubtless inadvertently—careless philoso-phizing about imaginary ticking bomb scenarios had given their [he means authors like me, who defend torture in certain circumstances] argument a starting-point which should never have been conceded" (Brecher 2008, 3).

The annoyance immediately became mutual, as it were, and resulted in this book. *I* am annoyed by the careless philosophizing that Brecher and many other absolutist torture opponents engage in. What particularly annoys me is the practice of many, if not all, of them to keep throwing stones while living in the glass house. For example, they collectively claim (and some of them make all of these claims at once) that absolutist torture opponents do not "immerse themselves into the empirical details," "do not know the psychological and medical literature on torture," "ignore the historical facts," "draw conclusions from idealized cases to completely dissimilar ones," "undermine rights with consequentialist fantasies," "commit intellectual fraud," and so on. In fact, however, it is they who commit these mistakes and many more, so this book will turn the tables on them.

Before going *in medias res*, however, let me make two points very clear. First, this is certainly not a "*pro*-torture" book. Most people think that killing in self-defense is justified under certain circumstances. However, this does not make them "proponents of killing"; they do not think that the world would be a better place with more killing. In the same vein, I am *against* torture in almost all circumstances. Hence this book is not *pro*-torture but is in favor of the *right to self-defense* (and, independent of this right, in favor of a liberty to produce an evil in order to prevent a very much larger one from happening, provided there are no other reasonable means). It is, thus, in favor of morality and rationality.

Second, my interest in the topic of torture was aroused by the German Daschner case, that is, by a child-kidnapping case, not by the "terrorist threat" the American debate is obsessed with. In particular, this book is not in the least intended to support "the war on terrorism" and the silly and often racist "us-versus-them" ideology that accompanies it. I simply do not belong to that camp. Thus, I would like to make clear that if, let's say, torturing an Islamic terrorist is justified to avert the explosion of a ticking bomb that would kill thousands of innocent Americans or Israelis, it then is obviously also justified to torture a Christian or Jewish state terrorist if by doing so one can avert a more or less indiscriminate bombing campaign by the American or Israeli air force that would (once again) kill thousands of innocent Palestinians, Iraqis, or Afghans. Thus, I prefer moral universalism to double standards. In this regard, at least, I am united with the absolutist opponents of torture that I will be criticizing in this book.

Acknowledgments

Chapters 1 and 7 and sections 2.1.1–2.1.2 draw on material originally published as "Justifying Defensive Torture," in *Torture: Moral Absolutes and Ambiguities*, ed. Bev Clucas, Gerry Johnstone, and Tony Ward (Baden-Baden: Nomos, 2009), pp. 39–60. Chapter 3 and the beginning of section 6.8 use slightly revised material from "Defusing the Ticking Social Bomb Argument: The Right to Self-Defensive Torture," *Global Dialogue* 12(1) (2010). Likewise, slightly revised material from "Torture Can Be Self-Defense: A Critique of Whitley Kaufman," *Ethics and International Affairs* 22(1) (2008) (online only) forms part of section 6.3. Revised parts of "Torture: The Case for Dirty Harry and against Alan Dershowitz," *Journal of Applied Philosophy* 23 (2006), pp. 337–53, appear in particular in sections 2.1, 4, 6.2, and 6.4. Chapter 5 is a slightly revised version of "Legalizing Defensive Torture," *Public Affairs Quarterly* 26 (2012), pp. 19–32.

The research presented in this book was partially supported by a grant from the Research Grants Council of the Hong Kong Special Administrative Region, China (Project No. HKU 752710). I am very grateful for this support.

I also thank the participants of the conference Torture and Terror at the University of Hull in November 2007 for comments on some of my thoughts on torture. Last but not least, I owe special thanks to Volker Erb and Gerhard Beestermöller for enormously helpful written comments on a first draft of this book.

Introduction

Is torture sometimes justified? This book answers, "Yes," and it will defend this answer against a host of objections. In doing so, it will provide the reader with a detailed and comprehensive overview of the current philosophical debate on torture. Moreover, this means that the book must also deal with topics of wider ethical (and sometimes legal) significance, namely, topics such as self-defense, rights-based morality, absolutism, consequentialism, Kantianism, human dignity, coercion, and freedom of the will. Since some of the analyses provided here contradict certain widely held (but, as will be shown, not necessarily warranted) assumptions, the relevance of this study goes well beyond the confines of the torture debate.

Chapter 1 will offer and defend a definition of torture. However, even if one does not accept this particular definition, this will not affect the ethical arguments of the later chapters.

Chapter 2 presents four different justifications of torture. The first two justifications, self-defense and the argument from the culpability for creating a forced choice situation, are purely rights-based arguments; the third justification, necessity, presupposes rights but combines this with consequentialist considerations, resulting in a "threshold-deontological" account. The fourth justification is utilitarian. I endorse the first three justifications but not the fourth.

Section 2.1 deals with the argument from self-defense. I will argue that there is something like self-defensive torture (which can include the defense of others) and that such torture is morally justified if certain general requirements for the justifiability of self-defensive violence/force are met. These requirements come under the headings of imminence, necessity, and proportionality.

In section 2.1.1 I will briefly discuss the English, American, and especially German legal regulations regarding self-defense. I will argue that the same moral reasoning that underlies these laws is also applicable to torture cases and that the necessity and the imminence requirements can be met in some torture cases.

In section 2.1.2 I will turn to the proportionality requirement and in that context discuss arguments that attempt to show that torture is worse than killing. I will argue that these arguments cannot hold water. Many forms of torture are definitely not worse than killing. In fact, I will show that there are cases where self-defensive torture is the morally preferable and more humane alternative to self-defensive killing. Moreover, I will also show that even if this were not the case, torturing a culpable aggressor in order to save his innocent victim from being further tortured by him can still be justified, for torture is not worse than torture. I conclude that if self-defensive killing is justified in some cases—and it is—then self-defensive torture is also justified in some cases.

In section 2.2 I discuss another rights-based argument, the argument from the culpability for creating a forced choice situation. Even if the self-defense argument, as some authors (mistakenly) argue, were not applicable to the child-kidnapping case or the ticking-bomb case, this argument still is, is intuitively compelling, and works just fine.

Section 2.3 discusses the necessity argument. This argument is not, as is so often erroneously claimed, a straightforward consequentialist argument, but one that combines consequentialism with deontology. While the first two arguments cannot be used to justify torturing innocent bystanders, this argument can under certain extreme conditions. However, contrary to its detractors, this is not a damning verdict on this justification. On the contrary, the fact that deontological antitorture absolutism prohibits torturing innocent bystanders under *all* circumstances is, as can be shown with suitable examples, a damning verdict on antitorture absolutism. Antitorture absolutism is immoral, irrational, and inhumane.

However, in section 2.4 I will remind the reader that the self-defense justification of torture is perfectly compatible with deontological rights absolutism, for example an absolutism about the right to self-defense. In other words, a deontological rights-absolutist can—contrary to the claims of absolutist antitorture opponents—consistently embrace the justifiability of torture.

In section 2.5 I will briefly discuss the utilitarian justification of torture. I do not subscribe to utilitarianism (since I am a threshold deontologist). Thus I only discuss the utilitarian justification of torture for didactic reasons, as it were, namely to counter certain absurd claims that have recently been made to the effect that torture cannot be justified in the real world by utilitarian considerations. It most definitely can.

In chapter 3 I will attack the habit many absolutist opponents of torture have of posing as the defenders of human rights or of deontological constraints against consequentialists intent on undermining those absolute rights and constraints by appealing to allegedly utterly unrealistic scenarios like "the ticking-bomb scenario." I will show that the specific version of "the ticking-bomb scenario" that absolutist opponents of torture incessantly attack is nothing but a straw man, that absolutist opponents of torture have no real deontological arguments against torture to offer, and that in fact it is they who undermine a fundamental right, namely the right to self-defense, with unrealistic consequentialist concoctions of their very own.

In chapter 4 I will argue that the *institutionalization* of torture (for example in the form of torture warrants or torture orders from above, torture training, torture camps, special torture squads, "applied" torture research)—which is to be distinguished from its mere legalization—is unnecessary and too dangerous and therefore unjustified.

In chapter 5, however, I shall argue that there is absolutely no evidence that the *legalization* of torture will lead to terrible consequences. Rather, there is evidence that under certain quite realistic and indeed real circumstances it will not do so. Those absolutist opponents of torture who have argued to the contrary have confused legalization with institutionalization and/or drawn sweeping conclusions from certain special cases to completely dissimilar cases—a practice they emphatically condemn when they criticize the version of the "ticking-bomb argument" they attribute to their adversaries.

Chapter 6 will examine and refute a host of objections, particularly, objections to the self-defense justification of torture.

Absolutist opponents do not like the self-defense justification of torture at all. (And some seem not even to have heard of it.) The reason for this is quite simply that the self-defense argument is the strongest argument for the justification of torture and not in the least vulnerable to certain criticisms absolutist torture opponents like to level, often rather triumphantly, against consequentialist justifications of torture. Not surprisingly, then, many absolutist torture opponents do not mention the self-defense argument to their readers. When they do, however, they try to quickly dismiss it. In section 6.1. I shall show that such attempts at quick dismissal display a lack of understanding as to what the legal and moral argument for self-defense actually is and involves, and thus they fail.

In section 6.2 I will demonstrate that there exists, contrary to an earlier claim of Henry Shue, no general moral side constraint against using force against the defenseless (which would normally rule out torture). I will also refute the additional argument that there cannot be self-defense against a defenseless person in the first place (such as against a child kidnapper who has been strapped to a chair in order to be tortured into disclosing the location of the child).

Section 6.3 will continue this discussion by considering and rebutting two particularly sophisticated, if not overly sophisticated, versions of this latter argument, namely, those provided by Whitley Kaufman and Daniel Hill.

In section 6.4 I will show that David Sussman's claim that torture forces "its victim into the position of colluding against himself through his own affects and emotions" and therefore "bears an especially high burden of justification, greater in degree and different in kind from even that of killing"[1] is wrong. First, not all forms of torture force their victims into such a position; second, some other types of acts that are widely and correctly considered to be perfectly justifiable do so; and third, as already demonstrated in section 2.1.2, killing definitely bears a higher burden of justification than most forms of torture. Death is and remains worse than most forms of torture.

In section 6.5 I will demonstrate that the popular maneuver of co-opting Immanuel Kant and his categorical imperative for an absolutist stance against torture does not work at all; indeed, it completely misinterprets and misrepresents Kant's philosophy. For Kant self-defense is the "most holy right" of human beings; and nothing in Kant's philosophy contradicts the justifiability of self-defensive torture.

Quite the opposite is true, as I will argue at the end of section 6.6. Before that, however, we will see that the popular claim that torture violates "human dignity" (or denies an individual her "subject status") by breaking the will of the targeted individual (or, more strongly and more mysteriously, by "breaking the inner freedom of the will" or by "abolishing the freedom of the will while maintaining consciousness")—which I will attack here in the paradigmatic form it has taken in articles by Heiner Bielefeldt and Gerhard Beestermöller—is nothing but empty rhetoric. Yes, interrogational torture aims at breaking the will of the person in an everyday sense of "breaking the will." However, there are countless obviously justified acts that also break the will of a person, and nobody believes that *they* violate "human dignity." The heavy weather made about "breaking the will" is, in fact, ill-considered and somewhat bizarre. If, however, "breaking the inner freedom of the will" or "abolishing the freedom of the will while maintaining consciousness" is supposed to be different from merely breaking the will, it remains entirely mysterious where this difference lies and what those phrases are supposed to *mean*. I will also argue that Hauke Brunkhorst's claim that torture is not compatible with democracy and "self-legislative rulership" does not hold water.

Section 6.7 refutes the claim, which Florian Lamprecht very much relies on, that torture is not compatible with the doctrine of double effect and therefore not justified. I will show that it is as compatible or as incompatible with the doctrine of double effect as killing or injuring in self-defense is. If self-defensive killing or injuring is sometimes justified, and it is, self-defensive torture is sometimes justified too.

Section 6.8 deals with the claim, repeated ad nauseum, that the ticking-bomb scenario is unrealistic. The ticking-bomb scenario attacked by absolutist critics is indeed unrealistic, but only because they have made it up themselves. They are attacking a straw man. Thus the intellectual dishonesty they accuse others of is their own. The actual ticking-bomb example, in contrast, is realistic, and it works just fine; those unrealistic assumptions of the "ideal" case (that is, of the straw man) that the critics of "the" ticking-bomb argument rave so much about are entirely superfluous and indeed not made by actual proponents of ticking-bomb arguments.

Section 6.9 tackles different versions of the claim that "torture knows no limits," including the claim that its justification will lead to the justification of all kinds of actually unjustifiable atrocities. I will show that this claim is mistaken and that some versions of the "torture knows no limits" reproach are in fact little more than rhetorical devices intended to silence adversaries rather than serious arguments.

Finally, in section 7 I will deal with the charge that justifying torture in some perhaps legitimate cases nevertheless somehow contributes to the spread of the illegitimate use of torture and that therefore publishing justificatory books like the present one is itself immoral. I will argue that such rather cheap charges have no rational basis whatsoever.

1

What Is Torture?

I shall define torture as follows:

> Torture is the knowing infliction of continuous or repeated extreme physical suffering for other than medical purposes.[1]

Some claim that torture has to involve the intent to break the will of the victim.[2] This might be true for interrogative torture, where the torturer seeks to get some information out of the tortured person. I say "might" because it is not entirely clear what "breaking the will" actually means, nor is it clear that the interrogative torturer must intend more than that the victim give the desired information. If the victim decides with an intact will: "I do not want to be tortured anymore, therefore I will give the information," this, it seems, should be fine with the torturer. Be that as it may, interrogative torture is not the only kind of torture; there is also punitive torture, which was widely practiced in the Middle Ages (and is, incidentally, still practiced today). Punitive torture, however, does not normally involve the intention to break the will of the victim. Whether his or her will is broken is completely incidental to the aims of this form of torture. The aim is simply to punish the victim by inflicting extreme physical suffering.

Some also claim that the victim has to be defenseless.[3] I agree that in many cases he or she will be defenseless, but this in itself is no reason to make this a definitional requirement. Consider this case: a robber breaks into the house of a jeweler, who has a safe with a lot of money in his house. The robber points a gun at the jeweler and says: "Give me the combination, or I'll kill you." The jeweler says: "Well, if you kill me, you won't get the combination." "Right," thinks the robber and draws something else, namely his pain-inflicting device, which when activated causes extreme pain (almost like drilling on the unprotected nerve of a tooth) to any person in a radius of ten meters, except for the person holding the device. He activates it. The jeweler writhes with pain on the ground, and the robber says, "Give me the combination," but the jeweler manages to reach for his own revolver. Because of the pain he cannot take real aim and can hardly hold the gun, yet he manages to shoot in the general direction of the robber, who dives behind a couch. "Let go of the gun!" the robber shouts, but the jeweler, still in extreme pain since the device is still activated, shoots in the direction of the couch, which offers no real protection, and the bullets go right through. The jeweler is obviously not defenseless. However, it seems that he was tortured nevertheless. Someone was intentionally inflicting pain on him nearly as intense as the pain inflicted by drilling the unprotected nerve of a tooth, and doing so in order to get some information or in order to have the person do something (let go of the gun)—how could this not be torture? The mere fact that the victim still has means of defense seems not to satisfactorily answer this question.[4]

At this point someone might object that this is a silly and contrived example that could not happen in the real world. Well, first, of course it could. Second, one might well see a taser as the equivalent of such a pain-infliction device. Thus there may already have been equivalent cases. Third, even if there never has been a real such case and never will be, that is not a counterargument against the definitional point. There is not, nor will there ever be, a Tyrannosaurus rex walking through the Black Forest in the years 2011 or 2017. However, that does not mean that by definition a Tyrannosaurus rex cannot do so. Whether one of them does is an empirical question, not a definitional one. A definition that simply stipulated that they cannot walk through the Black Forest in those years would be a *wrong* definition even if the Tyrannosaurus rex actually is extinct once and for all. Thus, if we would say about the case of the jeweler that it is (or would be) a case of torture, the alleged fact that such cases are not real is no counterargument to the claim that it indeed is (or would be) a case of torture.

The international conventions concerning torture seem to consider torture, for the purposes of those conventions, as something that can only be done by state agents. However, the legal usage of certain terms does not always coincide with the ordinary one. In any ordinary use of the term, torture can be practiced by private agents (for example the Mafia or a sadist).

Why is the knowing infliction of pain sufficient and specific intent not required? Consider the psychopaths that populate the movie *Hostel*. Let us assume that one of those people, who drill, for leisure, holes into their conscious victims or cut off their limbs, does not really have the specific *intent* to inflict pain or suffering. Rather, he just likes to drill holes into people and cut off their limbs. Are we, therefore, not dealing with a case of torture anymore? In other words, is the intent to inflict pain or suffering necessary for torture? Intuitively, of course not. If anything is torture, then those depraved acts depicted in *Hostel* are. It is therefore sufficient that the people engaged in these acts foresee the suffering of their victims and are not engaged in these acts in the course of providing medical help. This distinguishes the indifferent torturer "operating" on a nonanaesthetized victim from a caring doctor doing the same in order to help a patient.

A note on the expression "continuous or repeated": this is only meant to exclude isolated and single, extremely short "shocks" of intense pain. I find it hard to consider such "shocks" as torture (which is not the same as saying that they are quite all right). What counts as extremely short and what does not, however, might be debatable. Yet I do not think that this can be helped. Note, however, that what is relevant is the duration of the pain, not of the act that inflicts it.

What is "extreme"? That is contentious, but one kind of physical suffering that clearly is extreme is the above-mentioned pain produced by drilling on the unprotected nerve of a tooth. I will use this as a reference point throughout the book. This in no way implies that I think that lesser pains or certain other forms of pain and suffering are not also extreme.[5]

Finally, need torture be physical? Could torture not also occur via psychological suffering? Many people seem to think that torturing a person's child in front of this person also amounts to torture of that person. Mental or psychological suffering would be sufficient. I have doubts. Of course the person is made to suffer (and it is, all else being equal, a particularly despicable and monstrous way of making someone suffer), but is she being tortured? Consider a Nazi camp guard and artist who has produced what he considers to be his greatest painting yet, his legacy to the world; he would protect it with his life. Now, however, the painting is damaged in front of his eyes by the recently freed concentration camp inmates to make him suffer (or divulge secret information), and the Nazi artist indeed suffers immensely. Is he being tortured? Intuitively, I would say no. And what about someone who immensely suffers when people point out the absurdity of her religion to her? Suppose that somebody does do exactly that in order to make her suffer. Is this a case of torture? It would seem that if we allow the intentional infliction of psychological suffering to be torture, many things we would intuitively not consider torture would now be labeled "torture." I prefer to avoid this consequence. Thus, for the purposes of this book I use the term "torture" as defined above. This in no way prejudges the subsequent discussion. After all, if some forms of physical torture are permissible under certain circumstances, then obviously some forms of torture, period, are permissible under certain circumstances. Moreover, it is hard to see why some forms of psychological torture should not also be permissible under certain circumstances. Indeed, my moral arguments apply both to physical torture and to psychological "torture."

Thus, a *wider* definition of torture than the one provided here will for obvious logical reasons not be able to block my arguments for the justifiability of forms of torture that are *included* in such a wide definition. However, a *narrower* definition of torture might try to *exclude* things I consider as justified torture so that according to the narrow definition these things would not count as examples of justified torture anymore. Such a narrow definition would, for instance, be one that makes absolute unjustifiability a constitutive definitional element of torture. However, there is obviously no reason to accept such a definition. It is a dogmatic stipulation, not a rational contribution to a moral debate.

It should be noted, however, that some people simply insist—although the history of both the word and the phenomenon it designates clearly show that torture need neither be interrogational or coercive nor state-sanctioned—that torture must be defined somewhat along the following lines: "Torture is the coercive and state-sanctioned infliction of suffering on a person by a state official in order to make that person give away some information." According to this definition, the infliction of pain depicted in *Hostel* would not be torture. This implication of the definition is of course absurd. But be that as it may, even if we accepted this definition, this would still not block the moral argument provided in this book, since there are also many forms of torture in *this* sense that are not worse than killing. Thus, again, if self- (including other-) defensive killing is justified in some cases—and it is—then self-defensive torture (even in this narrower sense) is also justified in some cases.

2

The Moral Justification of Torture

In this chapter I will discuss the self-defense justification of torture (where the term "self-defense," as is usual in legal parlance, also comprises other-defense), the justification from the culpability for creating a forced-choice situation, the necessity justification, and the utilitarian justification. However, I only endorse the first three. The latter one I only discuss in order to counter certain claims that have recently been made to the effect that torture cannot be justified in the real world by utilitarian considerations. It most definitely can. I will also emphasize that the first justification (as well as the second, incidentally) is purely deontological and entirely compatible with rights absolutism.

2.1 The Argument from Self-defense

2.1.1 What Is Self-defense?

People have a right to defend themselves or others against wrongful aggression, in particular if the aggression is life-threatening. Here I would like to begin with a look at how German law (which is the law I am most familiar with) treats self-defense, in the course of which I will also draw some comparisons with British law and U.S. statutes before coming to a moral assessment.

Section 32 of the German penal code states (my translation):

(1) Whosoever commits an act that is required (*geboten*) for self-defense (*Notwehr*) does not act against the law.

(2) Self-defense is the defense necessary to avert a present (*gegenwärtig*) unlawful attack on oneself or others.

A few comments are in order.[1] First, the usual translation of the German term "*Notwehr*" is "self-defense." But the literal translation would actually be "emergency defense"—thus, there is no reference to any self. The statute applies as straightforwardly to self- as to other-defense. (Incidentally, U.S. and British "self"-defense statutes or common laws *also* comprise other-defense, in spite of the perhaps misleading term "self-defense.") Second, while the *necessity* requirement is supposed to *prevent excessive violence* (=violence that clearly goes beyond the amount of violence of equally promising alternative means that have not yet been tried), it is not intended to *guarantee minimal force*. In other words, the actual judicial interpretation prefers to err on the safe side—that is, it favors the defender, not the attacker. While the general idea is that the defender should select *among equally effective means* the one that harms the attacker the least, German courts have made it abundantly clear that the defender is not obliged to use less dangerous means of defense if the effectiveness of those means is doubtful. In addition, a person defending with milder means may escalate his or her defense if these milder means have proven unsuccessful. And of course, if no effective means are available, the defender is allowed to take his or her chances. A rape victim is not required to abstain from slapping the rapist merely because it is highly unlikely that this will have any effect. And although air rifles will hardly stop an aggressor (although it might slightly hurt him), I am completely within my rights to use them. Indeed, police would not prosecute a person according to the following logic: "Well, Herr Fritze, blasting the aggressor away with your shotgun was of course an effective means of self-defense, but you should not have first used the air rifle. There was practically no probability of success. So you are off the hook for the shotgun, but we are afraid that for using the air rifle we have to prosecute you for battery."

It is also important for the interpretation of the "necessity" requirement that German law does not require one to retreat from the aggressor if one could safely do so. A basic German principle of law is *Das Recht muß dem Unrecht nicht weichen* (roughly: *law/justice does not have to give way to the unlawful/ unjust*). This principle does not exist in U.S. law. However, it seems that there is no duty in U.S. laws to retreat from an aggressor threatening deadly force before defending with deadly force. As regards the UK, common law once contained a duty to retreat. This, however, is no longer the case.[2]

Thus, the "necessity" requirement is in fact very lenient, in the United States and the UK as well; and rightly so. Although the self-defense statute gives *some* protection (namely, against *excessive* violence) to the aggressor, its main task is to protect the defender. There is no moral symmetry between innocent defenders and culpable aggressors.

German law takes this asymmetry very far (which is a direct consequence of the principle that law/justice does not have to give way to the unlawful/ unjust). *There is no proportionality requirement in the German self-defense law.*

The necessity requirement *is not* a proportionality requirement! I emphasize this because necessity and proportionality are regularly confused by many people. This confusion is facilitated by the fact that we can say in *some* sense that the necessity requirement *is* a proportionality requirement. However, it is important to be clear in which sense it is and in which it is not. The "necessity" requirement prohibits excessive violence or force when using defensive measures against unlawful actions. It does *not*, however, weigh the severity of the attack or the value of the defended good against the harm inflicted upon the aggressor. In other words, it says that you are not supposed to kill a thief if you can also stop her by knocking her out. It does not, however, say that you shouldn't use lethal force at all in defending yourself against theft. It does *not* argue that human life is more valuable than property and that therefore defending property with lethal force is disproportionate. This latter argument would be a proportionality argument, which exists, for example, in English law. In Great Britain you are not allowed to use deadly force if this is the only way you can keep a thief from stealing your car. In Germany, you are *arguably* allowed to do so. To be sure, a growing number of scholars now claim that *killing* in order to defend *property* is not allowed (and other scholars contradict them),[3] but this special case would still not mean that there is a proportionality requirement in place (as the very same scholars who reject killing in defense of property of course acknowledge). Some *extreme* disproportionalities are now forbidden under German law (you are not supposed to shoot a thief in order to prevent him from escaping with an apple), but the fact remains that a principle that rules out *extreme dis*proportionalities is not yet one that demands proportionality.[4]

An attack is *present* according to German law if it is imminent, has started, or is ongoing. An *attack*, in German law, is every threat of violation or actual violation of an interest that is protected by law insofar as this threat stems from human action. Thus, the German law makes use of the term "attack" here in a way that does not necessarily follow ordinary usage, which associates attack with fists and knives and guns—with "action." If someone has been kidnapped and is now alone in a room, we might want to say that she is not *currently* under attack any more, but only was so when the gangster grabbed her and threw her into the car. For German law, however, the kidnapped person, stripped of her freedom, is still under attack.

It is already implicit in the foregoing, but worth emphasizing: self-defense can only be directed against the attacker, not against an innocent and non-threatening person!

In light of this brief exposition of German self-defense law, let us look at what I call a Dirty Harry case (there are real-life examples of Dirty Harry cases, the most recent one being the famous German Daschner case): a criminal kidnaps a child and puts her somewhere where she will suffocate if not rescued in time. There is not much time left, according to the kidnapper himself, who has been captured by the police. They ask him again and again where the child is. He refuses to tell. The police decide to torture the kidnapper in order to get the information they need to save the child. (In the Daschner case the kidnapper was only *threatened* with torture. Facing this threat, he gave up the location of the child. Tragically, the child was already dead.)[5]

This case falls under the German self-defense law. The kidnapped child is still under attack, in the sense in which German law uses this expression. And the necessity requirement—whether in the German, British, or American interpretation—in itself does not rule out the use of torture. The police had already tried normal interrogation, without success. In other words, the milder means did not work. So they were entitled to use harsher means.

At this point the usual objection will probably be heard, repeated like a mantra by many torture opponents: "Torture does not work to gain information." Actually, it sometimes does. In the real life Daschner case the threat of torture sufficed to make the kidnapper spill the required information. The child was already dead, but that was not some kind of metaphysical necessity. If he had still been alive, he would have been saved thanks to the threat of torture. Incidentally another case surfaced in the judicial proceedings of the Daschner case: In 1988 police had beaten up a kidnapper, who then gave up the information as to where he had hidden the child. The police were able to rescue the child alive from a wooden box.[6] I suppose that there are many more cases like these, but for obvious reasons police officers have an interest in denying that they used torture.

Moreover, even if torture were highly unreliable, this would not matter. As already explained above, the "necessity" requirement, which actually is a no-excessive-force requirement, allows you to use even "improbable" means to defend yourself if your (or another innocent person's) life is threatened by a culpable aggressor. And that is exactly how it should be. Even if it were an empirically well-proven and commonly well-known fact that stopping a serial murderer and rapist by ramming a sharp pencil deep into his ear only works one out of 10,000 times, the victim of a rapist would still be well within her rights to ram a sharp pencil deep into the rapist's ear if that is the only option remaining that has any chance of success.

Or consider this example: an innocent person is being attacked by an aggressor, who fires a deadly weapon at him (and misses him at first but keeps firing). The attacked person's only possibility to save his life is by using the One-Million-Pains-to-One-Kill-Gun that he happens to have with him. On average, you have to pull the trigger of this gun 1 million times in order to have one immediately incapacitating projectile come out of it (it incapacitates through the infliction of unbearable pain). All the other times it fires projectiles that only ten seconds after hitting a human target cause the target unbearable pain. Thus, firing this gun at the aggressor and hitting him will certainly cause the aggressor unbearable pain, but the probability that it will save the life of the defender is only 1:1,000,000. From the self-defense perspective (and any intuitively plausible moral point of view) the defender is allowed to use the gun against the aggressor. Yes, the pain inflicted by the weapon on the aggressor is extremely unlikely to secure the survival of the defender, but there still *is* a chance that it will, so why should the *defender* forgo this chance for the benefit of the *aggressor*? Clearly, there is no reason (at least none that I could see). Again, the application of this to the case of ticking-bomb terrorists and Dirty Harry kidnappers is obvious.

But—it is often said by torture opponents—couldn't the police have talked to the kidnapper longer? Maybe then he would have finally given up the information. Yes, maybe, but as already stated, if milder means—like talking—do not work in a self-defense situation, the defender is allowed to try harsher means. Besides, there are in fact cases where a rapist has been verbally persuaded by his victim to stop. However, hardly anyone would say to a rape victim: "Why did you ram the pencil into his ear after only 30 minutes of rape? Why didn't you endure some more rape, maybe half an hour more? Maybe your begging would finally have worked." Similarly, it should not be forgotten that the situation faced by the police is not one where the child is happily playing in a garden and would then, if the kidnapper does not give the required information, suddenly and peacefully die. While the kidnapper is not being tortured by the police, the child *is* being tortured, namely by the kidnapper. He is suffocating in a box the kidnapper put him in.

Thus in Dirty Harry cases torture is not ruled out by the "necessity" requirement, that is, the requirement that among equally promising methods of defense that have not yet been tried in that particular case the one that inflicts the smallest harm upon the aggressor has to be used. (Whoever wants to object at this point that torture is somehow "intrinsically excessive" only confuses necessity and proportionality again. I will come to proportionality shortly.)

From the perspective of German law the child is clearly in a situation that could justify self-defense. Is this also the case from the perspective of British and American law? The self-defense laws in these jurisdictions allow self-defense against the unlawful use of force only if the *imminence requirement* is met, that is, if the unlawful use of force is ongoing or imminent. Clearly, this requirement is fulfilled in the Dirty Harry case (as it is in ticking-bomb cases, incidentally). *The child is already a victim of unlawful force*, and not only at the moment when he dies. He is also already a victim of *deadly* force. Deadly force is not only force that has already killed you, but force that is typically capable of doing so. Someone who has been poisoned with something that will kill her in a month has suffered deadly force already at the moment she was poisoned, and not first at the end of the month. Thus, under British law and U.S. statutes as well, the child in the Dirty Harry case is in a situation that can justify self-defense.

However, for the sake of argument, let us take a look at whether it does morally make a difference—as is sometimes claimed—that in ticking-bomb cases or Dirty Harry cases *death* is not always imminent (while of course deadly *force* is). Some think it does. The underlying idea seems to be that if the expected harm (here in the form of death) is not imminent, there remains enough time to try all kinds of milder means to avert the danger. However, that is simply not always true. The fact that the ultimate harm might befall me late does not mean that I have much time to react. The incubation time of rabies can be up to 10 years, but after having been bitten one only has a couple of hours to get vaccinated. After that, everything is too late. Now consider this situation. Gina is in a jungle camp with Bob. A black mamba bites her. The poison will kill her in few minutes if she does not immediately get the antidote from the refrigerator. Bob wants Gina dead and blocks the refrigerator. She draws her gun and threatens to shoot him if he does not get out of the way. He does not, so she shoots him in the leg. If for some reason it were necessary to kill him in order to get him out of the way, she would even be allowed to do that. It is a clear case of self-defense.

Now imagine that she has not been bitten by a black mamba but by a dog with superrabies. It will kill her in five years, but she needs the antidote as quickly as she needed the one against the mamba poison. Again Bob blocks the way to the refrigerator. Is she now not allowed to shoot him in the leg or to kill him if necessary to reach the antidote? Of course she is. The difference in the time frame of the ultimate *harm* is normatively irrelevant. What is decisive is the time frame wherein *defensive action* to avert the danger is still possible. This is, incidentally, reflected by a large part of U.S. case law, by the Model Penal Code, and by the statutes of some U.S. states.[7]

Thus it seems that torturing an aggressor in order to save an innocent life from the aggressor's claws can be justified by self-defense law. To be sure, one might object that torture is still prohibited by international antitorture conventions, which are also binding for the national jurisdictions of the UK, the United States, and Germany. However, it seems that the antitorture conventions define torture as something undertaken by *state* agents. Thus, they might not be applicable to private defensive torture (for example, a Dirty Harry case where not a police officer but the father of the kidnapped child tortures the kidnapper). Second, for the German case, Volker Erb argues that a law or an international convention that protects the kidnapper from being tortured even where torture would be the last available means to save the innocent child violates the human dignity of the child.[8] The highest article of the German constitution, however, states that human dignity must not be violated. International conventions that violate that article would therefore be null and void under the German constitution.

Be that as it may, here I can set aside the question as to whether torture is *actually* legal in the three jurisdictions. I am dealing with the *moral* question. So why am I discussing self-defense *laws* in the first place? Because the self-defense law and its application in case law reflect intuitions many people have about self-defense. They also reflect the moral reasoning behind these intuitions.[9] My moral argument is that if injuring or killing a person in self-defense can be morally justified as long as the defense meets the so-called necessity, imminence and proportionality or no-gross-disproportionality requirements, the same is true for torture. To be sure, a legislator or an international convention could simply stipulate: "Never mind the self-defense law. We just want to rule out torture, even if it occurs in self-defense." (Or: "Never mind the self-defense law. We just want to rule out stabbing, even if it occurs in self-defense.") However, such a stipulation would not follow the previous legal reasoning nor especially the moral reasoning behind self-defense laws. It would be something externally imposed on the self-defense law and the moral reasoning behind it, something *contradicting* it. And since self-defense law is extremely plausible and the moral reasoning behind it very convincing, the contradiction would not show that self-defense law and the moral reasoning behind it are mistaken if they allow torture. Rather, it would show that the absolute prohibition of torture is wrong.

The only way out for the absolutist opponent of torture or the opponent of self-defensive torture would be to show that there is a normatively relevant difference between killing a person in self-defense and torturing him in self-defense that rules out the permissibility of the latter act. As I have already argued, appeals to the necessity and to the imminence requirements do not work. Yet, apart from the proportionality requirement (or the no-extreme disproportionality requirement), *there are no other requirements*.

This fact is often ignored. For example, sometimes it is considered to be a good argument against torture that you can never know *for certain* that the person tortured in the Dirty Harry case (or a ticking-bomb case) really is guilty. However, there is no certainty requirement in self-defense cases. In fact, in German law there is not even the requirement that the defender *reasonably* believes him- or herself to be under attack as long as he or she *is* under attack (a minority view states that under such circumstances defenders need not even *believe* themselves to be under attack *at all*). If the defender *is* under attack, then necessary and not grossly disproportionate countermeasures are justified, whether the belief of the defender to be under attack is itself reasonable or not. As regards American and British self-defense law, there is certainly no requirement that there be no reasonable doubt for the defender that he or she is under attack. Thus, the fact is that there are many cases of legally and morally justified killings in self-defense where the certainty that an actual attack was imminent was much lower than the certainty the policemen in the Daschner case had that they were dealing with a child kidnapper. The fact that the no-certainty argument gets repeated and repeated and repeated (for more on and against this, see section 6.8) does not make it any better. If self-defensive killing without certainty is justified, self-defensive torture without certainty is justified, too.

Thus, the fact remains that the last hope for someone who does not deny the permissibility of self-defensive killing or harming but nevertheless wants to show that defensive torture in Dirty Harry cases is impermissible can only lie in the proportionality requirement or the no-extreme-disproportionality requirement. Here, however, the proponent of defensive torture has a certain advantage. For the torture opponent to rule out the permissibility of torture, it would not be sufficient to show that it is somehow worse than killing. That one means of defense is harsher than another means of defense does not in itself show that the harsher means is unjustified. After all, killing someone in self-defense is harsher than merely knocking him out; still, self-defensive killing is justified in certain circumstances. Thus, even if torture were harsher than killing, torture might still be justified in certain circumstances. However, if the proponent of torture in certain cases can show that *killing* is worse than many forms of torture, then the fact that killing is sometimes morally justified demonstrates that torture can sometimes be morally justified too. With this in mind, let us turn to the question as to how bad torture really is in comparison to killing.

2.1.2 Proportionality, or: Many Forms of Torture Are Not as Bad as Killing

Now, why should we think that torture is always wrong? What is so bad about torturing people, anyway? People also kill people. Soldiers kill people, policemen kill people, doctors kill people, executioners kill people, and ordinary people kill people. Some of these killings are justified. So why shouldn't it be justified in some cases to torture people? After all, being killed seems worse than some forms of being tortured. Even most of the people experiencing torture seem to see it this way; otherwise they would kill themselves in order to escape further torture (yes, some do, but they are few). So, if killing is sometimes justified, torture too must sometimes be justified.

Of course, on the face of it,

(a) the intentional and continuous or repeated infliction of extreme physical suffering on a nonconsenting victim sounds like a pretty gruesome practice.

But how gruesome? After all,

(b) the intentional blowing out of someone's brain with a .44 Colt or

(c) the intentional chopping off of someone's head also sound like pretty gruesome practices.

In fact, practices (b) and (c) sound *much more gruesome* than practice (a). Yet, according to the principle of self-defense, most accounts of just war theory, and the overwhelming majority opinion of people around the world, these practices are permissible in some circumstances (for example in circumstances where they are the only promising defense of an innocent person against a culpable and life-threatening aggressor). Why, then, should torture not also be permissible in some circumstances (for example where it is the only promising means to save an innocent person from a culpable aggressor)? If *you* could choose to be the victim of practice (a), (b), or (c), which would you choose? It depends, of course. There are *some* forms of practice (a) that might be worse than any form of practices (b) and (c), but, for example, being subjected to a pain nearly as excruciating as that of an unprotected nerve maltreated by a drill for 15 minutes is not one of them (and it is still not one of them if this pain is inflicted by a state-sanctioned state agent for interrogational purposes). If this were the choice, most people would, no doubt, prefer being a victim of this form of practice (a) to being a victim of any form of the other two practices. The fact of the matter is that most people prefer extreme physical suffering to death. Death is *worse* than (most forms of) extreme physical suffering.

Once this is granted (and there is no *rational* way around granting it) the person who thinks that torture is never permissible is in a tight spot. So is the person who thinks that torture can only be allowed in certain extreme threshold cases, for example in ticking-bomb cases where the lives of hundreds, thousands, or even millions of innocents are at stake. After all, killing is permissible in a good many less spectacular cases; and if being tortured is not worse than death, the obvious question arises as to why torturing should be worse than killing.

However, to avoid this problem, certain absolutist opponents of torture insist that being tortured (or even having been tortured) *is* in fact worse than death. Such a claim, of course, flies in the face of reason and common sense. Nevertheless, let us have a look at how those absolutist opponents of torture try to back it up.

The last chapter of Bob Brecher's book on torture is entitled "Torture, Death, and Philosophy." He states:

> I shall argue that torture *breaks* people; and that "purely" interrogational torture, something that "leaves no lasting damage," is thus yet another fantasy. To allow torture at all, therefore—whether or not legally normalized, would be grotesque.[10]

What is actually grotesque here is the "therefore" in this quote. Blowing out somebody's brain in self-defense also leaves lasting damage; it lasts for eternity. Nevertheless, it is still entirely justifiable as a necessary and proportionate means to save an innocent life from the attack of an aggressor. The same holds for cutting off somebody's hand, gouging out somebody's eye, severely burning somebody's skin with a flamethrower, and many other forms of severely injuring an aggressor in proportionate and necessary self-defense. Besides, Brecher adduces no evidence that *all* forms of torture leave lasting damage; he just insists it does.

As regards the "breaking" of people, Brecher states: "The tortured person's capacity to act is broken."[11] Yet, this is of course simply wrong. A *dead* person's capacity to act is broken, that much is certain, and a person who has been knocked out in self-defense is likewise incapable of acting as long as she is unconscious—but interrogational torture that undermined the tortured person's ability to act would obviously be counterproductive. After all, one *wants*, one *needs* the person to act: namely to commit the act of disclosing the required information.[12] Disclosing it is an act, and omitting to disclose it is also an act. And after having been tortured, tortured people can do all kinds of things, for example going into a bar, having a chat with friends, and drinking beer. Dead people can't. They can only rot, but that is not an act.

Brecher also makes the following statement: "For some people death is preferable to torture, not just while being tortured, but afterwards too."[13] That is true, but it is also irrelevant. After all, for *some* people death might also be preferable to being publicly outed as homosexual. That proves neither that killing is always better than publicly outing someone as a homosexual, nor that outing someone as a homosexual is always unjustified.

Brecher criticizes Seumas Miller, who, like me, thinks that some forms of torture are preferable to death. Brecher claims:

> Miller forgets to tell us whether his assessment of what is preferable relates to the situation before torture begins or after it is over. If it is a matter of a person's preference before the torture starts, then they might well prefer—or judge—death to be better than *the risk* of one's will being broken and/or of one's life being irretrievably shattered. If the preference Miller has in mind is one expressed once the torture is over, then it is quite possible that neither preference nor judgement are any longer relevant. For these are components of a normal human life, not of an entirely shattered one. The inability in any everyday sense to prefer one thing to another, and/or to make everyday judgments, is precisely part of what it is for one's life to have been utterly shattered.[14]

First of all, if the "inability in any everyday sense to prefer one thing to another, and/or to make everyday judgments, is precisely part of what it is for one's life to have been utterly shattered," then very few torture victims' lives have been utterly shattered. Many torture victims are quite able to prefer, in an everyday sense, chocolate ice cream to vanilla ice cream or vice versa. Some people subjected to entirely justified nontorturous self-defense, however, are not, because the self-defensive measures taken inflicted far too much brain damage on them. Thus, what in Brecher's view is "quite possible" is also highly unlikely; thus the preferences after the torture are not irrelevant.

As regards Brecher's remarks about the preference for death before torture, they only show that he does not quite understand the position of his opponents. This lack of understanding is also revealed when he talks about "the assumption they make about torture being just obviously preferable to death."[15] No one who defends torture under certain circumstances makes any such assumption. Some of them only make the assumption that *some* forms of torture are obviously preferable to death. That assumption is certainly correct, and nothing Brecher says comes even near to refuting it.

J. Jeremy Wisnewski and R. D. Emerick, in their attempt to show that torture is worse than death, do not fare better than Brecher. For instance, they claim that it "is in torture's very nature to be capable of being worse than death."[16] This is as true and as irrelevant as Brecher's statement that some people prefer death to torture. It is, after all, also in death's very nature to be capable of being worse than some torture.

They also claim that "torture is inherently destructive of agency, and hence always impermissible."[17] I have already dealt with this claim in criticizing Brecher's mistaken assertion that "[t]he tortured person's capacity to act is broken."[18] There is nothing to add. This is also true for their claim, taken from Paul Améry, that "[w]hoever was tortured, stays tortured."[19] Whoever was killed, stays killed. Whoever was mutilated, stays mutilated. Whoever was deflowered, stays deflowered. None of this shows that they were unjustifiably tortured, killed, mutilated, or deflowered.

In a certain way Wisnewski and Emerick go even further than Brecher. They claim:

> The question that must be posed is . . . *not* what is to be preferred, torture or death; the question, more honestly, is as follows: what is to be preferred, an immediate death or torture, followed by the agonizing life of one who has been tortured?[20]

I find this question somewhat dishonest. This dishonesty is also displayed in the fact that Wisnewski and Emerick accuse others of a "seeming disregard paid to the actual literature,"[21] while their attempt to use it in support of their claim that torture is worse than death suggests that they do not really care about the actual findings of that literature. For instance, they quote Conroy saying:

> When Doctors Finn Somnier and Inge Genefke examined twenty-four torture survivors an average of 9.5 years after their torture (see "Psychotherapy for Victims of Torture," *British Journal of Psychiatry*, 1986, vol. 149), they found 71 percent had impaired memory, 75 percent had impaired concentration, 75 percent experienced fatigue, 50 percent suffered from persistent fear and anxiety, 38 percent experienced vertigo, 21 percent reported sexual problems, and 13 tremors or shaking.[22]

And they add three sentences later:

> As is obvious, the mental and physical state of one who has been tortured has significant implications for inter-personal relationships, and hence on one's ability to function in social and familial settings. This is often enough to wrench the last meaningful interactions from the lives of the broken. All that is left to do, it seems, is die.

At least it is somewhat refreshing that Wisnewski and Emerick are consistent enough to inform certain torture victims who are reading their book that death is the best these readers can hope for and that they are no autonomous agents anyway.[23] However, how that squares with their professed concern about human dignity, I do not know.

Anyway, not only "the mental and physical state of one who has been tortured has significant implications for inter-personal relationships"; obviously the mental and physical state of persons *generally*, tortured or not, has such implications. Besides, if "the mental and physical state of one who has been tortured" wrenches "the last meaningful interactions from the lives of the broken" only "often enough," then it does not *always* wrench it from the lives of those who have been broken by torture, let alone from those torture did not manage to break.

That is not surprising. For if you apply the method of subtraction to the Conroy quote Wisnewski and Emerick offer, you come to the following result:

When Doctors Finn Somnier and Inge Genefke examined twenty-four torture survivors an average of 9.5 years after their torture (see "Psychotherapy for Victims of Torture," *British Journal of Psychiatry*, 1986, vol. 149), they found 29 percent did *not* have impaired memory, 25 percent did *not* have impaired concentration, 25 percent did *not* experience fatigue, 50 percent did *not* suffer from persistent fear and anxiety, 62 percent did *not* experience vertigo, 79 percent did *not* report sexual problems, and 87 did *not* report tremors or shaking.

In contrast to this, empirical studies show that not 20, not 30, not 98, but *100 percent* of those who have been killed are dead. And the mental and physical state of being dead does not just "wrench the last meaningful interactions" from the dead "often enough"; it does so *always* and permanently. Maybe I am being pedantic, but to me it seems that this is a very significant difference between death and some forms of torture.

Wisnewski and Emerick also offer the following quote, this time from Sussman:

[U]nlike other kinds of unwanted imposition, pain characteristically compromises or undermines the very capacities constitutive of autonomous agency itself. It is almost impossible to reflect, deliberate, or even think straight when one is in agony. When sufficiently intense, pain becomes a person's entire universe and his entire self, crowding out every other aspect of his mental life. Unlike other harms, pain takes its victim's agency apart "from the inside," such that the agent may never be able to reconstitute himself fully.[24]

And they add:

This is sufficient, it seems, to demonstrate that death is not the greater of two harms. In fact, quite the contrary.[25]

Before drawing such a conclusion, Wisnewski and Emerick should perhaps first have *compared* torture with death. Let us do this now:

Unlike other kinds of unwanted imposition, death not only "characteristically," but *absolutely always* compromises or undermines the very capacities constitutive of autonomous agency itself. It is not only almost, *but absolutely always* impossible to reflect, deliberate, or even think straight when one is dead. Not only when "sufficiently intense," whatever that means, but *absolutely always* death *destroys* a person's entire universe and his entire self *once and for all*, *destroying* his mental life *completely*. Unlike other harms, death *destroys* a victim's agency *once and for all*, such that the agent not only "may" never be able to reconstitute himself *fully*, he is *definitely* unable to reconstitute himself *at all*.

This is sufficient, it seems, to demonstrate that not all forms of torture are a greater harm than death. In fact, quite the contrary.

Let us return to Wisnewski's and Emerick's accusation, leveled against people who defend torture under certain circumstances, of a "seeming disregard paid to the actual literature."[26] Richard Matthews[27] and Bob Brecher sing from the same hymn sheet. Brecher, for example, writes:

Let me start with a very obvious question. Why is it that none of the advocates of interrogational torture or of its legalization that I have come across make any reference at all to [Jean] Améry's testimony? His essay, "Torture," is, after all, the single best-known work of this sort. You might think that anyone discussing torture would need to say something about what it actually is.[28]

The obvious answer to this actually not so obvious question is that quite a few advocates of interrogational torture do say something about what torture actually is. They often even provide an explicit definition. You can do this quite well without making any reference to Jean Améry.

Another reason why some of them might not make any reference to Jean Améry is because many of them know what empirical research actually is. They therefore know that anecdotal evidence is of very limited value. In addition, those proponents of certain kinds of interrogational torture who have—unlike, it seems, certain opponents of interrogational torture—not only read the one chapter "Torture" from *At the Mind's Limits* but also the rest of the book and some other works of Améry's, including his *On Suicide*, also know that Améry provides particularly bad anecdotal evidence. Certainly he does not provide evidence justifying claims like this one:

> Améry's torturers, that is to say, turned his personhood against him, and in doing so made him into someone else. That is how he survived, as someone else; others do not. It is also why he eventually killed himself.[29]

First, Jean Améry was Jean Améry, and not someone else. Torture might change a person (so might certain kinds of self-defensive force or a vacation in India), but changing and becoming someone else is not quite the same. In fact, it is *logically impossible* to become someone else. Brecher is engaging in empty rhetoric here.

Second, *how does Brecher know* (or Wisnewski and Emerick, who suggest the same[30]) why Améry killed himself? The "Torture" chapter refers to several days in Fort Breendonk. However, after Fort Breendonk Améry was for two years imprisoned in the German concentration camps Auschwitz, Buchenwald, and Bergen-Belsen. Maybe Brecher, Wisnewski and Emerick, who interestingly all fail to mention this detail, think that two years of imprisonment in Nazi concentration camps is unlikely to have any impact on a person's "mental and physical state." Yet, the literature on camp survivors—of which the three authors, of course, might not be aware—suggests otherwise.

In addition, the chapter "How Much Home Does a Person Need?" shows that Améry, a Jew, greatly suffered from the alienation he felt from German culture. Thus, to take the example of a man who was tortured over a couple of days, alienated from his original culture, which suddenly treated him as less than human, and imprisoned for two years in concentration camps and to *then* claim that he killed himself *because* of the first factor, while not even mentioning the other two, seems to be a rather bold maneuver for authors who complain about the alleged methodological shortcomings of others.

Speaking of methodological shortcomings: the study by Somnier and Genefke cited in Wisnewski's and Emerick's quote from Conroy refers to exiled torture victims. They mostly came from countries with rather brutal military dictatorships. As far as I can see, all of these victims had been tortured over a period of days, weeks, months, or even years. It is inadmissible to draw, from an overview of the symptoms of victims of this prolonged torture, sweeping conclusions about what symptoms someone might show who is tortured for half an hour or several hours in order to make her reveal the location of a child she kidnapped. Absolutist torture opponents, who when criticizing the ticking-bomb argument cannot emphasize enough that one should not draw inferences from one kind of case to completely dissimilar cases, should certainly know this.[31]

No methodological shortcomings, however, are to be found on the part of Somnier and Genefke themselves. While Brecher, Wisnewski, Emerick, Matthews, and many other absolutist opponents of torture stress how enormously important the psychological research on torture is but, unfortunately, show absolutely no awareness of its methodological limitations (and thus may not quite understand this research), the psychologists themselves do:

> Most studies of torture survivors appear to be biased by complex selection factors which are often impossible to elucidate. Some survivors may choose not to tell about their torture experiences and their effect on them. Most surveys are conducted on exiled torture survivors, and only a few studies have been carried out in the country where the torture actually took place. Often torture survivors of different ethnic backgrounds are included for study. Structured interviews or other systematic procedures are only occasionally used, and usually no detailed information about the methods of examination is given. Psychometric methods, such as standardized neuropsychological tests or rating scales are rarely employed. Most reports [like Brecher's report on Améry] do not present a balanced assessment of the relative importance of the various aspects of the trauma such as torture, other stressful experiences and difficulties during imprisonment, and additional stress factors after release (e.g. further persecution or exile). Furthermore, many studies do not report adequate information about the time of onset of various symptoms following the traumatic experience.
> The paucity of controlled studies and of follow-up surveys precludes definitive conclusions concerning the long-term effects of torture. . . . Reports of various sequelae after torture may thus have limited generalizability to the "population" of torture survivors.[32]

And Metin Başoğlu, in the introduction to the collected volume from which the above quote is taken, states:

Most tortured individuals experience some degree of psychological distress after the trauma. Many, however, recover from these effects after a period of time.[33]

In light of this and similar passages in the psychological literature on torture, the actual "obvious question" is: why do absolutist torture opponents like Brecher, Matthews, or Wisnewski and Emerick not mention such passages? Did they perhaps not read the literature they hold in such high regard attentively enough, or are they misleading their readers on purpose? Given the accusations these authors wield against their opponents, it is also an entirely fair question to ask.

However, it also has to be said in all fairness that *meanwhile* Wisnewski seems to have come to a slightly better understanding of the literature and quotes passages referring to *recovery* from torture. Nevertheless, he still keeps making the entirely unwarranted claim that torture destroys agency at least in most of the cases and claims that this has been shown by what he refers to as "the literature." Let me point out that the torture victims in "the literature" he is referring to have not been unconsciously carried on a stretcher into the therapist's room; they have *gone* to the therapy sessions, *filled out* the forms and questionnaires, *driven cars, taken taxis or buses, have looked up the therapist in the Yellow Pages or asked around, called, made an appointment, etc.* Thus, they have *acted*. If the authors writing "the literature" are unable to infer from these empirical facts that the agency of their patients has *not* been "destroyed," then that speaks against the competence of those authors, not against the inference. (Incidentally, Wisnewski at least realizes that a torture victim's "act of suicide" is an "act of agency"—are there any other acts?—but he claims that "[m]any victims of torture feel entirely powerless, moving through life as through a fog, alienated and helpless. To act on suicidal ideation, in this respect, is not something we should expect—it would represent precisely the kind of exercise of agential control that torture destroys."[34] However, why giving up and killing oneself demonstrates more "agential control" than the decision to go to a therapist in order to improve one's life remains Wisnewski's secret. Moreover, being alienated and "in a fog"—and certainly not all torture victims are—is not the same as not having agency. In addition, someone who is quite able to drive to her therapist is obviously not helpless.)

Be that as it may, while Wisnewski now admits that torture does not necessarily destroy agency, he is entirely unwilling to draw the logical conclusions. Rather, he claims that "the argument that torture does not always destroy agency is a red herring (and it is actually generous to call this an argument—it is more realistically simply an empirical observation)."[35] That is correct. However, Wisnewski conveniently overlooks the fact here that his constant claim that torture destroys agency (in nearly all cases) is also not an argument, but more realistically simply an empirical observation—and a wrong one at that. He also does not mention here what he correctly identifies a few pages later as the actual argument of his opponents: "A final argument to be considered runs as follows: killing is worse than torture [of course, the actual argument is that killing is worse than *some forms* of torture]. It is sometimes permissible to kill. Therefore, it is sometimes permissible to torture."[36] This, of course, is the argument of this entire section of this book.

Wisnewski's first reaction to this argument is to deny the premise that killing is worse than torture. I have already dealt with this, and Wisnewski does not offer any argument I have not already refuted in the previous discussion.[37] His second reaction consists in the following claims:

> "[K]illing" is taken as a success term: that is, it is regarded as an action that has successfully been carried out. One attempted to accomplish a particular goal (to kill), and one successfully completed this task (hence, one killed). Unfairly, I think, torture is *not* regarded as a success term. One carried out particular procedures designed to accomplish a particular task (the destruction of agency . . .), but one *might not have been successful.*[38]

He then goes on to state that the following is the real question: "Is successful killing worse than successful torture?" And he opines that this question "is very much like asking if a life of total suffering that ends in death is better than simply dying."[39]

Obviously, it is Wisnewski who is being unfair here. "Torturing" is a success term in the same sense that "killing" is: after you have killed someone, that person has been killed; after you have tortured someone, that person has been tortured. But Wisnewski now claims that torture is only successful if it destroys a person's agency. However, as we have seen in section (1), the claim that torture necessarily aims at the destruction of agency is simply wrong. In fact, it seems that in spite of his professed hostility toward definitions of torture,[40] Wisnewski is not beyond surreptitiously importing a definition of torture if it suits his purposes. To wit, he now implicitly defines torture as something that necessarily aims at destroying agency; and thus, if an act of torture fails to destroy agency, it is not successful any more.

However, there is certainly no reason to accept such a definition. Waterboarding, after all, *is* torture. And if police waterboard a child kidnapper in order to find out where he has imprisoned the child, then if they do find this out, they will regard this as a success, whether the kidnapper's agency has been destroyed or not (they will, for example, after having freed the child, not necessarily say: "Damn, we have completely forgotten to destroy the kidnappers agency. Let's go back and try again.") Thus, successful torture certainly need not destroy agency. And therefore the above argument remains unrefuted.

Wisnewski himself has not provided an argument against torture. He remains in the realm of mere (and mistaken) empirical observation. For let us assume he is right and that torture is as bad as or even worse than killing. What would follow from this? Nothing. To see this, let me again repeat the argument for torture under certain circumstances: Killing is worse than some forms of torture. It is sometimes permissible to kill. Therefore, it is sometimes permissible to torture. Now, what is Wisnewski's argument? In analogy to the argument for torture, it could be formulated like this: Torture necessarily involves the destruction of agency, and the destruction of agency is at least as bad as killing. It is always impermissible to kill. Therefore, it is always impermissible to torture. Unfortunately, the second premise of this argument is obviously wrong.

Wisnewski would thus have to introduce something like the following premise: the destruction of agency is always wrong. And this is of course what he always assumes, but nowhere shows. Killing does destroy a person's agency, as Wisnewski admits, but it is, of course, sometimes permissible. So the destruction of agency cannot always be wrong. However, he mentions the following difference between killing and torture: "unlike death, torture leaves its victim to suffer through his or her own inability to act autonomously. Death is certainly a great harm, but it is not a harm that continues to be suffered by the person who dies."[41] First, again, the assumption that torture necessarily leads to an inability to act autonomously is wrong; second, even if true, again it would only be an empirical observation that torture victims suffer from that inability. It would still have to be shown that it is always wrong to make someone suffer that inability. Wisnewski shows nothing of that sort, which is not surprising, for it is not always wrong.

Consider, for instance, a psychiatrist who knows that attacking her patient Hannibal with a flamethrower will traumatize him in exactly the same way as he would be traumatized if one tortures him: thus, under the current assumption, it would make him suffer through an "inability to act autonomously." One day, Hannibal (whom the psychiatrist has recently discovered to be a cannibalistic psychopath disposed to kill and eat her) attacks her, with the obvious intention to kill her. As it happens, she can only defend herself with a flamethrower that will not kill the attacker, but burn him and thus traumatize him in the way torture does. Is she allowed to do so? She certainly is under the law. She also is under morality, and few would disagree. If Wisnewski thinks otherwise, the burden of proof is certainly on him. So far he has not even begun to shoulder it.[42]

Incidentally, since Brecher says (and since Wisnewski and Emerick clearly share his thought), "You might think that anyone discussing torture would need to say something about what it actually is," I will surely be forgiven if I point out that one might also think that anyone claiming that torture is at least as bad as death would need to say something about what *death* actually is. Unfortunately, however, Brecher, Wisnewski, Emerick, and many other absolutist torture opponents provide no reference whatsoever to the literature on death. Maybe that explains their deficient grasp of the phenomenon. So allow me to enlighten them:

> Death is the irreversible loss of the properties of living matter—that is to say, death is the cessation of life. It is when the body shuts down its machineries of life, never to start up again.[43]

And:

> Once death occurs, human decomposition takes place in stages. The process of tissue breakdown may take from several days up to years. At all stages of decomposition, insect activity occurs on the body . . .

Fresh

> The fresh stage of decomposition occurs during the first few days following the death. . . . At this point, the body enters algor mortis, the cooling of the body's temperature to that of its surroundings. When the body's cells reach the final stage of autolysis, an anaerobic environment is created, that is, an environment wherein oxygen is not present. This allows the body's normal bacteria to break down the remaining carbohydrates, proteins, and lipids. The products from the breakdown create acids, gases, and other products which cause volatile organic compounds (VOCs), and putrefactive effects. . . . Substances produced during the fresh stage of decomposition attract a variety of insects. Diptera insects begin to lay their eggs on the body during this stage, especially members of the Calliphoridae family of insects. If the body is on the ground or buried in soil there is also considerable insect activity by the insects that live in the soil around the body. The reasoning for this is simple: A dead human body serves as an excellent source of decaying matter to feed on, in a very hospitable environment.

Putrefaction

Odor, color changes, and bloating of the body during decomposition are the results of putrefaction. The lower part of the abdomen turns green due to bacteria activity in the cecum. Bacteria break down hemoglobin into sulfhemoglobin, which causes the green color. A formation of gases enters the abdomen which forces liquids and feces out of the body. The gases also enter the neck and face, causing swelling of the mouth, lips, and tongue. Due to this swelling and misconfiguration of the face, identification of the body can be difficult. Bacteria also enter the venous system causing blood to hemolyze. This leads to the formation of red streaks along the veins. This color soon changes to green, through a process known as marbelization. It can be seen on the shoulders, chest and shoulder area, and thighs. The skin can develop blisters containing serous fluid. The skin also becomes fragile, leading to skin slippage, making it difficult to move a body. Body hair comes off easily. The color change of the discoloration from green to brown marks the transition of the early stage of putrefaction to the advanced decompositional stages.

During the putrefaction stage of decomposition the majority of insect activity again comes from members of the Calliphoridae family, and includes Formicidae, Muscidae, Sphaeroceridae, Silphidae, Lepidoptera, Hymenoptera, Sarcophagidae, Histeridae, Staphylinidae, Phalangida, Piophilidae, Araneae, Sepsidae, and Phoridae. As with the fresh stage of decomposition if the body is on the ground or buried in soil there is also considerable insect activity by the soil-inhabiting arthropods.

Black putrefaction

After the body goes through the bloating stage it begins the black putrefaction stage. At this point the body cavity ruptures, the abdominal gases escape and the body darkens from its greenish color. These activities allow for a greater invasion of scavengers, and insect activity increases greatly. This stage ends as the bones become apparent, which can take anywhere from 10 to 20 days after death depending on region and temperature. This period is also dependent on the degree to which the body is exposed.

During the black putrefaction stage of decomposition, insects that can be found living in the body are Calliphoridae larvae, Staphylinidae, Histeridae, Gamasid mites, Ptomaphila, Trichopterygidae,

Piophilid larvae, Parasitic wasps, Staphylinid larvae, Trichopterygid larvae, Histerid larvae, Ptomaphila larvae, Dermestes, Tyroglyphid mites, Tineid larvae, and the Dermestes larvae. . . . The types of insects will differ based on where the body is, although Diptera larvae can be found feeding on the body in almost all cases.

Butyric fermentation

After the early putrefaction and black putrefaction phases have taken place, the body begins mummification, in which the body begins to dry out. . . . Insects that can be found on the body during mummification include most of the same insects as in putrefaction stage, but also include Acarina, Nitidulidae, Cleridae, Dermestes caninus, and Trogidae. The main soil-inhabiting arthropods include Dermaptera and Formicidae.

Dry decay

When the last of the soft-tissue has been removed from the body, the final stage of decomposition, skeletonization, occurs. . . . At the dry decay stage commonly found insects include Sphaeroceridae, Acarina, Nitidulidae, Cleridae, Dermestes caninus, Trogidae, Tyroglyphid mites, and the Tineid larvae. The soil-inhabiting arthropods are Collembola, Dermaptera, Heteroptera, Coleoptera and their larvae, parasitic Hymenoptera, Formicidae, Diptera larvae, Pseudoscorpiones, Aranae, Plectochetos, Acari, Pauropoda, Symphyla, Geophilidae, Protura, and Aphididae.[44]

Thus, it would appear that even if one granted Wisnewski and Emerick their semantically incorrect (just consult the dictionary!) and dramatic claim that "[t]orture *is* a kind of death,"[45] this would only mean that *some* kinds of death are preferable to others. For then those kinds of "death" that allow the victim to go on to see their children grow up, go to the movies and restaurants, write essays, go to bars, meet friends, travel around the world, visit museums and have sex, seem to be a very significantly better deal than the kind of death that immediately leaves the victim a slowly rotting feast for maggots.

Hence, not all forms of torture are worse than death (or than ten years of imprisonment, for that matter). This is one reason why self-defensive torture will not always be disproportionate. There is a second reason, though: *even if* all forms of torture were worse than death, logically not all forms of torture are worse than any form of torture. And some forms of torture are clearly worse than others. Thus, torturing a child kidnapper by waterboarding him for half an hour is certainly a proportionate means to save the kidnapped child from being tortured for many hours or even days more by being kept in a dark wooden box and slowly suffocating. The whole idea that self-defensive torture could be ruled out by its allegedly being disproportionate is a nonstarter.

Let me finally point to the utterly counterintuitive, indeed absurd implications of the view that all forms of torture are worse than death for third-party action. Surgeons sometimes amputate limbs of unconscious patients in order to save their lives. They do this on the very reasonable assumption that those patients would prefer life without a hand or a leg to no life at all. And if the patients do not, they still have the option to kill themselves afterwards. In the same vein, it seems to be justified to cut off someone's hand in the following situation: the victim's fingers have gotten caught in a machine that will slowly pull her in and crush her. A third person passes by. The victim is screaming in pain, unable to communicate and thus to consent to any action of another person. The only way to save the person's life is to cut off her hand with the axe the passerby has. It seems that he is entirely justified in doing just that. Cutting off the victim's hand is the lesser evil. It is for the victim's own good. In fact, all else being equal, the following seems to be true: if you can see to it that the smaller of two possible harms befalls a victim, you are justified in inflicting the smaller one if this is the only way to prevent the bigger one.

Now consider the following case: an innocent victim is about to be waterboarded for half an hour by some torturers (perhaps even by state-sanctioned state agents for interrogational purposes—if that should matter). Someone else comes along, and the only way she could possibly prevent the victim from being tortured is to shoot the victim. If one really thinks that all forms of torture are worse than death, it is unclear how absolutist torture opponents—unwarranted *ad hoc* claims aside—can avoid the conclusion that it is justifiable to kill the victim in this situation. I take this to be a *reductio ad absurdum* of the view that all forms of torture are worse than killing. Clearly, the absolutist torture opponent who, full well knowing that the victim will only be waterboarded for half an hour, kills him anyway to spare him a fate allegedly "worse than death" is quite simply morally insane.

This is of course no different if we consider aggressors rather than mere victims. To draw our discussion on proportionality to a close, here is *the case of the humane torturer and the bloodthirsty antitorture fanatic*:

> Bill works for a company that has a lot of trolleys on its enormous property to transport different goods. He is in charge of the maintenance of the trolleys. There is some kind of animal in the

region that often enters the trolleys from below and bites through the wires. Therefore, Bill planted several foot traps, which, however, can also trap humans. The traps have combination locks, and Bill knows the combination. In order to set in motion certain trolleys, one has to hold on to a lever well above one's head. Since Bill is very small, he has to jump to reach the lever. One day, Jeanette and Paolo, two completely innocent people, cross the tracks and both accidentally step into a foot trap. Jeanette shouts to Bill: "Help us!" "You wish," he shouts back. "I prefer to kill you." And he jumps up to a lever and sets in motion a trolley, which is slowly but fatally moving in Jeanette's and Paolo's direction. If not stopped, it will crush them. Jeanette has with her both her explosive projectile gun (these projectiles can blow people into small pieces but do not much affect trolleys) and her pain-infliction ray gun. Bill, for whatever reason, would rather die than let the two escape. Fearing that they might shoot at him with normal guns so that he lets go of the lever, which would stop the trolley, he handcuffs himself to the lever and throws away the keys, and shouts sneeringly: "I know the combination of your traps—but I won't tell you. I will watch you die." Shooting him with a normal gun would not stop the trolley since Bill would still be hanging on to the lever by the handcuffs. Jeanette draws her pain inflictor and shows it to Bill: "If you do not tell me the combination of the traps, I will torture you! This gun inflicts pain like a dentist drilling on an unprotected nerve." Bill remains silent. Jeanette sadly aims the pain-inflictor gun at him. "What are you doing?" screams Paolo now. "What am I doing? I am trying to save our lives!" "No, no, but you can't torture him. Torture is brutal; it's—the horror, the horror!" "So what am I supposed to do?" "Well, nontorturing self-defense is permissible. Draw your projectile thrower and blow him into small pieces!" "Are you crazy? That is not minimal force! Besides, maybe the guy is just having a psychotic break, or somebody's drugged him, and maybe he has family. If I get the combination by a few minutes of torture, maybe we can all still become friends. Why should I kill him?" "You like to torture, you like to torture," Paolo shouts, his face red in righteous indignation.[46] Two police officers approach from behind. They too step into traps and cannot interfere. They have overheard the loud argument. As Jeanette aims with the pain inflictor, one police officer shouts: "Don't do it! Torture is really bad. Blowing people into small pieces is much better." Jeanette is for a moment paralyzed by the sheer amount of idiocy and moral insanity she is confronted with. Paolo uses the opportunity and knocks her out, takes her explosive projectile gun, aims at Bill, and blows him into small pieces. The trolley stops. "Thanks," say the police officers. "You did the right thing. So good that we prevented torture." "My pleasure," says Paolo, while he is picking bloody pieces of Bill's flesh and bones from his jacket. "I'm always happy to uphold human rights and human dignity."

This elaborate example shows quite clearly that the whole idea that torture is worse than death or necessarily violates human dignity while at the same time self-defensive killing does not is untenable. Don't get me wrong: of course nearly all instances of torture in our actual world violate human rights and human dignity. But so do nearly all instances of killing (I use the term "killing" exclusively for homicide in this book). *Self-defensive* torture and *self-defensive* killing, however, as long as the general moral requirements of self-defense are met, do *not* violate human dignity or human rights. Therefore, the habit of many absolutist torture opponents of brandishing the concepts of human rights and human dignity as if they had a monopoly on them is quite inappropriate. The argument I am propounding here is a *rights-based* argument. It is not utilitarian or consequentialist at all. It is based on the *right* to self-defense. Self-defensive torture not only is justified; it is *just*.

2.2 The Argument from the Culpability for Creating a Forced-Choice Situation

I have argued (in section 2.1.1) that the self-defense justification for torture applies to both the Dirty Harry case, that is the child-kidnapping case, and the ticking-bomb case. If in these cases (a certain kind of) torture would be a necessary and proportionate means of defense against the aggressor, that kind of torture would be justified in that situation.

However, some argue that these cases are not cases of *self-defense* at all because the threat is, allegedly, not imminent or because the target of the torture is defenseless or because he is, allegedly, not engaged in an attack anymore (or for some other reasons). However, I have already dealt with the second objection, pointing out that nothing in the self-defense justification requires that the target of the defense not be defenseless himself, and I have also already dealt with the first and third objections.[47] (However, I will return to all of these objections again and in more detail in sections 6.1–3).

In effect, all these criticisms pretty much boil down to claiming that self-defense can only be directed against *attackers* or people *posing an unjust imminent threat* and that the child kidnapper and the ticking-bomb terrorist are *not* attackers or posing an unjust imminent threat. While I have already argued and will argue again below that the child kidnapper and the ticking-bomb terrorist *are* attackers, let us nevertheless assume now, just for the sake of argument, that they are not.

Would such an assumption give the absolutist torture opponent a break? Not really. To be sure, as already stated in the introduction, absolutist torture opponents react with panic to the self-defense justification of torture and try to dismiss it out of hand (some even preposterously deny that it exists in the literature) in order to then quickly move on to some partially consequentialist argument (like the necessity justification), promptly and triumphantly pointing out that on this justification innocents would no longer be safe; and in the light of this shocking result, they rest their case to their own satisfaction.

However, apart from the fact that the necessity justification is much less vulnerable to criticism than absolutist torture opponents make it out to be (as we will see in section 2.3), the possibilities of justifying torture are not exhausted with the two options of the self-defense justification (taken for now as something that can only be invoked against attackers or persons posing an unjust imminent threat), on the one hand, and some version of consequentialism, on the other. There is at least one additional option, namely *the argument from the culpability for creating a forced choice situation.*

The explicit formulation of this argument goes back to Phillip Montague and is in wide use today. Montague has pointed out that, in cases in which one cannot save oneself from the negative consequences of another person's acts in any other way than by diverting or inflicting them on this person, one is justified in doing so. Montague states the following conditions for this:

> (i) individuals X1 . . . Xn are situated so that harm will unavoidably befall some but not all of them; (ii) that they are so situated is the fault of some but not all members of the group; (iii) the nature of the harm is independent of the individuals who are harmed; (iv) Y, who is not necessarily included in X1 . . . Xn is in a position to determine who will be harmed.[48]

The infliction of harm (for example in the form of an attack or in the form of torture) on a certain person, thus, is not legitimized here by a *present* aggression but by the person's culpably causing or having caused the threat of harm. (Montague seems to think that mere responsibility is sufficient, and thus culpability not necessary. He might be correct, but I do not want to commit myself here to such a view. I am committing myself to the view that *culpability* is sufficient for the argument to work.) Thus, this cause can lie in the past. Montague adduces the example of a doctor who wishes for the death of a cardiac patient and therefore swallows the pacemaker the patient needs. The only chance to get the pacemaker quickly enough to save the patient's life is to perform a hasty operation on the doctor, which, however, would be fatal to him. Hence one faces a situation in which either the innocent patient or the malicious doctor has to die. If one has to decide who it is going to be, then, Montague says, one clearly should decide against the person who has culpably brought about this situation. That seems to be a pretty reasonable stance, and I agree with him. The application to the case of the terrorist who has hidden a bomb to kill innocents or to the child kidnapper is obvious.

A still clearer example might be needed at this point, since in some jurisdictions an attacker is simply someone posing an unjust threat; that is just what they mean by "attacker." Thus, Nozick's famous fat man falling from the cliff and threatening to crush the person below him could, it seems, count as an attacker. In my view, however, only *actions* (which, however, can sometimes come in the form of omissions or be partly constituted by omissions) can be attacks. The fat man's fall, however, is not an action (while the attack of a drugged aggressor would be an action). Thus, it would be worthwhile to see whether Montague's account works also for persons who really are merely what one could call Culpable Causes[49] and who are thus neither attackers (in my sense) nor unjust threats.

The ticking-bomb terrorist and the child kidnapper, however, *are* attackers. As I make clearer below, one completes one's action x at the last point where one could have prevented the intended effect from coming about. Thus the terrorist and the kidnapper are engaged in their attack on the child or the persons to be killed in the explosion for as long as they refuse to give the live-saving information. And arguably, although this is much less clear, the malicious doctor also could still *do* something to save the life of his victim: go up to the other surgeons and tell them: "Cut me open and get the pacemaker."

But now consider a clear-cut case where someone definitely is only a culpable cause and not an attacker or unjust threat.

The Slow Guillotine and the Unconscious Villain: Jane has been kidnapped by the serial killer Albert. Everybody knows, thanks to police investigations, that Albert kills his victims by fixating their heads under a slow guillotine. The blade of the guillotine then slowly moves downwards if a male voice says, "Start," and it stops (and can then not be restarted unless the whole device is taken apart) if the same voice that said, "Start," says, "Stop." Jane's head is shut into the device, but before Albert can say, "Start," he slips in the bathroom and dies. The landlord, Radovan, who had no idea about Albert's criminal undertakings, later enters the room with his own key for certain reasons. He finds Jane, sits down in front of her, cheers up, lights a cigarette and says, "Great, I always wanted to do that: START!" "Say stop," Jane begs. Radovan, to savor the moment, puts his head directly above hers, looks her in the eyes and says grinning, "No." Jane, whose arms are free and who is a martial artist, manages to knock Radovan unconscious with a karate chop. There is no chance of Radovan's waking up before the guillotine kills Jane. Jane, desperate, uses Radovan as a shield against the slowly approaching blade of the guillotine. The blade kills Radovan, but then comes to a halt. Jane is saved.

Radovan is no longer either an unjust threat (removing him from the scene would not save Jane, while removing the falling fat man from the scene would save the man beneath him), or an attacker, since, being unconscious and staying unconscious for too long, he can no longer *act* in a way that would save Jane. Thus, he has *already* completed the action that endangers Jane's life. Yet, Jane would clearly be justified in using the unconscious Radovan as a shield (thereby killing him) in order to save her own life from his past unjust and unjustified aggression.

Of course, this is still a case of self-defense, and I think one would be hard pressed to find any court in Germany, the United States, or the UK that would see it differently. The reason is that the relevant statutes are concerned with the perspective of the defender and thus with unlawful *attack*, unlawful physical *force*, or the prevention of *crime*, and not so much with *attackers*, *those who use unlawful force*, or *criminals*. Thus, although Radovan is no longer an (present or imminent) attacker in the last example, Jane still is *under attack*. Thus, the self-defense justification would still apply.

Yet the important lesson of this section is of course that even people who are not attackers or posing an unjust threat can be justly killed (or, for that matter, tortured) if this is a proportionate and necessary means to avert a threat that they themselves have culpably caused, whether one would call this self-defense or not. And if this argument applies even to the last case of Jane and Radovan, as it certainly does, it definitely applies to the cases of the child kidnapper and the ticking-bomb terrorist.

2.3 The Argument from Necessity

So-called defenses of necessity are known in several jurisdictions. Israel's Landau Commission, which claimed that torture might be justified under the defense of necessity, appealed in its assessment to section 22 of the Israeli Penal Law of 1977:

> A person may be exempted from criminal responsibility for an act of omission if he can show that it was done only in order to avoid consequences which could not otherwise be avoided, and which would have inflicted grievous harm or injury to his person, honour or property or to the person or honour of others whom he was bound to protect or to property placed in his charge, provided that he did no more than was reasonably necessary for that purpose and the harm caused by him was not disproportionate to the harm avoided.[50]

The U.S. Model Penal Code, which has informed the legislation of several U.S. states, says in section 3.02:

"Justification Generally: Choice of Evils"

(1) Conduct that the actor believes to be necessary to avoid a harm or evil to himself or to another is justifiable, provided that:

    (a) The harm or evil sought to be avoided by such conduct is greater than that sought to be prevented by the law defining the offense charged; and

    (b) neither the Code nor other law defining the offense provides exceptions or defenses dealing with the specific situation involved; and

    (c) a legislative purpose to exclude the justification claimed does not otherwise plainly appear.

(2) When the actor was reckless or negligent in bringing about the situation requiring a choice of evils or in appraising the necessity for his conduct, the justification afforded by this Section is unavailable in a prosecution for any offense for which recklessness or negligence, as the case may be, suffices to establish culpability.[51]

What is the difference between this kind of legal defense and that of self-defense? Miriam Gur-Arye states:

> The justification of necessity rests on the balance between interests of innocent persons. [This is actually not quite correct. Also the interests of noninnocent persons can be involved. Thus, it would be more appropriate to say that the defense of necessity rests on balancing rights violations.] The sacrifice of an innocent person's interests is justified when necessary to save those of another, when that other person's interests have a higher value. Therefore, if necessity is to apply to ticking bomb situations it will justify the use of interrogational force against the *innocent*. Taken to an extreme, necessity might prima facie justify the use of force against a terrorist's child in order to force the terrorist to reveal the information about the location of a bomb he has planted. Even to consequentialists the use of force against the child might seem "morally repugnant. No one should torture innocent children—even when done to produce a sizeable gain in aggregate welfare."[52]

However, Gur-Arye suggests that there might be a way around this:

> To rule out necessity in the case of the terrorist's child, we can introduce a limitation into necessity, similar to that in the German penal code.[53]

What does the German penal code say? Section 34 recognizes necessity as justification:

> Whoever commits an act in order to avert an imminent and otherwise unavoidable danger to the life, limb, liberty, honor, property, or other legal interest of himself or of another does not act unlawfully if, taking into consideration all the conflicting interests, in particular the legal ones, and the degree of danger involved, the interest protected by him significantly outweighs the interest which he harms. This rule applies only if the act is an appropriate means to avert the danger.[54]

An important feature of this formulation lies in the word "appropriate" (*angemessen*). For this term *could*, in theory, be used to prohibit certain means of avoiding the danger. However, precisely which means it would prohibit is open to interpretation. Yuval Ginbar, for example, thinks that he "found in the

German system a DoN [defense of necessity] that, while allowing 'lesser evil' calculations, 'caps' them with absolute prohibitions on acts undermining basic values, torture being one such act."[55] However, this assessment of Ginbar relies on a dubious interpretation[56] of the court decision in the Daschner case, and it does not take into account the influential new Maunz/Dürig commentary on Article 1 of the German Constitution (which states that human dignity shall be inviolable), arguing that the affliction of physical pain on a wrongdoer in a situation like the Daschner case or the ticking-bomb case does not necessarily violate human dignity in the sense of Article 1.[57]

Of course, we cannot go into a debate on German constitutional law here. There is also no need. Here, as in the previous discussion of self-defense, I only provide the legal statutes in different jurisdictions as a starting point for the *moral* discussion. And once we enter into this discussion, we can hardly escape the question *whether it might not indeed sometimes be morally justified to harm innocent bystanders: for example by killing or torturing them.*

Now, absolutist opponents of torture of course rely heavily on the moral "repugnance" of such a stance. Personally, I do not think, as the discussion in section 2.1.2 should have made clear, that torturing innocent bystanders is more repugnant than killing innocent bystanders. And innocent people are being killed on a massive scale in wars, including those some Western liberals regard as justified or even just.

Of course, the idea of torturing an innocent person, in particular an innocent child, surely *is* repugnant, but we should not let our moral judgment be clouded by emotional reactions.[58] That something is repugnant should not be ignored in our moral assessments, but it does not guarantee that the act or act type under scrutiny is necessarily unjustified.

After all, consider this example from Stephen Kershnar:

> Imagine two Bosnian Muslim siblings who are captured by a sadistic but honest Serb army sergeant. The sergeant tells the boy that he can torture his sister by ordering that she be gang-raped and then whipping her himself. The brother can refuse to order and participate in such treatment and the sergeant will honor his choice. However, if he does not order such torture, the sergeant will shoot the sister between her eyes. The brother, knowing that the sergeant is honest even if evil, orders the torture. It seems that the brother can order and participate in the torture without viewing his sister at any time merely as a means.[59]

Indeed, so it seems. Even more, while of course there still is something repugnant about the brother's decision (there would also be something repugnant about the opposite decision), it is anything but clear that he acts *unjustifiably*. This can perhaps be seen better if we provide a less extreme example than that of Kershnar. Consider this variation:

> The sadistic but honest sergeant gives a father of a twelve-year-old boy the option to either waterboard his son for 30 minutes or to have him executed by the sergeant.

In this case, in my view, the father's waterboarding and thus torturing his son for 30 minutes is *clearly* justified, precisely in light of the proportionality considerations already discussed above.[60] The father saves his son's life here. If indeed in this situation he did not choose the first alternative but instead the second (perhaps because he is an absolutist antitorture opponent who would rather sacrifice his son than his dubious principles), then *that* would be repugnant.

Another example of the justified torture of an innocent person is the case where the dictator gives prisoner A the choice of either killing 1 of 10 innocent prisoners or torturing 1 of them for 2 hours or having them all killed by the dictator.

Does my position here commit me to biting the rather daunting bullet of those who argue against the necessity defense of torture, namely, the "possibility of torturing V [the ticking-bomb terrorist] by threatening to torture, or actually torturing, an innocent person he deeply cares for"?[61] First of all, threatening a culpable aggressor with torturing an innocent person is not a harm inflicted on the innocent person himself. Actually torturing an innocent person, however, is. Does the necessity defense allow that?

The answer is: in theory, *but not in practice*. Absolutist torture opponents always claim that torture is quite unreliable. I agree (but I do not agree that it never works or is not a reasonable option under some circumstances). And there is no evidence that would suggest that torturing a person by torturing somebody he deeply cares for is more effective in retrieving the vital information than torturing the first person himself. But then there is no justification for torturing an innocent person.

But didn't I argue above that "even if torture were highly unreliable, this does not even matter"? Well, I argued this in the context of *self-defense*, and explained that

> the so-called "necessity" requirement, which actually is a no-excessive-force requirement, allows you to use even "improbable" means to defend yourself if your (or another innocent person's)

life is threatened by a culpable aggressor. And that is exactly how
it should be. Even if it were an empirically well-proven and commonly well-known fact that stopping a serial murderer and rapist
by ramming a sharp pencil deep into his ear only works one out
of 10,000 times, the victim of a rapist would still be well within
her rights to ram a sharp pencil deep into the rapist's ear if that is
the only option remaining that has any chance of success.[62]

Into the rapist's ear, not into the ear of the rapist's daughter! While in an
attempt to avert a danger you are allowed, if you have run out of options, to
inflict harms upon an *aggressor* that are quite improbable means of averting
the danger, as long as they at least have some chance of success, you are not
allowed to inflict such harms on an innocent bystander, precisely because she
is innocent.

Here an absolutist opponent of torture might be tempted to object: "The
fact that the *self-defense justification* does not allow that does not show that the
necessity justification does not allow that."

Actually, it does if the two justifications are integral parts of a moral
system that takes rights seriously. To see why this is so, let us take again a
hint from law. Both US laws and German laws take rights quite seriously.
The United States has a Bill of Rights, and Germany has its Basic Law, which
of course also contains a list of rights. Rights are treated in these systems as
"trumps," which cannot be sacrificed only because this would slightly increase
"social utility" and make some people happier. If the overall happiness or
satisfaction (or whatever unit of measurement utilitarians might wish to use)
in the world would increase in the long run by publicly torturing a certain
innocent individual because the happiness produced by the glee of the public
would outweigh the suffering of the innocent individual, this would not be
allowed on the basis of a law that takes rights seriously.

A *utilitarian* "necessity" or lesser-evil exemption is *not* compatible with
taking rights seriously, that is, with taking rights as "trumps."[63] Rights (or
"legal interests" or "protected interests" in the German necessity article), being
trumps, have a lot of weight in legal considerations within jurisdictions that
take rights seriously, and they can only be outweighed by necessity considerations if, as section 34 of the German penal code says, the interest that is
protected by an act undertaken out of necessity considerations *significantly*
outweighs the interests which he harms. (The fact that section 34 of the German penal code explicitly uses the qualifier "significantly" makes it in my
view superior to section 3.02 of the U.S. Model Penal Code, which sounds
unduly utilitarian.)

Thus, what we are dealing with here is not some utilitarian calculus, but *threshold deontology*:

> A threshold deontologist holds that deontological norms govern up to a point despite adverse consequences; but when the consequences become so dire that they cross the stipulated threshold, consequentialism takes over.[64]

Of course, one now has to "haggle over the price," that is, determine where exactly the threshold is; and one can have reasonable disagreement about this. It is a question of judgment, and it cannot really be decided in advance, nor can any explicit rule be given that could not, in the light of the actual situation of necessity, be overturned later. Nevertheless, case law can of course set some examples of what counts as acceptable. And German case law makes it clear that the protected interests of the innocent require a very high threshold indeed. In fact, while the German self-defense statute does not explicitly distinguish between attacks by culpable aggressors and attacks by innocent aggressors, case law actually does. The defender is much more limited in his defensive measures against innocent aggressors or threats. Obviously, then, the limitations will be even higher—much higher—in the case of innocent *bystanders*, which is the case the necessity defense is primarily designed to deal with.

This, I submit, holds equally for moral reasoning. The necessity justification of torture that I defend and endorse in this section is a *threshold deontological* justification that takes rights seriously (without absolutizing them) and is *incompatible* with utilitarianism. The necessity justification, as defended here, is a very plausible principle—a view obviously shared by the law in many Western jurisdictions. And on my interpretation it does rule out in practice (although not in principle) torturing the child of a ticking-bomb terrorist in order to make him give up the information sought, for example. The reason is simply that there is not enough evidence that would suggest that this works better than torturing the terrorist himself (and only him), and even if there were, the protection of the rights of innocents ranks very high in the threshold deontological account.

However, it does not rule out the torture of innocents in the quite realistic *Sophie's Choice*-circumstances above (as in Kershnar's example, the example of the father waterboarding his son to save his son's life, and the example of the ten prisoners)—and that they unfortunately *are* quite realistic (as even absolutist torture opponents sometimes grudgingly concede[65]), we know from historical experience, both recent and not so recent. However, since in at least some of these examples torture is *clearly* justified (as I think most people and most Western jurisdictions would agree), the fact that the necessity justification of torture allows the torture of innocent people in these examples speaks *for* the necessity justification, not against it. The fact, on the other hand, that absolutist torture opponents would require the father in the waterboarding example above to let his son be murdered by the sadistic sergeant rather than waterboard him himself for half an hour shows that antitorture absolutism is an inhumane and morally repugnant position.[66]

2.4 Reminder: The Justification of Torture Is Compatible with Rights Absolutism

I am a threshold deontologist—rights are trumps, but they are not absolute. But let me remind the reader that torture is quite compatible with rights *absolutism*. Instead of being an absolutist about the right not to be tortured, one would just have to be an absolutist about the right of self-defense. And the absoluteness of the latter right is much more plausible than the absoluteness of the former right. It is, for reasons already adduced at length, more plausible that an innocent child or people acting on its behalf have a right to save it from torture or death at the hands of a culpable aggressor by torturing that aggressor than that this culpable aggressor has the right not to be tortured, let alone to be shielded from torture.

I point this out because some people believe that deontological absolutism[67] must automatically come with a prohibition on torture. These people are wrong. Deontological absolutism can very well take a form that comes with an absolute prohibition of any interference in self-defense against unjustified aggressors—and thus with the permission of self-defensive torture.

2.5 The Utilitarian Argument

I am not a utilitarian (since I am a threshold deontologist), but for the sake of argument I will discuss utilitarianism anyway. That might seem to be somewhat superfluous, for what could be clearer than that utilitarian considerations can justify torture in a child-kidnapping or ticking-bomb case?

Of course, utilitarianism comes in different versions. I will deal here only with classic act utilitarianism. Walter Sinnott-Armstrong describes the position concisely:

> Classic utilitarians held hedonistic act consequentialism. *Act consequentialism* is the claim that an act is morally right if and only

if that act maximizes the good, that is, if and only if the total amount of good for all minus the total amount of bad for all is greater than this net amount for any incompatible act available to the agent on that occasion. . . . *Hedonism* then claims that pleasure is the only intrinsic good and that pain is the only intrinsic bad. Together these claims imply that an act is morally right if and only if that act causes "the greatest happiness for the greatest number," as the common slogan says.[68]

It seems absurd to claim that an act of torture that is the mildest means available in a given situation to prevent the explosion of a nuclear bomb in a big city would not, barring certain very exceptional circumstances, maximize human happiness. Whether it is the mildest means available, by the way, does not depend on whether the interrogators reasonably *believe* at the time they start the torture that it is the mildest means available or whether they reasonably believe that it is a promising means at all. The question is *whether in fact* this course of action contributes more to the maximization of happiness than any other available act would have done under the circumstances. If it is a fact—and nothing whatsoever excludes the possibility of its being a fact—then the act of torture *is* right or justified.

The same holds for the torture of a child kidnapper. If this torture was the mildest means to make the kidnapper disclose the location of the child, does not impose too terrible a suffering on the kidnapper, saves the child, thereby prevents the kidnapper from becoming a murderer (and going to jail for much longer), thereby making both the parents of the kidnapped child and the parents of the murderer much happier than they otherwise would have been, and so on, then all seem to be much better off than they would have been without the torture.[69] Again, this is an entirely realistic case, and any speculations about what people in that situation could or could not have known are, from the utilitarian perspective under discussion, entirely irrelevant to whether this act was justified under the conditions or not. The question is simply whether the act *actually* (not foreseeably) maximized happiness. Thus, torture is justified in such an entirely realistic case.

This is pretty straightforward, and I am certainly not picking out a version of consequentialism or utilitarianism that no absolutist opponent of torture would criticize. For example, Richard Matthews states that

there are only two variants present in the torture debate: act and rule utilitarianism. Act utilitarianism is the classical version of utilitarianism first developed by Jeremy Bentham. . . . Utilitarians assert that as moral beings we are obligated to maximize happiness and minimize suffering. Those actions are good that maximize the happiness of the greatest number of beings possible and that minimize suffering.[70]

However, Matthews' criticism of act utilitarianism misses the mark. Yes, Bentham states that before torturing someone we "must have good proof that the prisoner is able to do what the torture requires," but this is given as advice as to the circumstances under which "[t]orture might be made use of with advantage"[71]; it is given as advice as to how we should proceed in order to *increase the likelihood* of our actions being right; it is not, however, a necessary *condition* of our action's being right. Whether our actions are right or not, according to Bentham, depends on whether they *actually* maximize happiness.

As Sinnott-Armstrong notes, also with regard to Bentham:

> most consequentialists claim that overall utility is the *criterion* or *standard* of what is morally right or morally ought to be done. Their theories are intended to spell out the necessary and sufficient conditions for an act to be morally right, regardless of whether the agent can tell in advance whether those conditions are met.[72]

Thus, Matthews' claim that utilitarians "are committed to the belief that, if torture is to be justifiable, there must be a reasonable chance that it is effective" is wrong. Equally misguided in the context of a critique of the utilitarian justification of torture are all of Matthews' other claims (and he makes many of them) about the epistemic limitations of interrogators (he is also, in addition, wrong in claiming that those limitations are inevitable; see section 6.8). Whether they are so limited or not is irrelevant. Matthews simply misunderstands Bentham's act utilitarianism (and we will see later that he also misunderstands Kantianism).[73]

Does Matthews have any further argument for why torture should be absolutely prohibited in the two examples above? Well, one might say that he does not really try to show that. Rather:

> At stake here is the moral justification of state torture. Institutional behaviour is quite different from individual action and raises different moral considerations. . . . I argue that state torture must be institutional and that institutionalized torture cannot be happiness-maximizing.[74]

Of course, this leaves open the possibility that *private* torture can be happiness maximizing. Thus, his allegedly utilitarian arguments against *state* torture are not yet an argument against torture as such. Be that as it may, Matthews does not *argue* that state torture must be institutional so much as merely claim it again and again throughout his book.

His claim is difficult to evaluate since he (who complains that *others* use "unclear" or "vague" or "nonsense" terms—I will return to this below)[75] does not really inform the reader as to what "state torture" and "institutionalized" are precisely supposed to mean.

On my own account, torture is *state torture* if it is committed by a public official or a person acting in an official capacity *and* when such an act of torture is (or would foreseeably be) tolerated and hence not punished by the state even if the state is (or were) aware of this act.

I will not attempt to give a positive definition of what "institutionalization" means; instead, I want to distinguish institutionalization from mere legalization by way of examples. An example of an institutionalized practice is the request and the issuance of an arrest warrant. There are certain precisely regulated bureaucratic procedures that have to be followed by the police to request an arrest warrant and by the judge to issue it. In contrast, nose scratching by public officials, though legal in the United States, the UK, and Germany, is *not* an institutionalized state practice. It would, obviously, be downright ridiculous to claim that Germany or Great Britain had "institutionalized" nose scratching in their police forces merely because German or British police officers can scratch their noses with impunity, even *legally*.

The same holds for the practice of stabbing a pencil in a person's eye. A police officer can do this legally in the United States, the UK, and Germany if it is a necessary and proportionate defense against an attack—as it might well be under certain circumstances, including in circumstances where the police officer acts in official capacity (for example, when he tries to arrest a criminal, but the criminal surprisingly and viciously attacks). Yet, again, it would be ridiculous to say that in the United States, the UK, or Germany "state eye stabbing" is an institutionalized practice.

In the same vein, torture is not institutionalized merely by virtue of being legal or tolerated in the extremely rare cases of self-defensive torture. However, the practice of torture *is* institutionalized in a state if this state has bureaucratized it with a system of torture warrants, for example, or torture orders from above, torture training, torture camps, special torture squads, or "applied" torture research. I am adamantly against the institutionalization of torture. I am not against the legalization of torture.

With these terminological clarifications, let us get back to Matthews. If he uses the terms "state torture" and "institutionalization" the way I do, then his claim "that state torture must be institutional" or that it "is impossible to torture well [that means *effectively*, I suppose] if torture is made the exception"[76] is wrong, as the Mook case below and the Gachelin case show.[77] Of course, Matthews could be using "state torture" in such a way that it is *defined* as institutionalized torture, but then his claim is as trivial as pointing out that bachelors cannot be married, and it certainly accomplishes nothing for his critique of a utilitarian justification of torture.

The—rather obvious—fact is that even if the institutionalization of torture would have very bad consequences (and I agree that it would), this in no way shows that isolated acts of torture cannot be justified by utilitarianism.[78] I will have more to say about this in the next section that will confirm the result reached here.

Before moving on, however, let us have a look at some further remarks Matthews makes in the context of utilitarianism. Like his remarks on epistemic limitations, these further remarks also miss the point of utilitarianism. That is, even if they were correct, they would still not show that torture cannot be justified in the context of a utilitarian framework and of realistic assumptions, and hence they are irrelevant for the issue under discussion. Besides, they are *not* correct.

Thus, he claims, for example, that "torture is essentially terroristic and coercive" and that since "torture attacks identity, it will inevitably have a gender component, and where race is a relevant concern, torture will ineluctably assault that as well."[79] Yet, first of all, torture is not essentially coercive. Torture, for example, that is administered for pure sadistic or for pure punitive reasons needs not attempt to coerce the tortured person into anything. Interrogational torture, of course, does attempt to do so. Does that make interrogational torture bad or impermissible? Of course not. Death threats, for example, are also coercive, but they are often quite permissible. A woman, for instance, who manages to push the rapist off her and to reach her gun, aims it at him and threatens: "If you come a step closer, I will shoot you," also acts coercively. She also, however, acts permissibly. Does Matthews want to deny that?

In that context, let me make good on my promise to show that Matthews—who constantly complains in his book that those authors who think that torture can be permissible under certain circumstances don't understand this or don't realize that—obviously misunderstands, for his part, both utilitarianism *and* Kantianism. To wit, he says things like these:

> Since such [that is, political] torture is inevitably nonconsensual, torture is essentially coercive. As everyone will concede, this is absolutely incompatible with respect both for autonomy and for dignity.[80]

Or elsewhere:

> Everyone will concede that political suspects are not tortured con-
> sensually. Hence anyone in the Kantian tradition will already be
> opposed to torture on this ground alone.[81]

Actually, no reasonable person, Kant included, will concede that all non-
consensual and coercive actions are unjustifiable. Otherwise one would have to
concede that the woman in the last example, who threatens the rapist, violates
his dignity. What is she supposed to do in Matthew's opinion? Ask the rapist for
consent? "My dear fellow, do you consent to my threatening you with deadly
force in order to keep you from raping me?" What if he does not consent?
Is she then not allowed to threaten him? And what about killing or injuring
in self-defense? Does one have to ask the attacker for consent before one uses
defensive force? Kant would certainly reject such suggestions. He was definitely
not against all forms of coercion. After all, he was an absolutely staunch sup-
porter of the right of self-defense, and he supported the imprisonment of
convicts (although convicts normally do not consent to being imprisoned) as
well as the castration of rapists[82] (and one will also not find many rapists who
would consent to their being castrated). In short, Matthews' remarks on Kant's
normative philosophy are profoundly mistaken.

As regards Matthews' claims that "torture attacks identity, it will inevitably have a gender component, and where race is a relevant concern, torture
will ineluctably assault that as well"—they are all wrong. Of course, the first
claim is difficult to assess, for Matthews fails to explain what "identity" is
precisely supposed to mean (again he is more lenient toward his own vagueness than toward that of others). However, in any of the usual uses of the
term "identity" it is clearly not correct that torture necessarily attacks it. And
why the torture of a white male child kidnapper by white male police officers
should "inevitably" have a gender or race component remains Matthew's secret.
Nothing, by the way, will necessarily change by varying the race of either the
police officers or the child kidnapper. To suppose otherwise—is *that* not racist?

Let me finally come to Matthews' claim that torture is necessarily "terroristic." Well, in a *certain* sense of "terroristic" it certainly is, but so is—or
can be—the death threat against the rapist in the above example. When a
S.W.A.T team breaks into the house of a dangerous and armed criminal in a
surprise attack, loudly shouting, coming in with massive force, body armor,
and heavily armed, they also want to terrorize the target in order to undermine
his capability to offer coolly calculated resistance, but so what? Surely no one
will suggest that they send the criminal a card first in order to announce their

imminent arrival.

In another sense of terroristic, the one Matthews actually refers to, namely in Henry Shue's sense, torture is definitely not necessarily terroristic. Matthews quotes Shue saying:

> *Terroristic torture* is a pure case–the purest possible case–of the violation of the Kantian principle that no person may be used only as a means. The victim is simply a site at which great pain occurs so that others may know about it and be frightened by the prospect.[83]

Shue also says:

> The degree of need for assaults upon the defenseless initially appears to be quite different in the case of torture for the purpose of extracting information, which we may call *interrogational torture*.[84]

Matthews does not like Shue's distinction between terroristic torture and interrogational torture. Instead, he wants to argue

> that a pure concept of interrogational torture is incoherent and that the distinction between interrogational and terroristic torture cannot be maintained in principle. Rather, torture is, as Enrique Bustos (1990, 143–44) describes it, essentially a strategy of domination used to enhance control in the face of a crisis. . . . [T]he structure of torture is such that, by nature and design, it must disorient and create fear and terror in the mind of the given victim.[85]

Matthews misconceives or misrepresents Shue's concepts of terroristic as opposed to merely interrogational torture. Shue knows that interrogational torture (and certain other kinds of entirely permissible behavior, like certain threats or the shock and awe techniques of S.W.A.T teams) aim at terrorizing the target *in a certain sense* of "terrorizing." But Shue has defined "terroristic torture" as torture that uses the torture victim *so that others* may know about it and be frightened by the prospect. In this sense of the word, interrogational torture is certainly not necessarily terroristic. Police officers torturing a child kidnapper need not aim at intimidating others at all.

Admittedly, so far I have not yet shown that the various remarks of Matthews I just criticized are irrelevant for the issue of utilitarianism. I have only shown that they are wrong. So let me return to the issue of irrelevance. The irrelevance shows in the fact that a utilitarian could *accept* that "torture is essentially terroristic and coercive," "will inevitably have a gender component" and will, "where race is a relevant concern . . . ineluctably assault that as well" and *still* ask: "So what?" The reason is that a utilitarian cares about the maximization of human happiness. He will agree that being tortured reduces the happiness of the tortured person (whether it is "terroristic" or "coercive" or not). However, he will also point out that it could under certain circumstances actually be better if race or gender issues play a role, namely in cases where this leads to the torturer's enjoying the torture more and being happier. And he will ask how, especially in the case of the nuclear ticking-bomb example, the *one-off* torture of *one* ticking-bomb terrorist, even if such torture should be terroristic, coercive, racist and sexist, could, in terms of happiness maximization, possibly outweigh the survival of thousands, perhaps millions of people. That is certainly a very good question.

However, all that Matthews ultimately has to offer by way of an answer is this:

> The harms of torture are complex and extend long into the future life of the victim. Moreover, the resulting damage is widespread, affecting relatives and close friends of the victim as well as entire communities. It is a myth to think that harms of torture are suffered by the victim alone.[86]

That torture necessarily affects "entire communities" is wrong (unless there is a "community" of child kidnappers). However, it is entirely correct that the harms of torture are not suffered by the one tortured ticking-bomb terrorist alone (barring special circumstances). On the other hand, it is clearly also a myth that the harms of thousands or millions of people being blown up by a nuclear bomb are suffered by those thousands or millions of people alone. Not only ticking-bomb terrorists have friends and relatives. You do the math.

Defusing the Ticking-Social-Bomb Argument

Against Consequentialist Attempts to Undermine the Right to Self-defensive Torture

Human beings have a right to self-defensive torture against culpable aggressors. As we have seen, this is hardly surprising: since people even have a right to *kill* a culpable aggressor if under the circumstances this is a proportionate and necessary means of self-defense against an imminent threat, and since most forms of torture are not as bad as killing, people must also have a right to torture a culpable aggressor if this is under the circumstances a proportionate and necessary means of self-defense against an imminent threat.

However, we sometimes feel justified in violating the right of a person because the stakes are so very high. If we could save humanity only by killing one innocent person, thus violating her rights, we might well feel justified in doing so. In the same vein, the proponents of what I call *the ticking-social-bomb* argument argue that under certain circumstances it is justifiable to violate people's rights to self-defense (which also includes the defense of others) against a culpable aggressor by shielding this aggressor from torture (thus aiding and abetting him in his aggression), even if under the circumstances torture would have been a proportionate and necessary means of self-defense against the imminent threat posed by the aggressor. They say that this severe rights violation is justifiable in case such an act of self-defensive torture would have terrible social consequences. And they claim that acts of torture *always* have such consequences: *any* act of torture, according to them, leads to the *institutionalization* of torture, to a pandemic of torture, to a *social explosion of torture*, as it were.

This is the ticking-social-bomb argument. I will argue here that it is sheer fantasy and that we should not cede our right to self-defensive torture based on unrealistic consequentialist concoctions.

Many readers, especially those already familiar with the philosophical debate about torture, might rub their eyes in disbelief after these introductory paragraphs. After all, the structure and the style of this argument are quite familiar; however, the conclusion is different from what one might be accustomed to.

What happened? Well, I have mimicked—indeed mocked—the way quite a few absolutist opponents of torture deal with the so-called ticking-bomb argument (not to be confused with what I call the ticking-social-bomb argument): they like to pose as the defenders of human rights or of deontological constraints against evil or deluded consequentialists who are intent on undermining those absolute rights and constraints by appealing to allegedly utterly unrealistic scenarios. Yet, unfortunately for these absolutist torture opponents, it is rather easy to turn the tables on them, along the lines of the introductory paragraphs. This is precisely what I will do here.

No Deontological Foundation for an Absolute Moral Prohibition of Torture

Let me first note that practically all recent publications directed against the ticking-bomb argument do not provide *any* plausible deontological *argument* for the claim that there is an absolute right (as least as far as the real world is concerned) not to be tortured. For a plausible argument it is not sufficient to simply brandish the concepts of "human dignity" or of "ends in themselves" or "human rights"; rather it would have to show why torture in self-defense should be absolutely prohibited or violate human rights or human dignity even while *killing* in self-defense is not or does not. This is obviously a very difficult question, and in their desperation some absolutist opponents have resorted to insisting that all forms of torture are worse than death. Well, they are not, as we have seen,[1] and as a moment's reflection can easily show. Would you prefer death to 30 minutes of "waterboarding"? Or even a whole day of waterboarding?

The failure of several attempted deontological arguments—they fail because they all beg the question or make clearly mistaken empirical assumptions—is extensively discussed throughout this book, in particular in section 6. Nonetheless, let me here provide a particularly prominent example for my claim that recent critics of the ticking-bomb argument do not have much to offer by way of providing arguments for their deontological claims.

I take Henry Shue as my example. Shue has written an article on torture that is regularly referred to in the literature as "seminal" or "classic," and with good reason.[2] In that article he claimed that single acts of torture can be morally justified under extreme conditions. He has since rescinded this position and become an absolutist opponent of torture. However, in that older article he at least developed a deontological *argument* for why torture *might* always be impermissible even if killing is sometimes justified. I am critical of this argument;[3] it is clearly wrong, and Shue does not adhere to it anymore. But instead of providing a new *argument*, he now just begins his article "Torture in Dreamland"—a favorite among absolutist opponents of torture—with the *apodictic statement*: "Torture is wrong."[4] This short statement comes with a footnote that bears the whole argumentative burden: "David Sussman provides a powerful explanation of why torture is wrong in his article in this volume."[5] Yet Sussman not only provides no powerful explanation of why torture is wrong; he provides no explanation *at all*, nor does he claim to do so. Instead, he offers as conclusion merely: "If life calls for a special kind of respect or concern from us, then torture, insofar as it aims to transform life into a kind of anti-life, must be morally offensive in a way that is different from and perhaps greater than even killing."[6] Well, perhaps not.[7] But however that may be: *even if* torture were morally *more* offensive than killing—by which Sussman only means, as is clear from an important earlier article of his, that torture "bears an especially high burden of justification, greater in degree and different in kind from even that of killing"[8]—this would not show that it is always wrong (and Sussman explicitly says that he does "not here contend that torture is categorically wrong").[9] After all, killing someone is morally more offensive than breaking someone's finger, but that obviously does not show that it is always wrong to kill someone. It would suggest this, at best, if breaking someone's finger were always morally wrong—but it isn't. Killing someone is not always morally wrong, either. Therefore, the fact, if it were a fact, that torture is always morally more offensive than killing could not show, or even as much as suggest, that torture is always morally wrong.

In addition, Shue claims in his most recent article on torture (and other issues), again apodictically: "Clearly torture is morally wrong—no one seriously suggests otherwise."[10] Either Shue makes an entirely idiosyncratic use of the term "morally wrong," or else he ignores very important parts of the current debate—strangely enough for someone who vigorously takes part in it. Authors like, for example (completely aside those who have not published in English), Winfried Brugger, Stephen Kershnar, Fritz Allhof, Seumas Miller, Francesco Belvisi, Mirko Bargaric, Julie Clarke, Jeff McMahan, and me definitely do seriously suggest otherwise.

Thus, apart from dogmatic statements and an imagined consensus even a distinguished thinker like Shue has nothing really to offer on the deontological front against self-defensive torture. I think that this is quite revealing.

The Dreamy Criticism of the Ticking-bomb Argument

Henry Shue thinks that the ticking-bomb argument is unrealistic since it allegedly works with certain "idealizations" and "abstractions." We will come back
to his complaints in section 6.2, where we will also consider the "idealization"
arguments provided by some other authors. In this section, however, we will
focus on the "idealization" Shue detests most, and we also will deal with his
abstraction argument.

The supposed "idealization" Shue detests most is that of the rare, isolated
case:

> Once the original "right man" becomes too hysterical to provide
> coherent information, the torturers do not simply move on to, as it
> were, the second-best "right man." And the torturers do not, operat-
> ing on the principle that practice makes perfect, circulate from, say,
> Guantanamo to Bagram to Abu Ghraib to Romania to Poland.[11]

Shue, in contrast, proclaims that the ticking-bomb hypotheticals

> are not simply imaginary but unrealistic, like an imaginary alcoholic
> who drinks two beers only a night. There are former alcoholics, who
> do not drink at all, and active alcoholics. To think that there may
> be rare alcoholics who drink moderately is to fail to understand
> alcoholism. Similarly, history does not present us with a government
> that used to torture selectively and judiciously.[12]

The alcoholism analogy is representative of the ticking-social-bomb argument: if an alcoholic has one drink, he will have many. Similarly, if just one
act of torture is allowed to happen, many will follow—torture will "metastasize
throughout the body politic."[13] A single act of torture suffices to ignite the
fuse that will lead to the social explosion of torture.

Of course, it is Shue who fails to understand alcoholism—as much as
he fails to understand torture. He does not have any evidence for his claims.
While officially he stresses how important it is that "one immerses oneself in
the empirical details,"[14] it seems that he does not actually review the empirical
facts. True, in cheesy Hollywood soap operas and melodramas an alcoholic
cannot have only two beers a night. In reality, however, she can[15]—a fact Shue
could have easily discovered if he had checked reality instead of taking urban
legend at face value. Thus, one has to turn Shue's example upside-down: claiming that there cannot be rare, isolated cases of torture is like claiming that an
alcoholic cannot have only two beers a night. It confuses fact and fiction. It
is torture opposition in dreamland.

Shue seems to have a second argument, though, which he offers under the heading of "abstraction" instead of "idealization." Unfortunately, it is not quite easy to decipher what exactly the argument is supposed to be—Shue certainly is not particularly clear about it. However, let us take a look at the decisive passages:

> [I]t is simply dreamy to think that all of a sudden we are simply going to stumble upon someone who happens to have the skills to make a man who planted a ticking bomb reverse the direction of his life and assist us in defusing his bomb. But this is very bad news for my attempt in 1978 . . . to allow the exceptional case. Our . . . problem is abstraction: we have abstracted from the social basis—the institutional context—necessary for the practice of torture. For torture is a practice. Practitioners who do not practice will not be very good at what they do. . . . Either "torturers" are just thugs who have no clue what they are doing, in which case we need not allow for exceptional cases in which they rapidly and effectively extract invaluable catastrophe-preventing information, or some can have genuine expertise. . . . If we want it ready, we need to maintain, even nourish, the organizations and networks in which the expertise resides.[16]

This is an argument against torture based not on the bad *consequences* of acts of torture, but on the *preconditions* of successful acts of interrogational torture and the consequences of the *institutionalization* of torture. The argument seems to go like this:[17]

(1) In order to torture someone in a way that will actually retrieve the vital information, the torturer has to be skilled and experienced.

(2) Skilled and experienced torturers are only available if torture is *institutionalized*.

(3) Torture by unskilled and inexperienced torturers is always unjustified.

(4) However, institutionalizing torture has very bad consequences; it will mean that torture will metastasize instead of being limited to one-off cases of torture only.

Conclusion: Torture is never justified (one should never torture).

If this is not Shue's argument, I admit that I do not quite know what it is (and, again, the onus to make his argument clear is on Shue, not on others). Anyway, what should we make of this argument as stated here?

First of all, let me make clear that I whole-heartedly agree with premise (4). *Institutionalizing* torture—which is different from its mere legalization[18]— for example through "torture warrants," the training of torturers, the maintenance of torture camps, the production of torture instruments, and so on, is a very bad idea indeed. I absolutely reject the institutionalization of torture.

However, while I accept premise (4), I reject the first three premises. They are all wrong.

As regards premise (1), it is simply not true that in order to torture someone in a way that will actually retrieve the vital information, the torturer has to be skilled and experienced. In the famous German Daschner case, the mere *threat* of torture (and some think that threatening torture *is* torture) sufficed to make the child kidnapper, Magnus Gäfgen, disclose the location of the child (who, however, had already been murdered by Gäfgen—but that does not speak against the effectiveness of torture for retrieving the *truth* in some cases). He wanted to avoid *pain*. Pain is a very strong motivator. Even if he had withstood the threat of pain, the actual *infliction* of pain might very well have changed his mind. And it is simply not that difficult to inflict pain. It does not require long training and experience. To be sure, a skilled and experienced torturer will be more efficient in some cases, but in other cases he might not retrieve the information any quicker than an untrained torturer, and even if he did, the untrained torturer might still be effective enough to avert the danger in time. But we do not have to speculate: the eight-year-old Denis Mook was kidnapped in Bremen, Germany, in 1988. After the ransom payment, the kidnapper was arrested. He refused to reveal the location of the child. The police then beat him until, finally, he did reveal the child's location. The police retrieved the child alive from a wooden box (90x50x40 centimeters) in which the child had been caged for 13 days and 13 nights (a treatment that certainly amounts to torture, in this case the torture of an innocent child, and not of a culpable kidnapper). The child was alive and in relatively good health.[19] Thus, if we follow Shue's advice and immerse ourselves in the empirical details, we discover what he fails to see—for self-defensive torture to be effective, you do not need torture *experts*. (Besides, in spite of this act of torture, Germany has still not reintroduced a widespread use of torture more than 20 years later—as Amnesty International will confirm. This is further proof that Shue's claim that there cannot be isolated cases of torture is "dreamy," to use his word of choice.)

Premise (2) is also wrong. Even *if* it were correct that only a torture bureaucracy could produce torture experts (and it is not true, but I will not argue this point here), this still would not mean that you have to institutionalize torture, that is, that you have to create or to maintain a torture bureaucracy, in order to have access to torture experts. It is enough that there once *was* a torture bureaucracy somewhere in the not too distant past. This is the case, for example, in Argentina and Chile. Thus, if they faced a Daschner or Mook case (or a ticking-bomb case), they would have access to trained torturers without having to rely on the *existence* (now) of a torture bureaucracy, and there would be no metastatic effects involved.

That premise (3) is wrong already follows from the falsity of premise (1). However, it is worthwhile to note just *how* wrong premise (3) is. The idea behind the premise is of course that interrogational torture has to be likely to succeed in order to be justifiable. Sometimes Shue even sounds as though he thinks that torture actually has to succeed to be justified. That it does succeed is one of the "idealizations" Shue deplores.[20] However, interrogational torture does indeed succeed sometimes, as we just saw. Pointing out this fact is not idealistic, but realistic, while denying it is unrealistic. Moreover, it is not true that self-defense (self-defensive torture is no exception) has to be successful in order to be justified. If somebody tries to fend off a rapist with mace and fails, the use of the mace against the rapist was still justified. Might does not make right, and helplessness does not make wrong. Still further, there does not even have to be a *likelihood* of success in all cases. Indeed, success may be highly unlikely. To again recycle an example from above: "Even if it were an empirically well-proven and commonly well-known fact that stopping a serial murderer and rapist by ramming a sharp pencil deep into his ear only works one out of 10,000 times, the victim of a rapist would still be well within her rights to ram a sharp pencil deep into the rapist's ear if that is the only option remaining that has any chance of success."[21] There is simply no reason why the victim of an aggressor or the people who come to help the victim should forego their last hope only in order to make sure that the aggressor is not inconvenienced by defensive measures that in all likelihood will not stop him anyway. They are allowed to try to stop him with improbable means if they run out of probable ones.

"Hard Cases Make Bad Law": So Why Oppose Self-defensive Torture?

The attempt on the part of Shue and others to justify violations of our right to self-defensive torture with consequentialist arguments fails. Of course, Shue and others do not want to couch what they are doing in terms of a program for the consequentialist justification of rights violations. They want to pass that buck to the ticking-bomb theorist (or, in my case, the Dirty Harry theorist; while I think the ticking-bomb scenario is realistic, I do not believe that it has ever actually happened). However, that does not work.

Consider the fact that already in his original article on torture—where he still conceded the moral permissibility of torture in certain circumstances—Shue vehemently opposed the legalization of torture. "Hard cases make bad law" was his slogan, and still is.[22] However, Shue overlooks that this slogan cuts both ways.[23] As Volker Erb has rightly argued, someone who shields an aggressor from necessary and proportionate defensive measures by or on behalf of the victim (for example by making them punishable or by physically interfering with them) actually *aids and abets* the aggressor and violates the rights and the human dignity of the victim.[24] But this is precisely what Shue thinks should happen: the police and the law should keep a would-be torturer from defensively torturing the kidnapper of Mook, thereby providing important support for the latter's aggressive torture of the child. Thus, as far as these cases are concerned, Shue suddenly does want to make exceptions to the general rules that prohibit aiding and abetting child kidnappers, and, more generally, that allow for just self-defense and prohibit any attempt to hinder it. He demands that the victims' and their helpers' right to self-defense (and freedom and life) be violated and that the police and the law become the accomplices of the kidnapper. Whatever happened to "hard cases make bad law"?

The only justification Shue has for demanding that the child kidnapper and torturer be aided and abetted by legally shielding him from defensive torture, however, is his consequentialist ticking-social-bomb argument. Since that argument, as we saw, is spurious, we must reject it and uphold the right to self-defense, including the right to self-defensive torture.

Against the Institutionalization of Torture

Even if torture can be morally justified, this does not mean that it may or should also be institutionalized, as already pointed out. Indeed, I think it definitely should not be.

However, some think that legalizing *and* institutionalizing torture would be a very good idea. In particular, the lawyer Alan Dershowitz has made the infamous suggestion to introduce legal "torture warrants," issued by judges.

> [I]t is important to ask the following question: if torture is being or will be practiced, is it worse to close our eyes to it and tolerate its use by low-level law enforcement officials without accountability, or instead to bring it to the surface by requiring that a warrant of some kind be required as a precondition to the infliction of any type of torture under any circumstances?[1]

And he states:

> My own belief is that a warrant requirement, if properly enforced, would probably reduce the frequency, severity, and duration of torture. I cannot see how it could possibly increase it, since a warrant requirement simply imposes an additional level of prior review. . . . [H]ere are two examples to demonstrate why I think there would be less torture with a warrant requirement than without one. Recall the case of the alleged national security wiretap being placed on the phones of Martin Luther King by the Kennedy administration in the early 1960s. This was in the days when the attorney general could authorize a national security wiretap without a warrant. Today no judge would issue a warrant in a case as flimsy as that one. When Zaccarias Moussaui was detained after trying to learn how to fly an airplane, without wanting to know much about landing it, the government did not even seek a national

security wiretap because its lawyers believed that a judge would
not have granted one.[2]

A few things must be said concerning this argument. First, closing one's
eyes to the practice of torture is not the only alternative to the introduction of torture warrants. Unfortunately, Dershowitz seems to have difficulties
grasping the difference between closing one's eyes to torture and exposing and
condemning it. To wit, he criticizes William Schulz, the executive director
of Amnesty International U.S.A., who asks whether Dershowitz would also
favor brutality warrants and prisoner rape warrants. (Dershowitz answers with
a "heuristic yes," whatever that is supposed to mean.)[3] And he quotes himself
from an earlier text saying: "My question back to Schulz is do you prefer the
current situation in which brutality, testilying and prisoner rape are rampant,
but we close our eyes to these evils?"[4] Who is "we"? Certainly not Schulz or
Amnesty International.[5]

Second, Dershowitz admits that he "certainly cannot prove . . . that a
formal requirement of a judicial warrant as prerequisite to nonlethal torture
would decrease the amount of physical violence directed against suspects."[6] It
seems, however, that Dershowitz should offer something more than his personal
"belief" and two examples to back the quite grave proposal to institutionalize
torture. That he does not do so displays a flippancy about the matter that is
out of place. To be sure, he also adduces John H. Langbein's historical study
of torture,[7] and although he concedes that it "does not definitely answer"
"whether there would be less torture if it were done as part of the legal system," he thinks that it "does provide some suggestive insights."[8] However,
before drawing "suggestive insights" from Langbein's study and from history,
one should get both straight. Dershowitz does not.[9] In fact, Langbein leaves
no doubt that torture was *not* part of the judicial system in England. Not only
"law enforcement officers" but also the courts (and judges) could not warrant
torture. Langbein even states:

> The legal basis, such as it was, for the use of torture in the eighty-
> one known cases appears to have been the notion of sovereign
> immunity, a defensive doctrine that spared the authorities from
> having to supply justification for what they were doing.[10]

The facts, then, are that torture was never part of the English judicial
system (if it was ever legal in England at all), whereas it *was* part of the Con-
tinental legal system. Extensive (not to say epidemic) use was made of torture
on the Continent but not in England. Obviously, these facts suggest insights
quite different from those Dershowitz comes up with.

Moreover, it is also funny that Dershowitz thinks that his two examples *support* his case. What his examples show (if they show anything) is that an attorney general who is *authorized* to wiretap without judicial warrant is more likely to do so than an attorney general who does need a warrant.[11] However, the question to be answered is whether torture would be less likely under a requirement of a judicial warrant than *under a total ban*. To suggest a positive answer to this question by way of an analogy, Dershowitz would have to compare a legal arrangement in which the attorney general is *prohibited* from wiretapping with a legal arrangement where he is authorized to do so if he has a warrant. Dershowitz does not do that. It is he who engages in "tortured reasoning," to use his term,[12] not his critics.

Finally, why shouldn't state agents who do not get a warrant torture anyway? They cannot get a warrant as things are now, and some of them torture anyway. Dershowitz answers that

> the current excuse being offered—we had to do what we did to get information—would no longer be available, since there would be an authorized method of securing information in extraordinary cases by the use of extraordinary means.[13]

First, people who escape detection are not in need of excuses to wriggle out of punishment in the first place. Besides, the excuse *would* be available. It would be: "Since the judge didn't give us the warrant—he did not realize the seriousness of the situation (or there wasn't enough time)—we just had to torture under these circumstances without a warrant in order to get the information and to avoid a great evil."

In short, Dershowitz has not offered the slightest bit of evidence—not even anecdotal—for his bold claim that the introduction of torture warrants would reduce torture or even increase accountability. Yet there is very good evidence to the contrary. Since Dershowitz invited us to draw suggestive insights from history, especially on the basis of Langbein's study, it might be worthwhile to note what Langbein himself has to say:

> Another insight from history is the danger that, once legitimated, torture could develop a constituency with a vested interest in perpetuating it.[14]

And that, to draw the conclusion Dershowitz isn't able to draw, would hardly help to reduce torture or to increase accountability.

I do not, however (as will become clear in section 5), share the idea that the mere legal legitimization of torture already would have the nefarious consequences Langbein points to. Rather, it is the *institutionalization* of torture that worries me (and indeed Langbein's study deals with institutionalized and not merely legalized torture). Yet, in the first part of this book, I have argued that no compelling argument for an absolute moral prohibition of torture can be made—not even for a prohibition in Dirty Harry cases. I have also argued that torture is not worse than death and probably not worse than a decade of incarceration. So since we have institutionalized incarceration, why shouldn't we have institutionalized torture as well?

One very straightforward answer is: because we don't need it. The ticking-bomb case or the Dirty Harry case is a very rare case. In fact, it is safe to assume that all the torture that happened or happens in Abu Ghraib, Afghanistan, and Guantanamo simply has nothing to do with ticking bombs or hostages who are about to die. The same holds for the overwhelming majority of all other cases of torture. Ticking-bomb and Dirty Harry cases are *exceptions*. A self-defense article or an emergency or necessity article along the lines of section 34 of the German penal code could deal with such exceptions, and perhaps not even that is needed. If the stakes are high enough, and no other option is available, police officers or other state agents will probably use torture even if it means facing prosecution if caught (that is, incidentally, what Dershowitz himself claims). Besides, if punished, they might still be allowed the benefit of mitigating circumstances. In any case, *institutionalizing* torture to deal with such circumstances is serious overkill.

Second, that being tortured (or torturing someone) is not necessarily worse than being killed or incarcerated for a long time (or than killing someone or incarcerating her for a long time) does not imply that introducing a *wider practice* of torture is not worse than introducing or maintaining a wider practice of incarceration or killing. Dershowitz, for example, acknowledges:

> Experience has shown that if torture, which has been deemed illegitimate by the civilized world for more than a century, were now to be legitimated—even for limited use in one extraordinary type of situation—such legitimation would constitute an important symbolic setback in the worldwide campaign against human rights abuses.[15]

However, he thinks:

> It does not necessarily follow from this understandable fear of the slippery slope that we can never consider the use of nonlethal infliction of pain, if its use were to be limited by acceptable principles of morality. After all, imprisoning a witness who refuses to testify

after being given immunity is designed to be punitive—that is painful. Such imprisonment can, on occasion, produce more pain and greater risk of death than nonlethal torture.[16]

Indeed, it does not follow that we can never consider the use of non-lethal infliction of pain, but it does follow that *institutionalizing* torture—for example with torture warrants—is a bad idea. In particular, the analogy with the practice of coercing witnesses into testifying through imprisonment is mis-leading. The practice is designed to be punitive, yes, but that is not the same as being designed to be *painful*. Not every aversive treatment causes pain. It is important not to blur the distinctions. Further, the very fact that imprisonment only produces more pain and greater risk of death than nonlethal torture *on occasion* (although I would suppose that nonlethal imprisonment would carry no risk of death) shows that it is not designed to produce pain and death. After all, being released can also on occasion produce more pain and greater risk of death than nonlethal torture. But how is that supposed to support the case for torture or for torture warrants? Thus, by using imprisonment as a method of punishment we are *not* already on the slippery slope.

Even if institutionalizing torture puts us on a slippery slope, couldn't we stop the slide downward? Dershowitz proposes a "principled break":

> For example, if nonlethal torture were legally limited to convicted terrorists who had knowledge of future massive terrorist acts, were given immunity, and still refused to provide the information, there might still be objections to the use of torture, but they would have to go beyond the slippery slope argument.[17]

Actually, one argument that could be made here is that a *convicted* ter-rorist will hardly be a ticking-bomb terrorist, unless, of course, he has set the time fuse on a few months or even years in the future *or* his conviction was made without due process. Giving up due process, however, does not look very much like a "principled break," at least if the principle is supposed to be com-patible with the rule of law. That notwithstanding, it has to be admitted that "massive terrorist acts" must be planned long enough in advance that it would be possible for a convicted terrorist to have knowledge of them. Consequently, torturing him might in extremely rare cases be a means to thwart the attacks.

However, Dershowitz's talk about a "principled break" does not, in fact, address the problem of an "important symbolic setback in the world-wide campaign against human rights abuses" at all. The symbolic setback consists precisely in undermining the *absolute* prohibition on torture and cannot be compensated, probably not even mitigated, by recourse to alleged "principled breaks." (However, I nevertheless doubt that the effects of such a setback will be very severe in the case of the mere legalization as opposed to the full-fledged institutionalization of torture.) Moreover, the whole idea of a "principled break" in connection with "security laws" that cut down on civil liberties and individual rights is rather naïve. (I put "security laws" in quotation marks because cutting down on civil liberties and individual rights hardly increases an individual's security from the state—the political entity, it should be remembered, that has slaughtered more people than any other political entity in history and is certainly more dangerous than any subnational terrorist organization.) Experience shows that measures introduced against putative terrorists in alleged conditions of emergency tend to be doubly extended, namely, beyond the emergency situation and to crimes or offences of lesser seriousness. In the UK, for example, emergency antiterrorist measures, such as limitations on the right to silence, admissibility of confession evidence, and extended periods of prejudicial detention, have infiltrated ordinary criminal law and procedure.[18] After being advertised as targeting terrorists, they can now befall any citizen who gets involved in criminal procedure.

The dangers of the institutionalization of torture discussed here are very real.[19] This notwithstanding, it has to be admitted that there are different scales of institutionalization, and the idea that *any* kind of institutionalization will *inevitably* lead to a metastatic growth of torture in society is a sweeping claim for which there is actually *no* evidence. As Rainer Trapp rightly notes:

> For instance, the legalization of "life-saving final shots" [*finale Rettungsschüsse*, that is, shots by which a police officer, usually a sharp-shooter, intentionally kills a hostage taker, usually with a shot to the head] in constitutional states [*Rechtsstaaten*] did not lead to an increased trigger-happiness of the police even in less grave circumstances or under conditions that did not conform to the narrowly defined limits of police action in defense of others.[20]

In addition, this practice not only is legalized but also is *institutionalized*. Sharp-shooters are specially trained, and in most German federated states where this practice has been legalized, it is subject to the directive authority of superiors; that is, a superior officer can command a subordinate to shoot to kill in the relevant situation. Thus, "life-saving final shooters" normally belong to a specialized group (more specialized than the ordinary police officer), and there is some bureaucracy involved.

Applying this to the case of torture shows the following: as there is no indication that the rudimentary institutionalization that we find in the case of the "live-saving final shot" leads to its abuse by the police, there is no reason to believe that a similarly rudimentary institutionalization in the case of self-defensive torture would lead to such abuse.

Yet this is by no means a reason to relax one's opposition to the institutionalization of torture. Why not? Because, as I have already indicated, it is not clear what the point of such an institutionalization would be. Situations that justify the police in killing someone by a shot to the head are rare, but they are not *that* rare. Situations, however, in which it is justified for the police to torture someone *are enormously rare*. Institutionalizing torture in order to be equipped for such a rare occasion is like stationing a police officer at a lake somewhere in the wilderness because a parachutist might land in it and drown otherwise. And while there is nothing worrying or particularly off-putting about police officers on lakesides, there is something worrying and off-putting about torture specialists and a torture bureaucracy in police departments. Thus, given the rarity of the relevant circumstances, the exceedingly hypothetical benefits of a rudimentary institutionalization of torture are not worth the risks. They are, in fact, not even worth the bitter aftertaste.

These last remarks concerned the *rudimentary* institutionalization of torture. The case against a *full-fledged* institutionalization is, as we saw, infinitely stronger: fully institutionalizing torture in order to deal with the enormously rare Dirty Harry or ticking-bomb cases is not like using a sledgehammer to crack a nut. It is like cracking a nut by blowing oneself up along with it.

5

Legalizing Torture?

There are quite a few scholars who take the position that, while torture is morally justifiable under certain conditions, it should still remain *legally* prohibited.[1] Rainer Trapp, however, thinks that this is a "dishonest compromise,"[2] indeed, an "institutionalized hypocrisy."[3]

> The following form such an open hypocrisy could take, which is often recommended, strikes me as particularly unacceptable: that the officers follow their moral conscience, for instance in the ticking bomb case, and then—like Mr. Daschner—face the legal consequences of a life-saving interrogation [in the form of torture] that can only be conducted illegally. This would mean nothing more than to wash the legislative hands in the innocence of an ethics of conviction [*sich die gesetzgeberischen Hände in gesinnungsethischer Unschuld zu waschen*] and to impose the costs for this on the officers at the executive front or, in case these officers prefer their own career, even onto the crime victims who forfeit their lives.[4]

This point is well taken. However, Trapp is wrong in thinking that the position "moral legitimacy yes, legality no" involves an "evaluative inconsistency" (*Wertungsinkonsistenz*).[5] He claims:

> First, a person (= *x*) who regards an act *a* in [a certain situation] *S* as permissible or even as required for *moral* reasons and who therefore wants to see *a* executed in *S* cannot wish, already for reasons of *justice*, that the person *i* executing *a* be legally *punished* for this act. But this is just what this *i*—as *x* knows also—would have to accept if *a* were legally absolutely prohibited, and if *i*'s transgression of this prohibition would result in a legally determined sanction. . . . But also for *rational* reasons he cannot wish this. For a person who wants to see an action *a* executed by *i* in *S* because

of its good consequences must have an interest in there being as few reasons as possible for *i* *not* to execute *a* in *S*.[6]

I agree with Trapp that a person who tortures another person in necessary and proportionate self-defense would be *wronged* if he were punished. An *injustice* would be done to him. However, as already made clear, I am a threshold deontologist. Perhaps Trapp would be right if one accepted his avowedly consequentialist framework (given the peculiarities of his account, this is not even clear), but I don't—and most other philosophers will not either. In the light of threshold deontology, however, it is clear that there can be *morally justified* rights violations and hence *morally justified injustices*, and there is nothing inconsistent about allowing such things.

As regards Trapp's second claim, he actually contradicts himself in a footnote where he writes that while he thinks that stealing medicine in an emergency situation to save another person's life is morally permissible, his position "naturally" does not rule out that the person whose property has been stolen can sue the thief under civil law.[7] There is nothing "natural" about that. After all, the prospect of a civil law suit *is* a reason for not stealing the medicine; yet Trapp does not want to remove this reason.

Trapp is simply mistaken in claiming that it is irrational to want a person to do something and to simultaneously want that certain reasons that might keep her from doing it are kept in place. If, for example, the legalization of torture had not only the good effect that a police officer who tortured in just self-defense would not be punished, but also the bad effect that the amount of unjust torture would explode, then this latter bad effect might by far outweigh the good effect of the legalization of torture. This is, of course, the ticking-social-bomb argument applied to the issue of the moral permissibility (or prudential advisability) of *legalizing* torture (instead of to the issue of the moral permissibility of torture itself). If this ticking-social-bomb argument were correct, then wishing for torture to remain illegal *and* wishing for police officers (or others) to break the law in certain cases would be entirely rational. There is, contrary to what Trapp claims, nothing inconsistent about such a line of reasoning.

Yet not being inconsistent is not enough for being right: the ticking-social-bomb argument is not only a sheer fantasy if applied to the moral permissibility of acts of torture (as we have seen above); it is also a sheer fantasy if applied to the question of legalization.

Absolutist opponents of torture, however, think that history somehow proves that this metastatic effect is inevitable. Bob Brecher is a case in point. He refers to the situation of Israel in the aftermath of the 1987 Landau Commission report, when "torture became quasi-legal,"[8] and he quotes Anat Biletzki as saying that in Israel

> human rights organizations and their lawyers have unearthed the
> abusive and opportunistic use made of the ticking-bomb argument
> by the security services in order to obtain permission to torture in
> cases that are far removed from any kind of an immediate-danger
> scenario. The evidence amassed in the hundreds of suits and depo-
> sitions points clearly to a cheapening of the ticking time-bomb
> rationale.[9]

And Brecher then asks: "Why think that things would be different any-where else?"[10]

I can answer that question. In fact, Brecher should be able to answer it himself. After all, he quotes Shue approvingly as saying that "one cannot easily draw conclusions for ordinary cases from extraordinary ones."[11] This, of course, is the great mantra of the criticism of the ticking-bomb argument. The critics say that the situation of the idealized ticking-bomb scenario (that they themselves have made up, as we will see in section 6.8) is too special to allow any conclusions for the allegedly completely different real world cases.

Now, however, the case of Israel also looks to me like a pretty special case. Or, if it is not special, Israel is at least a case very dissimilar to that of, let's say, Liechtenstein. Israel is a colonialist and militarist state that treats a great propor-tion of its own citizenry, namely Arab Israelis, as second-class citizens, and that for decades and in defiance of a swathe of UN resolutions has militarily occupied the territory of another people as well as recklessly oppressed that people, with whom, of course, it is therefore engaged in an armed conflict. That in such a situation things can get out of control is not particularly surprising—but it teaches us very little about what will happen *in completely different situations.*

Besides, it is not even clear what exactly the case of Israel is supposed to prove in Brecher's view. As we just saw, all Brecher points out in the context of Israel is that the actual torture practice was not limited to ticking-bomb cases. But, as Ginbar (an absolute torture opponent) admits,

> the Landau model did not seek such limitation. This makes assess-
> ing the effectiveness of the governmental, parliamentary and other
> official review mechanisms difficult.[12]

In other words, the case of Israel (with regard to the Landau period) shows that in a situation where the law and legal practice *does not seek* to limit torture only to ticking-bomb cases, torture might not remain limited to ticking-bomb cases. Well, who has ever denied that, and what is that supposed to demonstrate about laws and legal practices that do seek to limit torture to cases of self-defense, for example?

Of course, after having admitted the problem, Ginbar nevertheless immediately adds:

> However, the huge number of those tortured, far outweighing those convicted or even charged of "security" offences, let alone of involvement in TBSs [ticking-bomb situations], and the fact that only in a single case were GSS agents charged (and convicted) of "excessive" use of force, point to rather limited effectiveness.[13]

Actually, that is not quite true, particularly in light of the concession he has already made. Perhaps Israel *effectively* limited the torture to those cases that were legally allowed; unfortunately, a lot of cases were legally allowed. As Ginbar himself states: "The Landau model allowed the use of 'pressure' methods far beyond TBSs."[14] Thus, the Landau model certainly teaches us absolutely nothing about what the consequences of legalizing torture *only in self-defense cases* would be.

Besides, the case of Israel is *not* a case of the mere legalization of torture; it is a case of its massive institutionalization. (In fact, much of the torture in Israel was doubtlessly done for terrorist reasons, that is, as a means to intimidate the Palestinian population.) But I reject institutionalization. Someone might insist that the Israeli case shows that the legalization of torture leads inevitably to the institutionalization of torture. But, again, for the reasons given, the Israeli case shows nothing of the sort. You cannot draw from certain special cases sweeping conclusions with regard to entirely different cases.

To put it by way of example: pointing to Middle Eastern colonialist and militarist states, to Latin American dictatorships of the 1970s and 1980s, to Nazi Germany, to the Roman Empire or to the Spanish Inquisition (all beloved examples in the arsenal of anti-ticking-bomb-theorists) in order to show what happens if you legalize self-defensive torture in the Federal Republic of Germany or in Liechtenstein is like pointing to the genocide in Rwanda or to a Nazi extermination camp in order to show what happens if you legalize self-defensive killing in Denmark. It is a *non sequitur.* Given that most anti-ticking-bomb theorists also like to constantly preach to *others* that one should not make inferences from special cases to completely dissimilar ones, it might also be intellectually dishonest.

It will also not do to point out, as Jeff McMahan does, that when "torture has been practiced, it has been unjustified far more often than it has been morally justified."[15] After all, the same is true for killing, injuring, and imprisoning people.[16] Yet McMahan does not advocate an absolute legal prohibition of these things. Apart from this, McMahan only repeats the ticking-social-bomb argument already made by others; and like those others he does not back it up with any evidence.[17]

While there is not only no evidence *against* the claim that the legalization of self-defense in stable, relatively peaceful liberal democracies under the rule of law would not lead to an unacceptable extension of torture to cases that have nothing to do with self-defense, there is actually evidence *for* that claim. We have already encountered it, of course: self-defensive killing is legal in Germany and Switzerland and Great Britain, yet there people do not run around constantly killing others in alleged but not real self-defense. Nor do police officers do that in these countries. They also do not constantly stab other people in the eyes with sharp pencils, although that is also legal in certain circumstances. And although the "life-saving final shot" is arguably an institutionalized police practice in Germany, there have yet to be cases of "car-saving final shots" to be reported: as of now, German police officers are not blowing away the heads of attempted car thieves. Nor are there any other abuses of the "lifesaving final shot."

One might object here that the training of snipers specifically for delivering a deadly shot and the regulation of the "life-saving final shot" in police law and practice in Germany *is* a form of institutionalization and that therefore self-defense does not constitute a relevant case in which there is legalization but not institutionalization.

But that is wrong. First the "life-saving final shot" has *not* been institutionalized in all jurisdictions where self-defense is legal (it has also not been institutionalized in all German *Länder*).[18] Thus, evidently legalization does not necessarily lead to institutionalization. Second, as already mentioned, the institutionalization of self-defensive killing in the form of the "life-saving final shot" has not led to any abuse. Thus, this kind of rudimentary, absolutely limited, and controlled institutionalization only proves that the legalization of a practice like self-defensive killing need not lead to the dreaded "metastatic effects." There is no reason to believe that this would be any different with torture. (On the contrary, I think that due to the extreme rarity of cases where self-defensive torture would be justified, there would be no pressure toward an even limited institutionalization.)

Of course, killing and nontorturous injuring in self-defense are not *precisely* the same as torture in self-defense, but no two cases are the same: otherwise they would not be two cases, but one. In order to draw conclusions from one case for the other it suffices that the second case is sufficiently or relevantly similar. And while the differences between the situation of Israel and the situation of Liechtenstein are enormous, the differences between self-defensive killing and self-defensive torture are not such that one could not draw conclusions for the case of legalizing self-defensive torture from the fact that the legalization of self-defensive killing does *not* lead to abuses on such a scale as to make the social costs of allowing self-defensive killing prohibitive. To claim otherwise seems to amount to nothing less than a belief in some kind of magical or addictive properties of torture that other forms of violence, apparently, do not have: once you taste it, you become addicted, and addicted people lose (in Hollywood melodramas) all control. But this is only the badly informed alcoholism metaphor all over again. It is mythology.

Jeremy Waldron has offered a very different and original explanation as to why and how the legalization of torture might have bad effects. He argues that the prohibition of torture is *archetypical* of the idea

> that even where law has to operate forcefully, there will not be the connection that has existed in other times or places between law and *brutality*. People may fear and be deterred by legal sanctions . . . [T]hey may even on occasion be forced . . . to do things or go places against their will. But even when this happens, they will not be herded like cattle or broken like horses; they will not be beaten like dumb animals or treated as bodies to be manipulated. Instead, there will be an enduring connection between the spirit of law and respect for human dignity—respect for human dignity even *in extremis*, where law is at its most forceful and its subjects at their most vulnerable.[19]

That the prohibition of torture is a legal *archetype* means that it has "a significance stemming from the fact that it sums up or makes vivid to us the point, purpose, principle, or policy of a whole area of law."[20] For example, Waldron shows that decisive court rulings against lesser forms of police brutality in the United States—lesser than torture, that is—were made with reference to torture. Similarities with torture were invoked to reject those other brutalities. This would not be possible, he argues, if torture itself became regularized and justified by law, for the similarity with a regular legal practice could hardly count against some other practice. As Waldron puts it:

> The idea is that our confidence that what lies at the bottom of the slope (torture) is wrong informs and supports our confidence that the lesser evils that lie above torture are wrong too.[21]

Thus, by undermining the archetype of the prohibition of torture one also undermines the prohibition of lesser forms of brutality. The whole set of injunctions against brutality would unravel, and the character of the legal system would be corrupted.[22]

I once thought that this is a very good argument. I still think that it is good, but I no longer think that it is correct. The problem is that not all forms of torture are at the bottom of the slope. Some forms of being tortured are simply not as bad as being killed. However, the fact that killing is justified by law in certain circumstances has not led to an unraveling of the prohibitions against killing in other circumstances. The fact that the nephew's killing of his rich uncle out of greed and the teenage girl's killing of the chainsaw killer out of reasonable fear for her life are *both* forms of *killing* has not yet led a judge in the United States to conclude that killing an uncle for his money is not that bad after all. Nor do U.S. judges seem to think that if killing in self-defense is justified then merely beating someone up for the fun of it is justified too.[23]

It helps very little, incidentally, to claim at this point that torture is simply not compatible with liberalism. David Luban, for example, claims that torture aims "to strip away from its victim all the qualities of human dignity that liberalism prizes" and that "torture is a microcosm, raised to the highest level of intensity, of the tyrannical political relationships that liberalism hates the most."[24] However, prisons are also "microcosms" of tyranny; yet most liberals do not find them incompatible with liberalism. Where is the difference? Maybe it lies in the fact that in torture tyranny is "raised to the highest level." But, first, it is far from clear that one hour of torture is more tyrannical than 15 years of prison. Second, even if torture were more tyrannical than prison, and liberalism abhorred tyranny, the fact would still remain that liberalism can accommodate quite intense forms of tyranny, such as incarceration for life (or for a decade and more). Why should it not also be able to accommodate the most extreme form of tyranny? "Because it is the most extreme form" is in itself no answer.

What is more important, liberalism is not so much about "dignity"—which is a quite elusive concept, anyway (in particular, I deny that the dignity of the culpable aggressor is violated by Dirty Harry's torturing him any more than it would be violated by Dirty Harry's killing him in self-defense)—but about liberty. It is called "liberalism," not "dignitism." It is also not about just anybody's liberty. It is about the liberty of the innocent. This is why there is no particular problem in liberalism with killing aggressors or depriving them of their liberty if this is the only way to protect innocent people from these aggressors. The core value of the liberal state is the protection of the liberty and the rights of *innocent* individuals against *aggressors*. The state can be such an aggressor, but the state can and must also protect against other aggressors. Thus to keep Dirty Harry from torturing the kidnapper in the situation described above (for example by restraining Harry with force or by threatening him with punishment) would run counter to the liberal state's own *raison d'être*. The state would be *helping*; it would be *aiding and abetting* the aggressor,[25] not the victim; it would facilitate the aggressor's tyranny over the innocent and therefore actually abet the relationship it hates the most.

Since my description of the core value of liberalism seems to me at least as plausible as Luban's (and I think it is historically much more plausible), the appeal to liberalism cannot help absolute opponents of torture. To claim that liberalism "correctly understood" absolutely prohibits torture is simply an attempt at persuasive definition and begs the question. Besides, why couldn't liberalism, "correctly understood," be wrong?

In addition, again contrary to Waldron, it also has to be pointed out that the prohibition on aiding and abetting aggressors is also a legal archetype, and certainly one that is much more fundamental than any prohibition of torture; "it sums up or makes vivid to us the point, purpose, principle, or policy of a whole area of law," in this case of penal law in a liberal state, if not of all law in a liberal state. The point, purpose, principle, or policy of law in a liberal state is, I submit, to protect the rights of people, and the innocent have a right against the state not to aid and abet those who attack them.[26]

Finally, we arguably *have* examples of liberal democracies not engaged in an armed conflict where torture indeed was allowed—*without* there being any "metastatic effects." Volker Erb argues that in the Federal Republic of Germany torture actually is legal under the German self-defense law.[27] His opponents object that while the German self-defense paragraph in itself might allow torture, nonetheless both Article 1 of the German Constitution, which claims that human dignity shall not be violated, and the fact that Germany is signatory to international antitorture conventions still make torture illegal in Germany. Erb has a very good counterargument to this objection, but this need not concern us now. My point is rather this: *even if* the objection worked in the case of the Federal Republic of Germany, it does *not* work in the case of the Weimar Republic. The Weimar Republic had the same self-defense law as the Federal Republic of Germany, but it did not have any equivalent to Article 1 of the current German Constitution, nor were there any international antitorture conventions. Thus, it would seem that torture was legal in the Weimar Republic. Incidentally, exactly the same argument can be made about Sweden and Finland between the wars. Yet in none of these three countries was there a particular problem with torture.

One might object here that while the actual written law might not have outlawed torture in these three states, the written law is not everything, and one would have to take into account how the law was actually interpreted. However, since we have no actual case law on torture for those three states for those periods of time, we simply do not know whether it actually was legal.[28]

I do not find this argument convincing. In the Federal Republic of Germany, to my knowledge, no one engaged in an unlawful attack has ever been killed with a crossbow. Do we therefore not know whether killing someone with a crossbow is legal under self-defense law if the act was necessary and not grossly disproportionate? I would say we do. It is legal.

One might argue that the case of killing with a crossbow is not as different from the case of killing with a gun as killing in self-defense is from torture in self-defense. Well, perhaps; perhaps not. In any case, the wording of the relevant paragraph clearly covers both cases. Of course, again, the wording is not the whole issue; how it is interpreted also matters. However, there can be no doubt that no judge today in Germany would, if a case of killing with a crossbow came up, simply state that killing with a crossbow cannot be self-defensive and must always be unjustifiable. If such an act were necessary and not grossly disproportionate given the circumstances, she would allow it. Thus necessary and proportionate killing in self-defense with a crossbow is covered by both the wording of the paragraph and the legal culture in Germany.

The situation is pretty much the same with torture in the Weimar republic (or Sweden and Finland between the wars).[29] Given the legal culture of the time (and the culture in general), it is hardly conceivable that any judge at that time would have denied a police officer the defense of self-defense if he tortured a child kidnapper to save the child, and torture was a necessary means to do so. And he would have had the wording and the spirit of the law on his side. Thus, a strong case can be made that torture *was* legal in Germany, Sweden, and Finland between the wars. Yet the metastatic effects and slippery slopes that the absolutist opponents of torture conjure up are nowhere to be seen.

Thus a convincing case against the legalization of self-defensive torture cannot be made. Quite the contrary.

6

Objections

6.1 Attempts to Quickly Dismiss the Argument from Self-defense and Other Rights-based Arguments

As mentioned above, absolutist opponents do not like the self-defense justification of torture. Very often, they do not even engage with it. Rather, they
try to simply dismiss it. There are at least three reasons for this: One is that
a few absolutist opponents of torture quite simply do not understand what
the legal (and moral) defense of self-defense actually is and involves. A second
reason is that the self-defense justification of torture avoids right from the start
a certain criticism absolutist opponents of torture heavily rely on: namely, that
the justification of torture also justifies the torture of innocent bystanders. This
criticism applies to the necessity defense (in theory) and to utilitarian defenses
of torture, but it definitely does not apply to the self-defense justification. Thus,
this latter way of justifying torture takes a lot of wind out of the sails of the
absolutist torture opponent. The third reason is that most people, including
most absolutist torture opponents, do not doubt that killing in self-defense
is justified under certain circumstances. But then for the reasons given in the
previous discussion this puts them in a very tight spot, since they have to
explain why torture in self-defense cannot also be justified. Thus they would
like to avoid that tight spot right from the start. We will see in the following
that they do not succeed.

Christopher Tindale, for example, writes about self-defense in a brief paragraph,
basically referring to a rather inane U.S. Department of Justice memo[1] and
briefly mentioning a rather intelligent article of Stephen Kershnar.[2] Instead
of actually engaging Kershnar's well-developed argument, however, Tindale's
complaints are pretty much summed up in his assertion that the "suggested
justifying circumstances are characteristically hypothetical."[3] Actually, they are
not. The justifying circumstances (like unjust threat, imminence, necessity,
proportionality, or no gross disproportionality) are either given, or they are

79

not. In the first case, self-defense by the means in question is justified; in the latter case, it is not. In certain hypothetical situations, the justifying conditions are given, ex hypothesi; in certain real situations, they are also given, de facto. Tindale, if he wants to show that the self-defense justification of torture is actually misguided, would have to show that torture can never be a necessary and proportionate means of averting the danger stemming from an unjust threat. He shows nothing of that sort, nor does he even try. Or does he? After all, he says the idea of proportionality

> involves the difficulty of identifying and then weighing the competing harms involved. If we believe, as many do, that permitting interrogational torture would cause deep and lasting harm to the society that does so, then a much different calculus is involved than that recognized by the proponents of justified torture.[4]

First, even if we believed, as many—correctly[5]—do not, that permitting torture in the sense of *legalizing* it would cause deep and lasting harm to society, this would neither imply that torture is legally absolutely prohibited, nor, more importantly for the present discussion, would it imply that all torture is *immoral*. For an isolated act of torture might not at all have those harmful consequences.[6]

Second, Tindale completely misunderstands what proportionality means in the case of self-defense. The justification of self-defense is based on rights. It is not utilitarian. Accordingly, the proportionality requirement in self-defense situations concerns the question of whether the *force* one uses against an attacker is or is not disproportionate with respect to the attack one seeks to avert or the harm one seeks to avoid.[7] As already said above, one is not allowed to kill someone to keep him from escaping with a stolen apple. The force used here, namely, *lethal* force, is grossly disproportionate to the harm one seeks to avoid. However, using lethal force against someone who is about to kill you *is* proportionate. Lethal force is pitched against lethal force. The fact that by killing this particular aggressor you also kill, let us assume, the only person who is able to cure a rampant disease that kills thousands of people in your society every year is completely irrelevant to the principle of proportionality as it is used in a rights-based justification of an act of self-defense. Although this particular act of self-defense causes "deep and lasting harm to the society," you would still be justified in committing this act. This is the case in law, and it is the case in morality. We are, special circumstances aside, not morally required to sacrifice our own lives so that others will live or not be injured or tortured.

Finally, Tindale also states that the requirement of necessity "acknowledges how the self-defense defense effectively reduces to the necessity defense
in most imagined circumstances."[8] It should be clear by now that this is, with
all due respect, blatant nonsense. The legal and moral self-defense defense only
justifies the use of violence against persons posing an unjust threat, not against
innocent and nonthreatening bystanders. This is a rather big difference that
most definitely cannot be "reduced."

Yuval Ginbar, in a 414-page book, dedicates three pages to the self-
defense justification of torture. He thinks that attempts to defend torture in
the ticking-bomb case by an appeal to self-defense

> have been half-hearted because the idea that a bound, immobilized
> prisoner is the attacker while another, for instance sticking needles
> under that prisoner's fingernails, is acting in self-defence defies
> common sense, in addition to exceeding the logical boundaries of
> the self-defence rationale. The justification of force in self-defence
> ends where the attacker ceases to use force, namely surrenders—but
> without such surrender . . . torture cannot begin.[9]

There have actually been justifications of torture in the ticking-bomb
case by an appeal to self-defense that have been anything but half-hearted. Be
that as it may, Ginbar's argument, if it were correct, would also apply to the
child-kidnapping case. Of course, it is not correct.

Ginbar is right in claiming that the "justification of force in self-defence
ends where the attacker ceases to use force," but then to continue "namely sur-
renders" is thoroughly mistaken and, if I may add, "defies common sense." The
rationale of self-defense is to *defend* (hence the name) oneself or others from an
attack, that is, *to stop the attack* of the aggressor, not to make him "surrender"
or to strap him to a chair. Yet, the child kidnapper, as we have seen[10] (and as
we will discuss further in section 6.2), has *not* yet ceased to use force; he is *still*
torturing the child he has left in the wooden box, whether he sits in a prison cell
or not. The same holds for the ticking-bomb terrorist.[11] The attack *has not yet
stopped* just because the terrorist is strapped to a chair. The attack may even be
imminent, and the terrorist can still succeed in blowing a lot of people up. If that
happens, it is, from a self-defense perspective, small consolation that the terrorist
has "surrendered." Thus, self-defense is obviously pertinent in both situations.

Ginbar also claims that "writers invoking [the concept of self-defense]
as justification for torture have actually tended (or been forced) to steer that
concept away from its original meaning and towards the 'lesser evil' justification." In addition:

The similar "stretching" of the legal concept of "self-defence" towards a "defence of necessity" ("lesser evil") one is described in Part IV. The result in both cases has been the blurring of any meaningful distinctions between the two concepts, rendering a detailed separate discussion unnecessary, the arguments above being valid equally against this variation.[12]

Actually, it is Ginbar who is doing all the stretching and the blurring here. I think it might be precisely the feeling (quite a correct one) that "the arguments above" (essentially that a consequentialist justification of torture opens the door to torture of innocent bystanders) will not work against the self-defense justification of torture that lead him to try to get rid of this justification as quickly as possible.

He does not succeed. While some defenders of torture may indeed have blurred the line between self-defense and necessity, the authors Ginbar actually mentions—Bargaric and Clarke[13]—have not. Rather, they claim that *both* the self-defense justification *and* the necessity (or another partially or completely consequentialist) justification can justify torture. I make the same claim. And this claim does not involve any blurring of boundaries. After all, the claim that certain acts of giving another person a certain amount of money can be justified either by an appeal to desert (the person deserves to get this money) or by an appeal to promises (one has promised the person to give her this money) or by an appeal to property rights (within limits one can do with one's money what one wants) also does not blur the lines among desert, promises, and property rights. Some acts are simply morally overdetermined. They are justified by more than one sort of justification. It is not confused to point this out; *denying* it is confused.

Let us now have a look at the discussion in "Part IV" that Ginbar mentioned. Here we are dealing with the legal concept of self-defense. Talking about lawyers for the U.S. Justice and Defense Departments, Ginbar claims:

> As these sources themselves recognize, however, the legal notion of self-defence as an individual defence to a crime cannot easily accommodate a situation where a prisoner who is bound and helpless, rather than attacking anyone, is beaten or otherwise deliberately and systematically made to suffer immense pain by one or more officials when neither they nor anyone near them is in any danger, immediate or otherwise. Thus, the August 2002 DOJ memo and the Pentagon Working Group concede that:

> . . . this situation is different from the usual self-defense justification, and, indeed, it overlaps with elements of the necessity defense. Self-defense as usually discussed involves using force against an individual who is about to conduct the attack.[14]

Ginbar is misleading the reader here (as do other absolutist opponents of torture in this context).[15] As the passage quoted from the DoJ memo (and a reading of the memo itself) confirms, "these sources" do not at all recognize what Ginbar claims they recognize. Of course, the legal notion of self-defense can indeed not accommodate a situation where "self-defense" is applied to someone who is not attacking someone or about to attack someone. However, as we have seen again just a few paragraphs above, the child kidnapper *is* attacking someone, and the ticking bomb terrorist who has actually planted the bomb *is* about to attack someone. And indeed, the memo does definitely *not* recognize that the legal notion of self-defense "cannot easily accommodate" *these* two situations.

Thus, when the memo states that "this situation is different from the usual self-defense justification" this does not at all say that the prisoner's being bound and helpless makes the difference. The difference lies elsewhere:

> In the current circumstances, however, an enemy combatant in detention does not himself present a threat of harm. He is not actually carrying out the attack; rather, he has participated in the planning and preparation for the attack, or merely has knowledge of the attack through his membership in the terrorist organization. Nonetheless, leading scholarly commentators believe that interrogation of such individuals using methods that might violate Section 2340A would be justified under the doctrine of self-defense, because the combatant by aiding and promoting the terrorist plot "has culpably caused the situation where someone might get hurt." If hurting him is the only means to prevent the death or injury of others put at risk by his actions, such torture should be permissible, and on the same basis that self-defense is permissible.[16]

Leaving aside the question of whether the situation described here is a self-defense situation in the legal sense or not, the fact remains that even if it is not, this implies *nothing* about the two cases I am concerned with: that of the child kidnapper and that of the terrorist who actually planted the bomb.

For these two agents *are* the ones "actually carrying out the attack," and obviously the DoJ memo recognizes that in *this* situation "the usual self-defence justification" does apply.

Ginbar also quotes Gur-Arye, saying that "[s]trictly speaking, the use of force in interrogation does not fall within the justification of self-defense."[17] Well, Gur-Arye is simply wrong here: the interrogation of the child kidnapper falls squarely within this justification. Her idea that self-defense strictly speaking can only be directed against acts (like planting a bomb) and not against omissions (like refraining from revealing the information)[18] is dubious to start with and even if correct relies on an ill-conceived distinction between acts and omissions. The arguments adduced below in section 6.3 against Daniel Hill's much more developed position apply also to Gur-Arye's reservations.

For now, however, it is more interesting to see how Ginbar continues after this quote:

> In order for it to qualify as a defence for torture in a TBS, these writers and officials acknowledge that there is no escape from what Gur-Arye calls "extending self-defense to include the use of interrogational force." I submit that such "extension" would have to be made in one of two directions.[19]

Obviously, I do not think that any such "extension" is required. And, as I have also pointed out already, nor does the DoJ acknowledge that such an extension is required in the two cases I am concerned with. Anyway, the two ways of extension Ginbar has in mind are one appealing to "collective self-defence"—I shall have nothing to say about this—and one where "the defence of 'self-defence' would inevitably have to 'overlap' with the 'defence of necessity,' and acquire its salient characteristics—enough to make the two virtually indistinguishable."[20] In alleged support of this conclusion he also quotes Gur-Arye again, this time concerning "what the right balance between the potential harms involved is."[21]

This Gur-Arye quote, however, is taken completely out of context; and I find it, quite frankly, unfair that Ginbar on the one hand quotes Gur-Arye about extending the self-defense justification but then fails to consider how she actually "extends" the self-defense justification to the interrogation case. This omission is not surprising, however, for Gur-Arye's extension fails to deliver the conclusion that Ginbar is so absolutely determined to reach:

> Even the innocent, then, would not escape harm under that version of "self-defence," and very little remains of what distinguishes it

from the DoN [defence of necessity]. The conclusion is that this approach does not offer a significant departure from the DoN model and as it is only the latter that has so far been actually applied, we need not be concerned with it any further.[22]

First, it is not only the latter that has been actually applied.[23] Second, we do need to be very much concerned with the former, as our discussion in section 2.1 has shown. Third, Gur-Arye's "extension" of the defense of self-defense (an "extension" that consists simply in allowing self-defense against culpable omissions) definitely excludes the justifiability of torturing innocent bystanders, as is absolutely clear from her discussion of the issue, which Ginbar, unfortunately, has chosen to ignore.[24] Fourth, the obstinate insistence that there can only be two theoretical possibilities when it comes to the justification of torture: either self-defense against attackers and threats (which is then dismissed in panicked haste) or some "consequentialist" justification (including the necessity justification) that then automatically makes room for the torture of innocent bystanders is misplaced, as we have seen in section 2.2.

In any case, far from showing that torture cannot be justified by an appeal to self-defense, Ginbar has only made dogmatic statements, misunderstood the actual requirements of self-defense (which do *not* include a requirement that the target of the defense not be helpless in the sense of being in custody or strapped to a chair—see also the next section), misrepresented the relevant literature, and ignored completely the case of the child kidnapper.

Seumas Miller (as well as *Fritz Allhoff*, to whom the following critical remarks also apply),[25] somewhat surprisingly, also thinks that torture cannot be a case of self-defense. In criticizing my opposing position, he states that torture of the child kidnapper, for example, would not constitute a reaction to an "imminent threat, as must be the case in self-defence." He claims:

> Either the kidnapper is not in custody in which case he or she cannot be tortured; or the kidnapper is in custody in which case the threat to the kidnapped child from the kidnapper in custody is not imminent (the child is either dead or is alive and no longer under threat from the kidnapper in custody).[26]

In fact, however, and as we have seen already, the kidnapper is not only an imminent threat; he is actually *currently attacking* the child, *currently grossly and brutally violating his rights*.[27] To say that the kidnapper is not currently depriving the child of his freedom, not currently torturing him, and not currently posing a threat to his life only because he is in police custody is like saying that a torturer in a dictatorship is not currently electrocuting her victim only because she has already pressed the button releasing the current and now has her hands in her pockets, gleefully watching. As long as she does not press the button a second time to stop the electrocution, she *is* torturing her victim (sometimes negative duties are discharged by positive acts, such as in cases where we have to counteract our previous harmful or dangerous actions).[28] As long as the kidnapper does not give the police the information they need to save the child, he *is* torturing and slowly suffocating him. Hence he may be stopped from doing so by self-defensive force—including self-defensive torture if need be.

Miller also claims that "torturing the guilty in self-defence is arguably something of a misnomer. . . . [I]t is not really self defence per se, but rather the saving of the lives of others. . . . I note that on many accounts self defence is a more readily acceptable moral justification or excuse for killing an attacker than is defending the lives of others (at least, others who are not members of one's family or close friends)."[29] Yes, of course it is a misnomer, but this "misnomer" is traditionally used both in law and by most moral philosophers writing on the issue as a term for *both* literal self-defense and other-defense. Therefore, in British, U.S. and German law (and, to my knowledge, also in Australian law, for that matter, as well as in the writings of almost all ethicists writing on the issue), the justification of other-defense (excuse is a completely different matter, and Miller should not run these two things together) is governed by *exactly the same* criteria as the justification of literal self-defense. Thus, Miller's point here is irrelevant and misinterprets what self-defense means in law and in the texts of most ethicists writing on the matter. In any case, if killing in other-defense is justifiable under certain circumstances (and it is), then torture in other-defense must also be justifiable under certain circumstances.

Richard Matthews, in a book that tries to explain over 238 pages why torture must be absolutely prohibited, dedicates little more than one page to the self-defense argument. His argument against the self-defense justification of torture is this:

> Self-defence will not work either. It will not protect the innocent. The problem is that interrogators are never going to know that the suspect is a perpetrator. . . . Although torture is supposed to avoid harming the innocent, a self-defence option cannot achieve this goal. . . . Public officials may well point to the unavoidability of killing and harming innocents in prosecuting a war or resolving a crisis and thus claim that they were acting in self-defence.[30]

This argument is badly confused. First, sometimes interrogators do know that the suspect is the perpetrator. Of course, they will not know it with *certainty*, but here as elsewhere certainty is neither possible nor required.[31] Second, that someone *claims* to have acted or to act in self-defense does not make this claim true. Third, the fact that some people might commit unjustifiable deeds under the *pretext* of self-defense does not make *genuine* acts of self-defense unjustified. If it did, then self-defense would have to be ruled out generally, and not only in the case of torture (a fact that seems to escape Matthews' attention). Fourth, the fact that there can be circumstances where a person *reasonably believes* that the requirement of the self-defense justification allows her to kill or to torture another person but is in fact *mistaken* does not at all make the self-defense justification of the use of force invalid. True, sometimes mistakes are made, in self-defense as in punishment, and innocent people will suffer. But often *no* mistakes are made, and a culpable aggressor is injured, killed, tortured, or sent to jail. And when no mistakes are made, the self-defense and the punishment *are* justified. Thus, in sum, yes, the self-defense justification—like all other moral and legal justifications, for that matter—can be abused and misapplied, but it is no less valid for that.

So far in this section we have looked at attempts to quickly dismiss the self-defense justification of torture. Let us now have a look at attempts to quickly dismiss deontological, rights-based, or justice-based justifications of torture generally.

Let us continue with Matthews. He wrongly claims, as do many other absolutist torture opponents, that "all the relevant arguments for torture are consequentialist."[32] However, he admits that there "are also a few rare rights-based arguments for torture." But, of course, he then immediately assures his readers that "the arguments are consequentialist despite their invocation of the language of rights." [33] He gives for this rather curious claim the following no less curious explanation, which I quote at length:

> The purpose of the torture, according to both Allhoff and Kershnar, is to acquire information to prevent an emergency, and it is this that generates the justification of torture. A suspect is classified as a "terrorist" and thereby loses his or her right not to be tortured. What justifies the torture is not an act already performed but imminent violence. In the case of state torture, there is no determination that a given individual has sacrificed his or her right not to be tortured, and there are none of the fairness procedures that would normally be in place to protect someone's rights. In state

torture, legal protections cannot exist because they are incompatible with the imminence condition of the arguments used to defend torture. The deontological tradition is fundamentally concerned with issues of fairness and justice, neither of which is possible in state torture. . . . State torture . . . is consequentialist. It has to do with perceived preservation of national security or with perceived preservation of the laws, rights, and structure of the state. But preservation is a consequentialist, rather than deontological, concept. Since everyone accepts that torture is evil, and since everyone agrees that all human beings have a prima facie right not to be tortured, the debate has to be handled on consequentialist grounds.[34]

That an explanation of why Kershnar's (Allhoff is a different matter) "arguments are consequentialist despite their invocation of the language of rights" would have to be staggeringly convoluted was of course quite clear from the outset, and Matthews certainly does not disappoint expectations in this respect. Let me set a few things straight.

First, nowhere does Kershnar (and Allhoff for that matter)[35] say that the terrorist "sacrifices" his rights (why does Matthews come up with such out-of-place terminology?) And he (along with Allhoff) most certainly does not make the downright idiotic claim—contrary to what Matthews unfairly suggests—that *by being classified* as a "terrorist" the suspect loses his or her right not to be tortured. Rather, Kershnar claims that the terrorist *forfeits* his right not to be tortured *because he culpably caused a lethal threat* that can only be averted by torturing him.[36] It does not matter how he is "classified"; it matters what he has done or is in the process of doing. This reasoning, by the way, applies not only to "terrorists" but also to the child kidnappers in my examples.

Second, what exactly is it supposed to mean that "there are none of the fairness procedures that would normally be in place to protect someone's rights"? I suppose that it means that there is no court hearing before the suspect will be tortured. That is quite correct, of course. However, there are also no court hearings before people are injured or killed in self-defense. And that *is* an issue of justice and fairness: it is unfair and unjust to require an innocent person facing an imminent threat by a culpable aggressor to have a court hearing first and shoot later. Because this means in practice requiring the innocent person to sacrifice—and here the word is in order—her own life for the sake of a culpable aggressor. What could be more unfair and unjust?

Here it might be countered that court procedures are not so much designed for the sake of the guilty but for the sake of the innocent. Similarly, someone who *believes* herself to be under attack might not actually be under attack but face an innocent person she only mistakes for an aggressor. Here certain "fairness procedures" would thus protect the innocent person alleged to be an attacker.

The response is obvious: there are (at least) *two* innocent people involved in this scenario, and to ask innocent people who reasonably believe themselves to be under attack to patiently wait for court proceedings and death instead of responding promptly is unfair to them, as it shifts all the burden onto their shoulders while the real or alleged attacker has all the advantages on his side. This is a plainly unjust distribution of risks—even more so since most people who believe themselves to be under attack get it exactly right: most people who believe themselves to be under attack *are* under attack. Of course, this does not mean that all "fairness procedures" have to be thrown overboard. Quite the contrary: the reasonability requirement inherent in the necessity requirement in particular *is* just such a fair and just constraint intended to protect the innocent.

Besides, it should also be noted that even if an innocent defender does not *reasonably* believe that she is under attack and needs to shoot the attacker in order to save her life, she still does not act *unjustly*; she still does not *wrong* the attacker in shooting him as long as her belief is *true*, for this attacker, qua unjust aggressor, simply does not have the right not to be killed if this is the only way to stop him from killing an innocent person.

Third, "state torture"—unfortunately, Matthews nowhere clarifies what exactly that is supposed to mean, but I suppose it refers to state-sanctioned torture by state officials—can be applied to save innocents, pure and simple. It does not have to be concerned with "national security" at all.

Fourth, to claim that "preservation is a consequentialist . . . concept" is like claiming that "chipmunk is a consequentialist concept." "Preservation," like "chipmunk," is in and of itself neither a consequentialist nor a deontological concept. Besides, neither Kershnar nor Allhoff talks about preservation.

Fifth, a justification of torture that says, as Allhoff's and Kershnar's justification does, that a culpable aggressor has *forfeited* his *right* not to be tortured by posing a threat to the *rights of innocents* is definitely deontological; there is absolutely nothing consequentialist about it.

Sixth, the last sentence in the long quote above is a rather obvious *non sequitur.* Even if everyone agreed that torture is evil and that all human beings have a prima facie right not to be tortured, it would certainly still not follow that the debate has to be handled on consequentialist grounds. Matthews, like other absolutist torture opponents, cannot handle rights-based justifications of torture; that is why he denies their existence even when they jump right out at him.

While *Bob Brecher* accuses *others* of not having read the relevant literature, he nevertheless makes astonishing claims (astonishing, at least, to anyone who does know the literature) like this: "All those who advocate interrogational torture, whether legalized or not, simply assume some variety of a utilitarian understanding of morality."[37] A lack of acquaintance with the philosophical and legal literature on self-defense or the just distribution of unavoidable harm would also explain his following comments on Seumas Miller. (Ironically, Miller clearly does not assume some variety of a utilitarian understanding of morality, which is precisely what seems to motivate Brecher to dismiss Miller's approach right on the very first pages of his book. But then it is quite strange to insist a few pages later that all those who advocate interrogational torture "assume some variety of a utilitarian understanding of morality." This looks to me pretty much like an intentional attempt to mislead the reader.)

> If they [the ticking-bomb terrorists] tell the interrogators right away where the bomb is, there will be no torture; if they delay, the torture will end as soon as they confess. In short, it is *their fault* they are being tortured. But this reasoning is appalling. . . . Or consider Seamus Miller's bizarre argument that "the terrorist is forcing the police to choose between two evils, namely torturing the terrorist or allowing thousands of lives to be lost," because in refusing to say where the bomb is, "the terrorist is preventing the police from preventing him from completing his (joint) action of murdering thousands of innocent people." In shifting responsibility onto the person under torture in those circumstances, Miller's position would allow blame for how anyone deemed guilty was treated to shift from those actually treating them in that way to the allegedly guilty party. "She made me do it" the woman's husband could legitimately say to anyone objecting to his assaulting her: by refusing to reveal her lover's name, she was preventing him from preventing her from doing something wrong. *And* he had warned her what would happen if she were ever "unfaithful."[38]

Apparently, on Brecher's account, a mother who surprises an intruder while he is strangling her baby and who asks him to stop and then, when he does not, starts stabbing him with her pocket knife should later not claim: "He forced me to do it. All he had to do was to let go of my baby. He did not. Therefore, he forced me to choose between his health and life and that of my baby. My baby is innocent; he is not. By not letting go, he brought his death upon himself." Brecher finds the mother's reasoning appalling. However, it should be quite obvious whose reasoning is actually appalling here.

Or maybe he *would* rather allow the mother to stab the baby strangler. But then he would have to answer why and also why torturing the ticking-bomb terrorist would not be permissible for the same reasons. The legal and philosophical self-defense literature—which, again, Brecher ignores—explains the permission for the mother's act with precisely the idea that the strangler is an unjust threat, in this case even a culpable one, and that he therefore does not have the right not to be attacked in self-defense. The literature—and common sense, for that matter—for good reasons sees nothing appalling in the idea that it is the *aggressor's fault* when he is severely injured or even killed in a situation where this was the only way to stop his aggression.

Incidentally, Brecher, like Matthews, practices unfair and misleading rhetoric. As we saw, Matthews claims that on Allhoff's and Kershnar's accounts the terrorist loses his right not to be tortured by being *classified* as a "terrorist." And Brecher now claims that "Miller's position would allow blame for how anyone *deemed* guilty was treated to shift from those actually treating them in that way to the allegedly guilty party." In fact, however, Miller's account talks about what may happen to a person who *is* guilty of being in the process of murdering innocent people, and not about what may happen to someone who is *deemed* guilty.

More important still, Miller's account (and the rights-based account generally) definitely does not have the weird implications Brecher sees fit to ascribe to it. First, while Miller does not explicitly mention proportionality considerations, they are certainly implicit in his account. Thus, his claim that torturing one terrorist to save thousands of innocents is justified certainly does not suggest that a husband can beat up his wife to get her lover's name. The former course of action, after all, is proportionate, while the latter is not.

Second, as Jeremy Waldron has pointed out, people can have a *right* to commit certain wrong deeds:

> If P has a right to do A, then it follows that it is wrong for anyone to try to stop P from doing A. Thus the assertion, "I have a moral right to do A," is entirely appropriate when my act is challenged in the sense that somebody threatens to interfere coercively.[39]

I do not think that this account is quite correct. That P has a right to do A does not mean that some other person cannot *permissibly* stop her from doing A. It only means that some other person cannot stop her *without wronging her*. After all, there can be *permissible* rights violations.[40] For example, innocent bystanders have a right not to be injured by others, but sometimes injuring an innocent bystander is permissible in light of what is at stake (perhaps many other innocent people would otherwise be injured or even killed).

This account of a right to do something wrong can be easily applied to the cases in question: the wife in Brecher's example has a moral right to refuse to tell her husband the name of her lover, even in the case that not telling him would be morally wrong. And since nothing in this example suggests that her refusing to tell would have such terrible consequences that violating her right not to tell would be justified, such a violation is *not* justified in these circumstances. The terrorist in Miller's example, in contrast, does not have a right to refuse to give the information, *for he does not have the right to kill thousands of innocent people.*

Thus, the wife is morally protected against the assault of her husband by both her right not to tell her husband the name of her lover *and* by the proportionality requirement. The terrorist in Miller's example, in contrast, neither has a right to keep quiet about where the bomb is, nor would torturing him to find out be disproportionate. Thus, if something is "bizarre" here, it is not Miller's argument but Brecher's.

6.2 The Defenselessness Argument

We have already dealt briefly with the defenselessness argument when I criticized Ginbar's attempt to quickly dismiss the self-defense justification of torture. However, it is worthwhile to tackle the argument again in the renowned version presented by Henry Shue and, given the popularity of the defenselessness argument, to make some further comments on it.

Shue does not directly refer to self-defense, but he thinks that the argument is weak that if killing is sometimes justified, torture must sometimes be justified too. Referring in particular to the legitimate killing of people in war, he states:

> Even if one grants that killing someone in combat is doing him or her a greater harm than torturing him or her . . . , it by no means follows that there could not be a justification for the greater harm that was not applicable to the lesser harm. Specifically, it would matter if some killing could satisfy other moral constraints (besides the constraint of minimizing harm) which no torture could satisfy.[41]

In principle, Shue is indeed right about this. The mere fact that death is worse than many ways of being tortured does not logically imply that killing is worse than torturing. Losing most of your property in a poker game nobody compelled you to take part in is worse than many forms of being stolen from;

this, however, does not show that winning most of another person's property in a poker game nobody forced the other person to take part in is worse than stealing a rather limited amount of money from him. Nevertheless, the mere fact that a particular answer to the obvious question—why should torture always be prohibited if killing is sometimes justified, and death is worse than some forms of torture?—is not logically impossible does not make the question go away. It still has to be answered. In the case of stealing and winning, it is not too difficult to point out essential differences between the two cases and then to demonstrate that they are normatively relevant (such explanations, for example, would involve reference to the presence and absence, respectively, of consent to the poker game and to being stolen from).

In the case of torture, however, such explanations are much more difficult to provide. Shue attempts to give precisely such an explanation. The moral constraint he has in mind is the prohibition of assaults upon the defenseless. However, it can be doubted whether this is a valid constraint at all. Shue's idea that it is valid is based on the fact that one "of the most basic principles for the conduct of war (*jus in bello*) rests on the distinction between combatants and noncombatants and requires that insofar as possible, violence not be directed at noncombatants."[42] One fundamental function of this distinction, according to Shue, is "to try to make a terrible combat fair." While the opportunities may not be anywhere near equal—it would be impossible to restrict wars to equally matched opponents—at least none of the parties to the combat should be defenseless.[43]

To be sure, Shue admits that this "invokes a simplified, if not romanticized, portrait of warfare," but he explains that

> the point now is not to attack or defend the efficacy of the principle
> of warfare that combat is more acceptable morally if restricted to
> official combatants, but to notice one of its moral bases, which,
> I am suggesting, is that it allows for a "fair fight" by means of
> protecting the utterly defenceless from assault.[44]

It is true that the fact that the prohibition of assaults upon the defenseless is not always obeyed in war does not pose any problem for Shue's argument. What does pose a problem, however, is that this principle is no *jus in bello* principle at all, and it does not, *pace* Shue, underlie the principled distinction between combatants and noncombatants.[45] This can be seen quite easily. Suppose an army that possesses superior artillery advances upon the enemy trenches. It has two options. It can shell the enemy trenches from a safe distance with artillery fire. The enemy would be entirely defenseless against such an attack; his weapons do not have the range for fighting back.[46] (This was pretty much the situation in the first and the second Iraq wars.) Or it can advance without shelling the enemy first. Here the enemy would be able to fire upon the advancing troops and to inflict heavy casualties. The point now is that there is simply no article in the laws of war (and no constraint in just war theory, for that matter) that would rule out the first option as such. Of course, if the objectives of the war could be achieved without shelling the enemy in its death-trap trenches *and* without inflicting higher casualties on one's own forces, this alternative course of action would have to be adopted. But the reason for this is the *jus in bello* principle of proportionality.[47] An alleged principle of the immunity of the defenseless plays no role here.

To be sure, I do not deny that there is something fishy about attacking the defenseless. What is fishy about it might be captured very well in this passage:

> The pilot of a fighter-bomber or the crew of a man-of-war from which the Tomahawk rockets are launched are beyond the reach of the enemy's weapons. War has lost all features of the classical duel situation here and has approached, to put it cynically, certain forms of pest control.[48]

Judged from a traditional warrior's code of honor, a code that empha-sizes, among other things, courage, there is nothing honorable in killing off defenseless enemies (whether it is therefore already *dis*honorable is yet another question). But honor and morality are not the same, and honor and the laws of war are not either. In short, the prohibition of assaults upon the defense-less is neither an explicit nor an implicit principle of the laws of war or of just war theory.

Moreover, it is not even clear what is supposed to be unfair about killing the defenseless in war in the first place. If the rules of war allowed both sides to kill defenseless prisoners of war, for example, what would be unfair about that? Both sides are in the same situation. And if the laws of war allowed the torture of POWs, the same would be true. Principles of fairness cannot be invoked as an argument against either of the two practices.

The situation with domestic self-defense is not any different from the situation with war. Here as well defenseless people can be attacked. This can be illustrated with another example. In self-defense theory talk about the fat innocent man falling off a cliff is ubiquitous. Let us say Jeanette is at the bottom of the cliff, and for whatever reason she is unable to move out of the way of the falling man. When he lands on her, she will be crushed (but he will survive due to the cushioning effect). She has a ray gun, though, with which she can vaporize the man (who is himself unarmed). This man, thus, is completely defenseless; in vaporizing him Jeanette would be attacking a defenseless person. Yet, on the accounts of most moral philosophers (Shue included, as far as I can see), vaporizing the man would be justified. It would also be justified under British and German law and under most self-defense statutes of the United States.

Consider also the following example:

Gina, who has recently had an accident that makes it impossible for her to use her legs or her voice for two weeks, is lying in the hospital. She is visited by her sister and her small niece. The sister leaves the room for a while, and the niece plays around. She happens to end up between the movable steel backrest and the steel bed frame of a paraplegic patient in the room. Gina has once seen how a very thick wooden stake was accidentally crushed between the backrest and the frame. "I'm stuck," the niece says. The normally grumpy paraplegic lightens up. "Oh really?" he says, smiling at Gina: "You know, I haven't told anybody here, but I'm a serial child murderer. I thought I would never be able to kill a child again. But this—oh God, this is my lucky day." And then he bites on a button in front of his mouth—he can only move his head—making the backrest move down very slowly. If it goes down all the way, the niece will be decapitated. Gina, who cannot leave her bed or scream for help, grabs the .357 Magnum she has under her pillow at all times (a wise precaution, as it turns out) and, hoping that this will suffice, shoots the poor, absolutely defenseless, paraplegic serial child murderer in the leg. For a moment he lets go of the button, but then he bites it again. The backrest is only an inch away from the child's neck. Gina fires a bullet into the paraplegic's chest, killing him. He lets go of the button. The child is saved.

Gina's actions were both legally and morally entirely justified self-defense. The claim, repeated by many absolutist torture opponents *ad nauseam*, that self-defensive action cannot be directed against defenseless people is clearly false. We should note that this is even conceded by David Sussman, whom many like to quote when arguing *against* torture:

We can do anything we like to him [the terrorist is in our power], and there is nothing he can do to resist or shield himself against us.

But such helplessness means neither that the terrorist has ceased to engage in hostilities against us, nor that he is no longer an active military threat. His placing of the bomb was the beginning of an attack on us; his silence, although not any kind of further overt act, is nevertheless voluntary behavior undertaken for the sake of bringing that act to completion. His continued silence thus might well be considered a part of his attack, understood as a temporally extended action.[49]

Thus, self-defense can perhaps not be directed against "attackless" or "threatless" people; that is, it cannot be directed against people who are not attacking or posing an unjust threat, but neither morality nor the law requires that the targets of self-defensive action not be *defenseless*.

The situation of the paraplegic child murderer is not relevantly different from the situation of the child kidnapper who has put the child into a small wooden box and is now being tortured by the police who want to know where the child is. Both are defenseless with regard to Gina or with regard to the police, but they are also simultaneously attacking a child, by torturing it or by being in the process of decapitating it. Thus, the assertion that self-defense against them, be it by killing or by torturing them, is not allowed since they, in turn, cannot defend themselves against such self-defense is mistaken from the perspectives of both law and morality.

6.3 But Is It Really Self-defense?
Whitley Kaufman and Daniel Hill

Anglo-American philosophers and lawyers arguing for an absolute prohibition on torture hardly ever consider the child-kidnapping case. This is somewhat ironic. It is ironic because they like to claim, as Shue does, that the "advocates of torture love a ticking bomb."[50] Actually, however, it is they who love it, or, more precisely, who are obsessed with it—so much so that they can hardly see beyond it. For the most part they labor under the illusion that by "defusing" the ticking-bomb argument one defuses "the" argument for torture.[51]

Therefore it is hardly surprising that two recent critics of the idea that torture can in some cases be justified by an appeal to the right to self-defense focus exclusively on the ticking-bomb case. The arguments they advance are different from the ones so far considered.

Whitley Kaufman's criticism relies on the distinction between what he (basically following Jeff McMahan)[52] calls Aggressor and what he calls Culpable

Bystander. The latter is "a person who has committed a wrongful act, but is not *now* committing a wrong."[53] The former is *now* committing a wrong, or is posing an imminent threat. Kaufman thinks that the captured ticking-bomb terrorist is only a Culpable Bystander and that violence to avert pending unjust harm may only be directed against Aggressors.[54]

Even if this line of criticism were correct, though, it is, nevertheless, completely inapplicable to the child-kidnapping case since, as Kaufman himself admits, a "kidnapper . . . is an aggressor simply by virtue of his holding you hostage."[55] Thus a child kidnapper, by holding the child hostage in a wooden box, thereby depriving her of her freedom and torturing her, *is* an aggressor, whether in custody or not. He is, after all, torturing the child right now *while* he is in custody.[56] Thus, torturing him to save the child would be a case of self-defensive torture even under Kaufman's own assumptions.

Moreover, Kaufman's line of criticism is not correct. The ticking-bomb terrorist *is* committing a wrong: not disclosing where the bomb is in order to execute his plan to kill a lot of innocents (assuming, as the example does, of course, that he is not justified in killing them). In fact, not only is Kaufman's criticism incorrect, but it is confused to the uttermost degree. To demonstrate this I will first quote Kaufman's decisive passage at length and then analyze it. Kaufman rightly asks:

> But might it be argued that at least in some cases (the ticking bomb) the terrorist is not a mere bystander but a continuing aggressor, insofar as his act of violence has been set in motion but not yet completed, and he has the power to prevent it by revealing the location of the bomb? There are two ways of interpreting this argument. First, the claim might be that against a Culpable Aggressor, *any* sort of force is permissible so long as it helps prevent the harm that is being defended against. But this claim is patently false. The doctrine of self-defense permits only force of a certain kind: force that is defensive, that wards off or literally fends off the threatened harm. It has never been interpreted to permit using a person—even a Culpable Aggressor—as a means to escape harm—that is, to use instrumental force. Thus, Suzanne Uniacke rightly points out that one may not invoke self-defense to "forcibly use" an aggressor as a human shield against his co-conspirators. Characterizing the captured terrorist as a "continuing aggressor" is already a highly questionable assumption, given that he is in custody and incapable of causing any more harm. . . . But even if he [the captured terrorist] were considered a "continuing aggressor," it would not follow

that any force against him is permissible. There would have to be evidence that the force being used is genuinely defensive, and not instrumental force used as a means to a further goal.

The argument, therefore, would have to show that this sort of force—the use of torture to get the terrorist to reveal information—was genuinely defensive. But this would be equally implausible. The use of torture to achieve a further goal, however laudable that goal, is a classic example of instrumental rather than defensive force. It is force used as a means to prevent future harm, just like using an innocent bystander as a human shield. Indeed, torture is often seen as the paradigm case of force that violates the ethical imperative not to use people as a means to achieve one's goals. . . . That torture is not defensive but instrumental force can also be seen in that it is in practice irrelevant who one tortures so long as one achieves one's goal; for example, one could try to get the terrorist to reveal the information by torturing his wife or child in front of him.[57]

The following are some of Kaufman's confusions (I do not claim that my list here is exhaustive):[58]

1. That the "doctrine of self-defense permits only force of a certain kind" does not imply that an argument intended to show that torturing the captured terrorist is *permissible* has to show that torturing him is a case of self-defense. There might be other valid moral doctrines that allow the use of force, including torture, even in cases to which the doctrine of self-defense does not apply.

2. This is confirmed by Suzanne Uniacke's own stance. Kaufman misrepresents what Uniacke is actually saying on the pages of *Permissible Killing* he is referring to. One finds her there denying that it is a genuine case of self-defense when in a situation where "I am exposed to a grenade about to go off which you have just triggered" and which "is no longer under your control. . . . I push you on top of it in order to protect myself." However, she does *not* deny that it is a *justified* act.[59] Besides, it is not clear that this example of Uniacke's has too much to do with the case we are discussing. After all, the ticking bomb of the captured terrorist still *is* under his control: he can see to its deactivation by just telling the police the location. In the

grenade case, however, there is nothing "you" can do to prevent the grenade from exploding.

Moreover, Uniacke does not at all point out "that one may not invoke self-defense to 'forcibly use' an aggressor as a human shield" against his co-conspirators. Instead she says this: "Whereas if you have (say) informed gangsters of my where-abouts and they come looking to kill me, I am clearly not acting in self-defence against you if I forcibly use you as a shield against these gangsters' bullets." Why not? Because the threat is not "a direct effect of your conduct" (you might be a completely innocent person).[60] The threat in the ticking-bomb case, however, obviously is a direct effect of the conduct of the ticking-bomb terrorist.

3. Why is "[c]haracterizing the captured terrorist as a 'continuing aggressor' . . . a highly questionable assumption, given that he is in custody and incapable of causing any more harm"? After all, Kaufman informed us that the "kidnapper . . . is an aggressor simply by virtue of his holding you hostage." However, he can still hold you hostage while "he is in custody." And he does cause you further harm by keeping you or the child in a wooden box where you slowly suffocate. However, the ticking-bomb terrorist, in turn, can cause even more harm by not telling the police where the bomb is.

4. There is no "ethical imperative not to use people as a means to achieve one's goals." I will deal with this alleged imperative separately, in section 6.5. Yet it also comes up in point 6.

5. Kaufman just *assumes* that "instrumental" force cannot be defensive. But there is no reason to accept such an assumption. Quite the contrary. When a defender shoots an aggressor, he does this for *instrumental* reasons: he does not do it because shooting people is for him an end in itself; rather, he shoots the aggressor *as a means* to save his own life.

6. But probably Kaufman means with instrumental force something else. Instrumental force is force that uses *a person* as a means to one's goals (which brings us back to point 4). Of course, using someone as a means to my goal of finding out what time it is by asking him for the time seems to be quite

all right. The same is true for my using a terrorist as a means to my goal of finding the bomb by asking him where it is or of my using the person sitting next to me in a restaurant as a means to get the salt that is out of my reach. I ask him: "Could you please give me the salt?" And he does, so he is my means to get the salt.

But maybe with force it is different. Thus, may I apply force to use someone as a means to my goals? Of course I may. Consider the thief who has stolen my medicine, which I need in the next minutes in order not to die. I manage to catch the thief before he can escape (in fact, his plan was to murder me this way). My goal is to get the medicine into my possession again. I twist the thief and would-be murderer's arm, causing him pain, telling him to hand the medicine over. He does so in order to avoid further pain. Thus, he is my means to get the medicine back (as the person in the restaurant was my means to get the salt)—after all, he is handing it over. I cannot imagine any American, British, or German court—or any reasonable person, for that matter—not considering this justified.

7. To claim, as Kaufman does, that "force used as a means to prevent future harm" is "just like using an innocent bystander as a human shield" is bizarre. If innocent Jane is shot at by culpable Bill, who tries to kill her, then Jane's using force by returning fire is also a means "to prevent future harm," namely her future death or serious injury. Three seconds or minutes from now is future too, not only three hours or three years from now. And there is a very obvious difference between Jane shooting back at the culpable aggressor on the one hand and her grabbing her neighbor's baby as a shield on the other. There is also a very obvious difference between this latter course of action and torturing a ticking-bomb terrorist in order to keep him from blowing up the city or torturing a kidnapper in order to keep him from suffocating a child.

8. No less unwarranted is Kaufman's claim: "That torture is not defensive but instrumental force can also be seen in that it is in practice irrelevant *who* one tortures so long as one achieves one's goal; for example, one could try to get the terrorist to reveal the information by torturing his wife or child in front of him." On this logic Jane's shooting Bill is not a case of self-

defense, for she could have tried to save her life by shooting Bill's daughter, hoping that he will then immediately abort his attack on Jane and rush off to the hospital to save his daughter. Obviously, Kaufman's logic is flawed.

There is yet another problem with Kaufman's approach I would like to mention, but it is more convenient to discuss it after the next criticism of the idea that interrogational torture can be a form of self-defense.

This next criticism is offered by *Daniel Hill*. He assumes (without argument) that if you cause a person to perform a very specific action, then the action by which you cause this is not self-defensive. Self-defensive actions, according to him, are only those that *prevent* a person from doing something. I see absolutely no reason why one should accept this assumption. It is certainly not part of the *meaning* of self-defense. Even if it were, though, this would not affect the argument for torture—unless one interprets the phrase "to prevent a person from doing something" in such an unnatural way as Hill in fact does. We come to that in a moment.

Hill thinks in addition that there is a big moral difference between preventing someone from doing something and making him do something specific. He offers the following two examples, which I quote at length:

Holding Case: A police officer spots a known terrorist about to detonate a bomb, which, if it goes off, will illicitly inflict serious harm and serious pain on many innocents. The detonator button needs to be held down for ten seconds for the bomb to go off. The only way the terrorist can be prevented from holding down the detonator button for ten seconds is if he is caused such pain that he will choose to take his finger off the detonator button in order to get the pain to stop. The officer shoots the terrorist in the foot, intending to cause no serious lasting harm but so much pain that he will make a conscious decision to stop priming the bomb and turn his attention to nursing his foot.[61]

Hill contrasts this with the following case:

Withholding Case: A police officer spots a known terrorist about to detonate a bomb, which, if it goes off, will illicitly inflict serious harm and serious pain on many innocents. The detonator button needs to be in the down position for ten seconds for the bomb to go off. The device works in such a way, however, that once pressed

the button will remain depressed unless pulled up by someone with
the terrorist's fingerprint. The only way the detonator button can
be prevented from remaining depressed for ten seconds is if the terrorist is caused such pain that he will choose to pull the detonator
button up in order to get the pain to stop. The officer shoots the
terrorist in the foot, telling the terrorist that he can expect more
pain in the other foot unless he pulls up the detonator button.[62]

And he concludes:

Withholding and Holding are superficially very similar, but there
is one crucial difference: in Holding the terrorist is prevented from
performing an action (holding the button down) and in Withholding the terrorist is not prevented from doing anything—instead
he is (just) caused to perform an action, the action of pulling the
button up. It would seem that this makes a moral difference. Intuitively, it is not permissible to inflict pain in Withholding in order
to compel the terrorist to pull the button up, but intuitively it *is*
permissible . . . for pain to be inflicted in Holding in order that
the terrorist might be prevented from pushing the button down.[63]

The reader will not be surprised that I do not share these intuitions at all.
Of course, I think that to shoot the terrorist in the foot as a start is probably
excessive, but we can account for that by postulating that he is—like Gina
in the paraplegic child murderer case—for certain reasons unable to use any
other methods; maybe he is separated from the terrorist by iron bars and thus
cannot come closer to him. In that case, I think that he is clearly allowed to
use such force; and I think that many will share this intuition. The philosopher
who actually came up with the Withholding case certainly did.[64]

Let me add a further case, one involving private citizens rather than a
police officer. It is a variation of the example of the slow guillotine and the
unconscious villain above:

The Slow Guillotine and the Conscious Villain: Jane has been kidnapped by the serial killer Albert. Everybody knows, thanks to
police investigations, that Albert kills his victims by fixating their
heads under a slow guillotine. The blade of the guillotine then
slowly moves downwards if a male voice says "Start," and it stops
(and can then not be restarted unless the whole device is taken
apart) if the same voice that said "Start" says "Stop." Jane's head is

shut into the device, but before Albert can say "Start," he slips in the bathroom and dies. The landlord Radovan, who had no idea about Albert's criminal undertakings, later enters the room with his own key for certain reasons. He finds Jane, sits down in front of her, cheers up, lights a cigarette and says: "Great, I always wanted to do that: START!" "Say stop," Jane begs. Radovan, to savor the moment, puts his head directly above hers, looks her in the eyes and says grinning: "No." Jane, whose arms are free and who is a martial artist, manages to sling one arm around the would-be killers neck and with her other hand to ram her switchblade into his genitals, causing him severe pain. "Say STOP!" "No." She twists the knife in the wound, until finally he says: "Stop."

On Hill's view, Jane's actions are unjustified here. Again, I think that this is utterly counter-intuitive—and I think that it is inhumane. In fact, Jane would even have been justified in killing him after he said "Stop" in order to prevent him from murdering her later in some other fashion. And she would have been permitted to use his head, whether he was dead or still alive, as a shield against the blade.

With these remarks let me make good on my promise to return to Kaufman. If Kaufman thinks that *any* court in the United States, Canada, the UK, or Germany would find that Jane's hurting Radovan in order to make him say "Stop" was *not* justified under self-defense law, then he is completely and entirely out of touch with the legal realities in these jurisdictions. Since, however, his views on self-defense effectively rule out that this is a case of self-defense or a case of justified use of force, and since he also claims that a valid theory of self-defense "must successfully account for the current principles and practices of self-defense, including our moral intuitions,"[65] we can safely discard his views on self-defense.

Not only are Kaufman's and Hill's views completely counterintuitive, but they also lack any sound theoretical underpinning. We already saw this in the case of Kaufman. However, some further remarks on Hill are in order. After all, he himself recognizes:

It might be responded that the terrorist in Interrogation and With-holding and similar cases *is* still performing an evil action, viz., the causation of the terrorist atrocity, and that, therefore, the torturer *is* preventing the terrorist from performing an action, and so there is, after all, a similarity with Defense and Holding and similar cases.

However, he thinks:

> This raises the big metaphysical question of when one completes an
> action, (a) when its effects come about, or (b) when one finishes
> the *basic* actions (i.e., the bodily movements) that ultimately lead
> to the effects. Intuitively, only (b) is tenable, as if (a) were correct
> one would continue performing lots of actions long after one's
> death. Admittedly, (b) does have the counter-intuitive consequence
> that a killer kills the victim before the victim dies, but this is less
> counter-intuitive than the view that one might kill someone after
> one's death. . . . . It follows, further, that the torturer in Interroga-
> tion and Withholding etc. is not preventing the terrorist from
> performing an action of terror but preventing him from *having
> performed* an action of terror, and this difference between such cases
> as Interrogation and Withholding on the one hand, and Defense
> and Holding on the other hand, seems to make the difference
> between the licensing of the intentional infliction of severe pain
> or severe harm in Defense and Holding, but not in Interrogation
> and Withholding.[66]

I have three observations to make. First, again Hill and I have different views on what is more counterintuitive and what is less counterintuitive.
Second, the formulation "preventing him from *having performed* an action
of terror" looks suspiciously like sophistry and legerdemain. Third, this last
impression is confirmed if one realizes that there is an obvious alternative to
the options (a) and (b) Hill mentions: *one completes one's action x at the last
point where one could have prevented the intended effect from coming about.* This
account nicely fits our intuitions, the legal reality and the facts about comply-
ing with one's negative duties.

These latter facts are decisive, for since Hill endows it with such great
importance, he clearly owes us some explanation concerning "the basis of this
moral difference between preventing someone from performing an action that
will cause a tragedy and causing someone to cause a tragedy not to occur."[67]
It lies, he says, in the difference between *negative* duties (*not* to do something)
and *positive* duties (to *do* something). He elaborates:

> It seems permissible, then, in some circumstances to inflict pain to
> force people to comply with their negative duties, but it does not
> seem permissible to inflict pain in order to force people to comply
> with their positive duties, even extremely important positive duties,

such as the duty to avert an atrocity that the people in question have set in motion.[68]

The problem is that Hill has a remarkably simplistic—indeed mistaken—view of negative duties. To be sure, one can discharge negative duties by *never doing anything whatsoever*, but once one starts to do something one might only be able to discharge one's negative duties by doing something. As Richard Louis Trammel notes:

> Drivers must correct the movement of their cars, and waiters and waitresses must hold on to hot dishes passing over their customers. Thus the requirement of the commands not to kill or injure is not that the agent refrain from initiating any causal processes tending toward death or injury, but rather that the agent not initiate any such causal processes without continuing to intervene to counteract the tendencies he has previously initiated.[69]

Thus, for the ticking-bomb terrorist and the child kidnapper, the positive action of revealing the location of the bomb or of the child, respectively, is an obvious way to discharge their negative duty not to unjustifiably kill or torture innocent people. If they do not discharge this duty voluntarily, they can be forced to discharge it in self-defense—by self-defensive torture, if need be.

Thus, I conclude that Kaufman's and Hill's attempts to show that interrogational torture cannot be self-defensive fail. Self-defensive torture is both possible and justifiable.

6.4 David Sussman's Complicity Argument

David Sussman has recently attempted to give another explanation of why torture, allegedly, "bears an especially high burden of justification, greater in degree and different in kind from even that of killing."[70] However, he also cautions that this "is not to say that when torture is wrong, it is worse that [sic] wrongful acts of maiming and killing" or that "it is more important for us to prevent torture than it is to prevent murder, or that torturers should be condemned or punished more severely than murderers. The moral differences between torture, killing, and maiming may not always make a difference in such third-personal contexts."[71] But why, then, should torture bear an "especially high burden of justification"? Does it bear such a higher burden only in second-personal or first-personal contexts? But what is that supposed to mean?

That whereas one does not need a better justification for allowing others to torture or for not condemning torturers than for allowing others to kill or for not condemning killers, one does need a better justification for torturing (and perhaps also for risking being tortured) than for killing? Sussman argues that

> torture forces its victim into the position of colluding against himself through his own affects and emotions, so that he experiences himself as simultaneously powerless and yet actively complicit in his own violation. So construed, torture turns out to be not just an extreme form of cruelty, but the pre-eminent instance of a kind of forced self-betrayal, more akin to rape than other kinds of violence characteristic of warfare or police action.[72]

He elaborates:

> What the torturer does is to take his victim's pain, and through it his victim's body, and make it begin to express the torturer's will.[73]
> . . . Torture does not merely insult or damage its victim's agency, but rather turns such agency against itself, forcing the victim to experience herself as helpless yet complicit in her own violation. This is not just an assault on or violation of the victim's autonomy but also a perversion of it, a kind of systematic mockery of the basic moral relations that an individual bears both to others and to herself. Perhaps this is why torture seems qualitatively worse than other forms of brutality or cruelty.[74]

But all this can hardly explain the alleged difference between "third-personal" and other contexts. In fact, it would seem rather natural to assume that, if torture isn't worse than killing from a third-personal perspective, it isn't worse from a second- or first-personal perspective either. If Sussman sees this differently, the high burden of justification, it appears, would be on him. That burden, however, cannot be met. Assume a dictator confronts prisoner A with the following choice: either to kill one of ten prisoners or to torture one of them for two hours (all these prisoners are innocent and have no special relation to the first prisoner).[75] If A refuses to choose and to act on his choice, all ten prisoners will be killed. If he decides to choose (and it seems plain to me that he is justified in choosing, even though he may not be obliged to do so), should he kill one prisoner rather than torture one of them for two hours? This is to be strongly doubted. However, there can hardly be any doubt that the ten prisoners would prefer him to opt for torture if he asked them what to do—to refuse to choose, to choose to kill, or to choose to torture. He is not permitted to ask them (if he did, all ten prisoners would be killed). However, in light of the fact that it is reasonable to assume that they would prefer two hours of torture to being killed for good, he should honor that preference if he decides to choose. It seems, then, that some forms of torture are easier to justify than killing even from a first-person perspective.

Moreover, the feature that in Sussman's eyes makes torture so bad is by no means unique to torture. We find it, in fact, even in armed robbery. If a robber points a gun at a victim and threatens to kill him if the victim does not give her his money, the robber, if successful, also turns the victim's agency against the victim himself. She makes the victim's fear express her, the robber's, will; and the victim, in handing over the money for fear of death, is "complicit" in his own violation.

It is important to note here that the victim will also normally not react to the threat with a utility/risk-calculation, that is, with rational deliberation. If, especially at night in a dark alley, one finds a gun pointed at one's head and hears: "Give me your f——ing money or I'll f——ing kill you," one will hardly engage in deliberations of the following sort: "The probability that his threat is meant seriously lies around x; my options to defend myself or to escape are this and that, with this and that probability of success; if, on the other hand, I give him the money, this will cost me certainly y money units, which in turn leads with probability z to my not being able to pay in time for this and that thing, which in turn . . . and therefore I will . . ." Rather, many people threatened with deadly violence will think: "Oh my God, he wants to shoot me. He wants to shoot me . . . I'll give him the money!" Thus, the sudden death threat and the perceived time pressure will in many if not most cases severely disturb the ability to deliberate rationally if they do not completely undermine it. In short, fear may overwhelm one just as pain overwhelms the victim of torture. There may be differences of degree but no qualitative ones. Besides, at least some forms of torture will undermine the ability of some torture victims to think rationally less than some forms of death threat would that of some threatened people.

Thus, Sussman is not able to show that there is a higher burden of justification on torture than on killing; and thought experiments like those of the ten prisoners strongly suggest that it is the other way around.

Of course, it is true that *emotional reactions* to displays of torture, for example in movies, are much stronger than those to displays of killing. And I suspect that much of the conviction that torture is somehow more terrible than death is sustained by these immediate emotional reactions. In fact, however, very little of moral relevance follows from them. After all, the emotional reactions to scenes involving large amounts of faeces or cockroaches, for example, are also stronger for the most part than to scenes involving killing, at least when it is a quick killing. When the killing is prolonged the reactions are stronger, but then they are prompted by the suffering on display—sometimes simply in the form of fear—rather than by the impending death itself. The point is that *we simply cannot empathize with the dead*. There is nothing we can empathize *with*. We do not know how it is to be dead, and there is certainly no possibility of *feeling* dead (in any nonmetaphorical sense). We do know, however, what it is to feel *pain*. Thus if we see how pain is inflicted on another person, we can quite literally feel *com-passion*. There is no such compassion possible with the dead (we can only feel sorry for them, but that is a completely different and far less intense feeling). In other words, our emotional reactions to displays of either torture or killing are distorted by certain limits of empathy. What are not distorted are our emotional reactions to the prospect of our *own* death. Most of us fear it more than torture (for a restricted length of time). Whether killing is worse than torturing, then, should be measured by the preferences of people facing the alternatives of torture (for a certain limited time) and death; most prefer torture. To measure it by emotional reactions to displays of torture would by extension also mean that it is better to shoot someone dead than to push her into a bathtub filled with cockroaches. But such an implication obviously reduces the premise to absurdity.

6.5 Kant's Categorical Imperative: The Three Kantian Formulas

Many absolutist opponents of torture rely on Immanuel Kant—in vain, it has to be said. He offers three formulations of his "categorical imperative," that is, of what he sees as the fundamental principle of morality. We do not have to discuss here whether all three formulations have the same implications (I do not think they do). Let us just look at them separately.

The "Formula of the Universal Law of Nature" goes like this:

Act only on that maxim through which you can at the same time will that it should become a universal law.[76]

It is, of course, not particularly clear what this is supposed to mean. There are different interpretations in the literature (many of them not clearer than the original formulation), and while Kant gave indeed some examples, these are unfortunately not as illuminating as one might wish them to be. Anyway, this is not the place to go into a Kant exegesis, and there is no need to.[77]

The reason is simple: Kant thought that the categorical imperative (and thus this formulation of it too) is compatible with punishing the guilty, with waging war, and, most important for our purposes, with self-defense.[78] But since some instances of torture *are* instances of self-defense, they must be compatible with the categorical imperative. If absolutist opponents think they are not, the burden of proof is on *them*. So far none of them has met it, or even tried to. One wonders why. (By the way: the maxim "I will torture a culpable aggressor in cases where this is a necessary and proportionate means to defend an innocent person from his aggression" is clearly one that one can will, without contradiction, to become a universal law.)

The "Humanity Formula" goes like this:

> Act in such a way as to use humanity, whether in your own person or in that of anyone else, always as an end and never merely as a means.[79]

Again, it is not quite clear what this formulation is supposed to mean, and there are different interpretations in the literature. For one thing, it is unclear what it means to *use* a person as an end.[80] Since I cannot use a person as an end, I can only *use* persons as means. What is wrong with that?

Perhaps Kant means that we should never only use persons merely as means, but we should *treat* them also as ends. Still, this is not much clearer. If I ask someone for the time, I certainly use this person in order to find out what time it is (unless my asking is only a pretext for socializing or something of that sort), but in what way do I also treat her as an end? What does it mean to treat a person as an end?

One possible interpretation is that not treating a person as an end involves treating her as though she had no rights. But just as killing an aggressor in self-defense does not involve treating this aggressor as not having any rights, torturing an aggressor in self-defense likewise does not involve treating this aggressor as not having any rights. On the contrary, the self-defense requirements demand that the aggressor not be treated in ways that are not necessary for the purpose of self-defense or that are disproportionate in light of the threat to be averted. That an aggressor has no right not to be tortured in certain circumstances and is treated accordingly does not imply that he has no rights whatsoever and is treated accordingly.

There can of course be other interpretations,[81] but the general question they all have to answer is why injuring or killing someone in self-defense is compatible with a given interpretation, while torturing a person in self-defense is not. Such an answer, in order to count, must not be question-begging (simply brandishing concepts like "humanity," "human dignity," "inner freedom of the will" and so on certainly does not count, as we will see below in section 6.6). Yet such an answer has been absent so far. This is hardly surprising.

However, let me consider Rainer Trapp's interpretation of the *Humanity Formula*:

A human being is used as a *mere means* if and only if one uses him for some ends without giving him the opportunity to in any way codetermine by some acts of self-determination the ends of his use and/or the beginning, the ending or the way of his use as a means.

He illustrates this with some examples:

A person who is knocked out on the street from behind and brought to a "Mafia-hospital" in order to take out his kidneys for the benefit of a don would be a crystal-clear case of a complete instrumentalization of a human being. The same would be true for a woman who is drugged with so-called knockout drops in a discotheque, brought to some apartment, raped there, and then abandoned somewhere . . . [These persons] are used as pure *passiva*, as mere objects.[82]

However, as Trapp plausibly shows, this interpretation of the Humanity Formula is perfectly compatible with self-defensive torture. Here the person can influence what happens to her by giving up the needed information,[83] and, as already said above, her right not to be treated in a way that is disproportionate or unnecessary for the self-defense purpose is respected.

A point Trapp does not consider is whether it is always wrong to treat a person as a mere means in his sense. It clearly is not. Jane, in the Slow Guillotine example from above, would clearly have been justified in knocking Radovan unconscious and in then using him as a shield against the blade (in addition, it would also have been *just*, that is, it would not have violated Radovan's rights). This would have been using him as a mere means, but it would have been justified. Let me give yet another example:

Dictator A, who likes to publicly kill his opponents in a huge Plexiglas gas chamber, sometimes stops the gassing process by jumping on a huge scale in front of his balcony in the coliseum (always cheerfully frequented by his loyal death squads). Only his exact weight in full uniform can stop the extermination. He hopes thereby to also symbolize his political weight. One day a revolution breaks out, and just when the dictator has started the process of exterminating 2,312 opponents, a revolutionary sneaks up on the dictator from behind, knocks him out with the first volume of Marx's *Capital* and throws him onto the scales, thereby saving 2,312 innocent people by using the poor dictatorial mass murderer as a mere means.

Was that justified? Of course it was! For that matter, it would also have been justified if just *one* innocent life had been at stake here instead of 2,312.

Incidentally, it is also sometimes justified, and quite easily justified, to use completely *innocent and nonthreatening* persons as mere means. Let us vary the dictator example: he escapes, but his mentally disabled and completely innocent half-brother, who to everyone's knowledge happens to weigh the exact same as the dictator, remains behind, unconscious, for whatever reason. The revolutionary tries to wake him up, but when that fails, he grabs him and puts him on the scales, thereby saving 2,312 innocent people. This act was not only justified; it was highly commendable.

Finally, it should be noted that the whole effort to find some independent criterion for what it means to treat people merely as means might overestimate the role the talk about "treating people merely as means" plays in Kant's philosophy. The fact of the matter is that Kant's talk about "treating people merely as means" does not do any explanatory work in his philosophy. For him, treating people merely as means *means* simply treating them unjustly. There is absolutely no independent criterion (independent from the question of justice) in Kant's philosophy that would specify what treating people merely as means is. And, importantly for our present question, he would certainly not believe that torturing people in self-defense is treating them unjustly.[84]

The third formulation is the *Kingdom or Realm of Ends Formula*:

Act in accordance with the maxims of a universal-law-giving member of a merely possible realm of ends.[85]

This looks pretty much like a variation on the first formula. If that is correct, what I said there applies here too. If it is not correct, then absolutist opponents of torture would have to explain why not and how this formula permits self-defensive injuring and killing but not self-defensive torture. They have not provided any such explanation. In fact, I found no absolutist opponent even mentioning the Kingdom of Ends Formula.

In sum, the Kantian formulas of the categorical imperative do not prohibit self-defensive torture. The constant claims to the contrary are simply dogmatic and entirely unwarranted. Finally: the idea that Kant himself would have objected to self-defensive torture is rather silly. Kant had no qualms allowing, in fact, *demanding* castration as punishment for "rape as well as pederasty or bestiality."[86] Similarly, Kant would have had no qualms permitting the torture of a child kidnapper to save the child. Indeed, as we will see below,[87] this permission *logically follows* from his account of self-defense and human dignity.

6.6 "Breaking the Will" (and "Dignity," "Subject Status," and "Self-legislative Rulership")

Invoking the allegedly ultimate horror of breaking someone's will is another popular maneuver among absolutist opponents of torture. *Heiner Bielefeldt* argues as follows:

> The point of torture is not merely, as it is for example in coercive detention or in many other coercive measures of the state, to impose unpleasant consequences upon a person's actions (or non-actions) that are supposed to *influence* his voluntary decisions [*Willensentscheidungen*] without directly [*unmittelbar*] breaking the will. Nor is the point to limit his external freedom of action . . . through such police measures as for example tying him up, or to completely eliminate it in the extreme case—through a fatal shot. Rather, the intent of torture is precisely to strategically use the physical and psychological vulnerability of a person for *directly breaking his inner freedom of the will.* For this reason torture is the direct negation of the subject status of the human being and hence of his dignity.[88]

Really? I doubt it. First, I already noted at the beginning that I am quite skeptical about the notion of "breaking the will." What precisely does that mean? I took the liberty to google the expressions "Wille gebrochen," "gebrochener Wille," "broken will," "will was broken" in connection with different sports. Judging from this, it seems that in football, boxing, and other sports the wills of persons are broken quite often. Is the person's status as a human being negated in such cases? Do sports violate human dignity? One might indignantly object that in these contexts the expression "his will was broken" is only being used metaphorically. Indeed, it is. However, my contention is precisely that there is no nonmetaphorical use of the expression. All one typically means by saying that someone's will is broken is that after having for a while resolutely endured in some undertaking she has finally given up in light of obstacles or some kind of attrition or because all hope was gone or because she was finally too exhausted to go on. What "breaking the inner freedom of the will" means, in contrast, is entirely unclear.

Besides, in criticizing Rainer Trapp, Bielefeldt complains:

> Well-nigh cynical is the claim that the person [namely the kidnapper of a child who has put him in some hole to let him suffocate and is asked by the police for the location] subjected to the painful interrogation procedure would merely suffer the "disadvantage of being confronted with the choice between the voluntary and the coerced exercise of his duties." For the alleged freedom of choice in this situation can be nothing else but the freedom to collapse; and the collapse will sooner or later occur nearly inevitably either because of unbearable pain or because of the fear of unbearable pain.[89]

One might wonder, of course, whether Bielefeldt's suggestion that the threat of a fatal gunshot does not violate the threatened person's freedom of choice is not also well-nigh cynical. Be that as it may, although I agree with Bielefeldt that Trapp's use of language is unduly euphemistic, I definitely do not agree that the kidnapper's only option is collapse. For example, faced with the threat of torture (Trapp is referring in particular to the famous German Daschner case), the kidnapper could say: "Hey boys, slow down, take it easy . . . I had no idea that you guys take the life of that child so seriously. I certainly don't. So, what the heck: here's the address." Where is the collapse here?

More important, however, it that Bielefeldt says that even just the *fear* of unbearable pain can break a person's will. This undermines his position. Since, as argued above, nearly all people fear death more than some forms of torture,[90] it follows that fear of death can break the will of nearly all persons *more easily* than fear of some forms of torture. Then, however, the police shouting to a criminal who fears death more than some forms of torture, "Don't move, or we'll shoot!" or, "Put down the gun, or we'll shoot!" would "negate" the criminal's "inner freedom of will" and his human dignity. In fact, however, such warnings and threats are completely legitimate, and it seems that Bielefeldt does not want to deny this. But then "breaking" someone's will is not always illegitimate, and hence torture is not always wrong.

One could try to avoid this conclusion by taking back the claim that even just the threat of torture is capable of "breaking" a person's will and instead claim that only real torture can achieve this. Yet, there still remains the problem of what "breaking the will" is supposed to mean. Why is the case of someone who after fifteen minutes of torture says, "Please stop it, please stop it, I'll tell you what you want to know," a case of broken will, while the case of someone who after fifteen months of coercive detention says, "Please let me out, please let me out, I'll tell you what you want to know," is not? Without providing some phenomenological account of what breaking the will means and some empirical evidence that it is caused by all forms of torture but not by coercive detention or death threats, the whole talk that torture breaks the will while those other forms of coercion do not is nothing but empty rhetoric.

In that context, consider a few pretty straightforward examples of breaking the will. One example is the above case of the mother who stabs the child strangler. Of course, she wants to make him let go of the child. If the strangler is determined to hold on, then her stabbing becomes an attempt to break his will. Is such an attempt justified? Of course it is! Or consider a police officer who twists the arm of someone who has unjustly attacked him with a knife. The officer uses the so-called pain compliance hold (the name says it all), asking the attacker to let go of the knife, and twisting the arm further until the attacker can't take the pain anymore and indeed lets go of the knife. Is that unjustified? Of course it is not! Or consider further a woman strangled from behind in her car by the serial killer who has waited for her on the back seat. The attacked woman cannot reach the gun she put into the glove compartment shortly before the killer's attack, but she can reach the cigarette lighter that has just become hot. The serial killer strangling her is determined not to let go of her because he fears precisely that she might then reach the gun. She presses the hot cigarette lighter hard onto the back of his hand; the man tries to bear the pain, tries to bear it, tries to bear it—but finally can't and lets go. The woman, thus, succeeded in breaking his will. Was she justified in doing so? Of course she was. Did she thereby violate his "dignity"? Of course she did not (and Kant certainly would agree). Thus, the whole idea that breaking someone's will is necessarily unjustified or even a violation of human dignity is quite simply wrong. Or does Bielefeldt really want to suggest that the woman has to allow the serial killer to strangle her to death instead of breaking his will? If that indeed is his position, then it is certainly him and those who share his attitude who have a seriously confused account of human rights and human dignity.

Besides, it should also be noted that some people *hold out under torture.* They do not give up the information. Furthermore, as already said, punitive torture does not even *aim* at the will of the victim, hence it does not aim at breaking his will either. Bielefeldt claims that Jörg Splett has proffered the "most succinct" definition of torture by designating it as the "abolition (by physical or psychological means) of the freedom of the will while maintaining consciousness."[91] For the reasons already adduced (unsuccessful interrogational torture is still torture, as is torture that does not even aim at the will, for example punitive torture), this definition is not so much succinct as confused, as is any critique of torture that relies on it.

Last, but not least: even if there were anything to this whole talk about "breaking the will," it by no means answers the question at all as to *why* torture is worse than killing. Bielefeldt has quite correctly identified a difference between killing and torture—the first one, if successful, necessarily eradicates the consciousness of the target person, whereas the latter does not. But *why* does that make killing worse? *Why* is torture "the direct negation of the subject status of the human being and hence of his dignity," while killing is not? In the example above, could Paolo say: "Well, true, I blew Bill into small pieces against his consent, but at least I didn't negate his subject status as a human being"? Isn't this statement downright idiotic? And if it is not—could Jeanette not claim to be much more respectful of Bill's subject status, a status she, after all, does not want to destroy once and for all by killing him? The answer can only be yes. Thus, Bielefeldt has certainly not provided any *argument* that would demonstrate that torture is worse than killing. He has only made a dogmatic claim.

This dogmatism, for the record, can also be found in the statements of one of the most outspoken opponents of torture at the 2007 torture conference in Hull, *Massimo la Torre*. He claims:

> Torture defeats any attempt at bringing it under a principle of universal material application: No one who accepts infliction of torture on others will accept it on oneself; this is not a standard that anyone would advocate and at the same time choose to *live by*. And it stands to reason that no one should do so, because torture is experienced by those on the receiving end of it as an act of extreme, *intolerable* violence, as an abuse and an excess—and it *must* be so experienced if it is to qualify as torture, as an *unbearable* torment, as a method for effectively obliterating another's will. Torture could never pass the test of universal acceptability that acts more or less as a final criterion of morality, for it is defined as an excess and an abuse even by those who use and apply it.[92]

First, torture is *not* defined as an excess and an abuse even by those who use and apply it. If la Torre thinks it is, his knowledge of the history of torture is very limited indeed. Nor is there any reason to define it this way, as should be clear from my above remarks on the definitional issues. After all, there is also no reason to define self-defensive killing as an abuse even though most people would rather be tortured for a few minutes than killed for good. Second, as already said, not all torture is unbearable. Some people do bear it and do not break. Unsuccessful interrogative torture is still torture (why is that so difficult to understand?). Third, interrogative torture does indeed to some extent *aim* at being "unbearable," but so does coercive detention. "Unbearable" coercive detention, however, can still be justified. So can "unbearable" torture. Besides, for both interrogative torture and coercive detention limits can be accepted by those who use these methods. Fourth, the criterion of universal acceptability is not a final criterion of morality; rather, it is itself unacceptable—and perhaps universally so. The norms "Do not abuse children for your sexual pleasure," "Do not suppress free speech only to keep yourself in power," and "Do not torture for fun" are not universally acceptable, for they are not acceptable to dedicated rapists, child abusers, and sadistic dictators. However, that obviously says nothing against their validity. Fifth, will anyone who accepts that others are killed in self-defense also accept that she herself be killed in self-defense? Perhaps not, in the act, but what does that say against the permissibility of self-defense? Nothing. Moreover, one might still (and most people do) accept a maxim that allows self-defensive killing, in the full knowledge that this maxim might lead to oneself being killed in self-defense. And again there is no difference here to the case of self-defensive torture. Many people, myself included, *do*, after all, support a moral maxim allowing self-defensive torture. It does not help matters here, by the way, to claim that at least in principle one might accept *even in the act* being killed in self-defense (thinking, with the bullet entering the heart: "I had it coming, I accept it"). I suppose that is indeed *possible*, but it is of course also possible in the case of torture. To be sure, some definitions of torture rule out that a person could be tortured with her consent, but one can still *accept* things one did not *consent* to. Since most people would prefer being tortured for a few minutes to being killed, the case in which someone accepts being tortured is, all else being equal, more likely than the case in which someone accepts being killed. Besides, I can define a special kind of self-defensive killing, namely, "unaccepted self-defensive killing," which by definition only takes place when the person killed in self-defense does not accept being killed in self-defense. Obviously the same would be true of this form of self-defensive killing that la Torre thinks is true of torture: no one who accepts that others be killed in unaccepted self-defensive killing would herself accept being killed by unaccepted self-defensive killing (if she did, it would obviously no longer be unaccepted self-defensive killing). However, unaccepted self-defensive killing (practically all actual self-defensive killing is of this kind) is certainly justified in certain circumstances. So is unaccepted self-defensive torture.

Hauke Brunkhorst seems to accept that torture can be morally justified. Yet he thinks that the legalization of torture would contradict the very conditions of democracy:

[T]here can be no doubt that the principle of democratic inclusion and the idea of *self-legislative rulership of all ruled individual human beings* (of all human being [*sic*] affected by collectively binding decisions) categorically *excludes* torture . . . [T]orture . . . would destroy the democratic self-determination because legalized, and *only legalized torture* oppresses the opportunity of subjects to the law of torture, to intervene *every time* into the public issue on this law once [I suppose what is meant is: "whenever"] it is applied to her or him. Thus, the most elementary method of the individual affected by law to participate democratically in its making—namely to be able to interfere with an argument about its validity at every time, as the chain of democratic legitimacy demands it—would cease to exist. A law to [*sic*] which *both*, the torturer and the tortured could accept or reject, no longer would be possible. As opposed to legal torture, not even the otherwise barbarian death penalty destroys that option. The condemned individual can agree or disagree with it until the very last second in order to continue the egalitarian argument about its validity even beyond his own death.[93]

A couple of observations are in order here. First of all, talk about "the idea of *self-legislative rulership of all ruled individual human beings*" is a rather big and misleading way to express the idea that "everybody who is affected by a legally binding decision has to have sufficient and equal access to the discussion, creation and implementation of legal norms."[94] In any case, if this is Brunkhorst's position, he should be against not only the legalization of torture, but also the legalization of restrictions on citizenship (for example in Germany), because the vast majority of those affected by these restrictions (namely non-Germans) do not have the same access to the making of those laws as others (namely Germans). However, Brunkhorst sees no difficulty here.[95] Anyway, if all you can say against legalized torture is that it might be as "bad" as legalized immigration restrictions against people who did not have a say in those restrictions, then this might not be the most impressive argument against torture.

Second, it is simply not correct that "everybody who is affected by a legally binding decision has to have sufficient and equal access to the discussion, creation, and implementation of legal norms." Immigration laws are a case in point (which is not to say that current immigration laws are quite all right). There are other cases. Germany was certainly affected by certain laws that Great Britain made during the Second World War. Does Brunkhorst think that it was unjust of Britain not to give Hitler a chance to participate in the British decision-making process?

Third, even if this premise were correct: how is it supposed to undermine the case for torture? After all, the torturer can also disagree (or agree, for that matter) with being tortured while he is being tortured. He can continuously, or intermittently, scream: "I am against torture." (However, the child kidnapper who is torturing the child he has put into the wooden box only seems to be opposed to being tortured himself.) And someone being waterboarded could make it clear beforehand that his showing "the finger" should be read as a sign of disagreement. Thus, while being tortured, he could demonstrate his disagreement.

Maybe Brunkhorst would counter (though he says nothing to this effect; thus, it is very unclear how his argument is to be understood in the first place) that while someone is being tortured he cannot really rationally disagree (or agree) to anything. That, however, is not necessarily true; besides, there are other acts that can sometimes undermine the ability of rational agreement or disagreement but be perfectly justifiable. Consider again the examples I mentioned in the context of breaking the will: the woman stabbing the child strangler might by this stabbing undermine the strangler's ability to engage in rational agreement or disagreement; so might the woman burning the serial killer's hand with the cigarette lighter; as well as the police officer using a painful armlock to disarm his attacker. All these acts are legal. And their legality is perfectly unobjectionable, *even if* those acts should undermine the capacity of rational agreement or disagreement of those being subjected to them. And to give a final example: it is justifiable to kill an attacker with a flamethrower if this is a proportionate and necessary means to stop his attack (which it can sometimes be); however, somebody being burned with a flamethrower will certainly be seriously compromised in his ability to take part in democratic decision-making processes or to formulate his rational dissent or consent. In short: if the legalization of these kinds of acts is justifiable (and it is; indeed these acts already are legal under certain circumstances), then the legalization of torture is justifiable as well.

Fourth, why should it be a *conditio sine qua non* of democracy that an individual can intervene in the public discussion of a law *every time* it is applied to him or her? That is entirely mysterious.

Fifth, let me note a perfectly legal practice that, unlike torture, *always and definitely* undermines an individual's capacity to intervene in the public debate of a law *every time* this law is applied to her. This is the legal practice of not waking up a sleeping person. If we exercise our right of abstaining from waking up a certain sleeping person, then this person cannot at that time intervene in our exercise of this right or in the public debate about it. After all, while a person is sleeping, she can hardly participate in the legislative discussion and say: "I object to the law that makes it legal not to wake me up right now."

It is also legal, by the way, to induce a coma in an already unconscious person for medical reasons. The unconscious person, however, obviously cannot agree or disagree with that treatment or otherwise interfere.

According to Brunkhorst's logic, all these legal regulations and permissions would be incompatible with democracy. That only shows that something is severely askew with Brunkhorst's logic.

Brunkhorst also says:

> While the reasonable [*einsichtig*] delinquent can (with Hegel) see the punishment as the exercise of his own, legislative will, the tortured person—whatever he says—, whose capacity to will anything at all is supposed to be destroyed by the legal permission of torture, *cannot* understand himself anymore as the author of the law that is executed on him.[96]

This seems only to repeat La Torre's claim that no one "who accepts infliction of torture on others will accept it on oneself; this is not a standard that anyone would advocate and at the same time choose to *live by*." This claim is as wrong (or irrelevant) here as it was there. Besides, not all torture is directed at the will in any way. Punitive torture, for example, does not necessarily aim at the will; nor does sadistic torture. Interrogative torture does, of course; but it certainly does not aim at *destroying* the target's capacity to will something. After all, that would be entirely counterproductive. Instead, interrogative torture aims to *make* the target will something: it aims to make him will to disclose the required information.

Furthermore, at some point the torture is over, and the tortured person can then will things without being under duress or pain. Death, on the other hand, really destroys one's ability to will something—permanently. Thus, it is rather strange when Brunkhorst distinguishes torture from the death penalty by claiming that the "condemned individual can agree or disagree with it [the death penalty] until the very last second in order to continue the egalitarian argument about its validity even beyond his own death." It is equally strange that Brunkhorst has no problem with lethal self-defense or with "the shooting down of a full-to-capacity passenger plane being steered by terrorists into a skyscraper or nuclear plant."[97] For contrary to his bizarre assurances, nobody can do anything beyond his own death. If you are dead, you are dead.

And what does it mean that a person being killed can "agree or disagree" with his being killed "until the very last second"? What is the last second? If it is the second of the person's actually being killed (that is, the second of the person's death), then Brunkhorst's claim is actually not quite right. For example, the death penalty is often administered such that the condemned is often unconscious long before she dies; and a person whose brain is damaged by a bullet entering it might not be dead that very second but, thanks to the brain damage, still be quite incapable of agreeing or disagreeing with anything. The same is true of a person being strangled to death in legal self-defense or being killed in legal self-defense by a method that is so painful as to undermine the person's capacity of agreeing or disagreeing to anything. The big difference Brunkhorst sees between torture and certain (completely legal and justifiable) forms of killing and injuring is entirely fictional.

Finally, it also has to be noted that if the child kidnapper who is tortured by the police cannot consider himself to be the author of the law that legalizes his torture and cannot agree or disagree to the torture while being tortured, *then the kidnapped child* (or a kidnapped adult, for that matter) who is still being tortured by the kidnapper who refuses to disclose the location of the box he has put her in *also* cannot consider herself to be the author of a law that by prohibiting the torture of the kidnapper prolongs her own torture, nor will *she* be able to agree or disagree with that law while it prolongs her torture. Thus, the question is not whether we should have a law that someone being subjected to cannot regard as an expression of his self-legislation; we will have this situation anyway even if Brunkhorst is right about torture. Rather, the question is whether, all else being equal, it is better to have a law that a culpable aggressor cannot consider a result of his self-legislation *or* to have a law that an innocent victim cannot consider a result of his self-legislation. I would submit that the answer is obvious. It is deplorable, however, that Brunkhorst does not even raise the question.

Moreover, even if the tortured child could somehow, in some mysterious fashion, regard herself as author of the law that prolongs her aggressive torture, while the tortured kidnapper cannot regard himself as the author of the law that leads to his defensive torture—why should that be an argument against the legalization of torture? Even if such a law would in some sense contradict the conditions of democracy (which is an unwarranted assumption anyway), why should it be more important to *never ever* have *any* law that somehow contradicts the conditions of democracy or the idea of strict self-legislation than to save the lives of innocent victims from the crimes of culpable aggressors? Again, Brunkhorst does not even raise the question. The answer, however, is that it is certainly *not* more important.

Incidentally, it is quite clear that for Kant, restricting self-defense so as to prohibit the necessary and proportionate self-defense against a culpable aggressor in some cases would amount to restricting the rule of law itself—and thus the rule of *justice*.[98] And I do not see why we should follow Brunkhorst in making a fetish out of some overblown and unrealistic idea of democracy to the detriment of justice, the rights of the innocent, and the rule of law.

In any case—and despite whatever Brunkhorst says—if someone who is being legally killed or severely injured in self-defense can see himself as the author of the laws at issue, then someone who is being legally tortured in self-defense can see himself as the author of those laws too. But even if he can't, that would make no difference to the justifiability of self-defensive killing or self-defensive torture. The just defender simply doesn't need the consent of the unjust aggressor.

Gerhard Beestermöller is yet another absolutist antitorture critic who seems (I will return to the "seems") to rely on the entirely unwarranted—indeed, as I have shown, quite absurd—assumption that breaking someone's will can never be justified. Beestermöller, like Bielefeldt (but unlike Brunkhorst, it seems), appears to think that breaking someone's will violates his human dignity. And also like Bielefeldt, he thinks that Jörg Splett's definition of torture is particularly commendable. Here it is again:

> I define torture as the abolition (by physical or psychological means) of the freedom of the will while maintaining consciousness.[99]

As I have already pointed out, there is a lot of torture that does not even aim at breaking the will or at abolishing "the freedom of the will"; while other forms of torture do aim at breaking the will (in the same sense as coercive detention does) but *fail* to break it. Yet both forms of torture, including unsuccessful interrogational torture, are still torture. If Splett, Bielefeldt, and Beestermöller do not realize this, I can only conclude that they do not quite understand what torture actually is. Their definition declares certain things nontorture that definitely are torture. In addition, their definition also declares quite a few of things torture that are definitely *not* torture.

I will return to this latter problem in a second. But let me first try to elucidate what Beestermöller's argument actually is. He explains:

> The concept "moral act" [*sittliche Handlung*] possesses a certain ambiguity. In one sense the talk about a "moral act" can designate the morally good act in opposition to the morally bad act. In another sense it can refer to the *actus humanus*, to the act to which the distinction between good and evil applies, in contrast to the pre-moral behavior, the *actus hominis*, for which the human being does not bear any responsibility, for example for the things he does unconsciously. The morality [*Sittlichkeit*] which is common to both morally good and morally bad action, which continuously underlies them, I want to call here proto-morality [*Proto-Sittlichkeit*]. This proto-morality possesses a claim to absoluteness that is violated by torture.[100]

Why is that?

> They [the tortured persons] experience themselves also in relation
> to the acts that are forced out of them under torture [*der erfolterten
> Handlungen*] under the demand to direct their action-guiding will
> towards the good. But torture makes this impossible. To this extent
> the moral demand is not only not met in morally bad acts, but
> also not in acts forced out of people under torture [*in erfolterten
> Handlungen*].[101]

The idea here is that an action a person was forced to do under torture
cannot be morally good or bad. Even if that were true, an obvious question,
of course, is: "So what?" After all, why should it be more important to allow
a child-kidnapper to do *moral acts* at all times, in the first sense, than to make
him engage at a certain time in behavior (or "acta hominis") that saves an
innocent child from the results of his previous absolutely immoral acts (in the
second sense)? To say, "Because it violates his human dignity," is not quite an
answer. First, one can doubt that it does (as we will see shortly); and second,
why should a culpable aggressor's "human dignity" be more important than
an innocent child's survival (and human dignity)?

Beestermöller, like so many German theologians (and quite a few lawyers
and philosophers), might be laboring under the assumption that once you claim
that a certain act violates "human dignity" every defender of such an act has
to sink to his knees crying, admit defeat, and repent. Unfortunately, however,
the concept of "human dignity" is anything but clear, and therefore its argumentative value is somewhat limited, to put it mildly. I, for one, think that
if the torture of the child kidnapper in order to save the child should violate
the child kidnapper's human dignity, then this only proves that human dignity
can be justifiably violated and that its value might be severely overestimated.

But Beestermöller faces even more questions and problems. The last quote
ends with a footnote in which he refers to Friedo Ricken, whose account, as
Beestermöller explicitly says, "can very well be understood in line with the
position endorsed here" (that is, by Beestermöller). He quotes Ricken saying:

> The ability to set oneself ends is the necessary, albeit not sufficient
> condition of the good will. Thus, whoever hinders another person
> from setting herself ends at all and realizing them, completely
> impedes the good will and its realization. Thus every intervention
> in the freedom of decision and action of a human being offends
> against the absolute value of the good will.[102]

But here a little problem arises, as Beestermöller concedes:

> If one reads this literally, and thereby presumably against the intentions of the author, then nobody can be sent to jail or be killed. Likewise, nobody can be drafted to collaborate for genuinely collective goods like, for instance, military service, dike watch or jury duties. These things also involve limitations of freedom. However, if we read the sentence more narrowly as referring to the setting of ends to one's conscious acts, then an offence against the setting of one's own ends would occur exactly when one deprives a human being of the possibility to direct his consciously produced acts towards ends he has chosen himself. This and hence torture would then always be an offence against a human being's ability to set his own ends [*gegen die Selbstzwecklichkeit des Menschen*].[103]

Actually, if you kill someone, you do deprive her of the possibility to direct her consciously produced acts toward ends she has chosen herself, for you deprive her of the possibility to produce any acts, consciously or otherwise. Thus, in order to be consistent, Beestermöller would have to be against lethal self-defense. He is not against lethal self-defense; nor is he consistent.

By torturing someone, however, you do not deprive the tortured person of the possibility to direct his consciously produced acts toward ends he has chosen himself. For the tortured person obviously not only has the *possibility* to direct his consciously produced acts toward ends he has chosen himself, but he actually *is* doing precisely this: if interrogative torture is to be successful, the tortured person has to set himself the end of avoiding pain (an end, incidentally, most people set themselves even before ever being tortured), and on the basis of this he has to set himself the end of ending the torture, an end he can achieve, in the context of strictly self-defensive torture, by disclosing the life-saving information.

Thus, Beestermöller's claims about interrogational torture are simply wrong. Interrogational torture does not abolish "proto-morality," the ability of a human being to set his own ends; it *presupposes* it.

Of course, by *successfully* subjecting someone to aversive stimuli (like pain) and to threats (for instance, of continuing the infliction of pain) in order to make him execute an act he would not otherwise execute you are putting him under pressure: when he then executes the desired act, this act is an expression of his will, but not of his *free* will in the sense of a will that was *not* influenced and bent by aversive stimuli and threats. But, so what? If Beestermöller is against this, he again immediately faces the problem of the literal interpretation of Ricken's statement: sending people to jail, drafting them into military service, and deterring them with legal sanctions from murder and rape would be impermissible. But Beestermöller really wants to permit these things. So why not permit torture, which is, after all, entirely compatible with protomorality?

In that context, let me come back to my claim that according to Splett's (and thus Bielefeldt's and Beestermöller's) definition a lot of things that in fact are not torture would count as torture.

I already noted that according to their definition a lot of things that quite clearly are torture do *not* count as torture. Remember that according to Splett torture is "the abolition (by physical or psychological means) of the freedom of the will while maintaining consciousness." Thus, if for hours and hours terrible pain is inflicted upon a person by giving electrical shocks to his genitalia or, alternatively, by slowly burning away his hand with a blowtorch, then as long as the person does not do what the torturers want him to do, it is not torture at all, for obviously it did not abolish the tortured person's freedom of the will. Rather, this person only gave an impressive proof of the enormous *strength* of his will.

When would this procedure become torture, in Splett's sense? Well, when (while maintaining consciousness) the freedom of the will of the tortured person is abolished. But when does that happen? How do you find out? In fact, what does that *mean*?[104] (Here I make good on my promise to return to the word "seems": Beestermöller can argue, and in fact does argue,[105] that he is not against breaking of the will as such, since coercive detention already does that, but only against something different: the "abolition of the freedom of the will." But then he would have to explain what that *means* and how we can *recognize* such an abolition of the inner freedom of the will. He does neither.)

Let us assume that the tortured person (I use the word "torture" in my sense, not in Splett's sense) at some point does disclose the information the torturers are looking for. Is this a sign that her freedom of the will was abolished? Well, why should it be? For example, let us suppose that the tortured person knows that she would be immediately released once she gives the required information. But she is really enormously tough and in fact wants to prove it. And she knows that she can still take much more pain. She is determined to endure the torture longer. However, suddenly she remembers (she has, understandably, forgotten because of the whole business of her arrest and torture) that she has not yet mailed an important letter. If she does not do so within the next hour, this would mean a disastrous financial or personal loss for her. So she says: "Okay, here is the information: the password is grwlwrompf802. Can I go now?" The torturers check the information, find out that it is correct, and let her go. Has the tortured person's freedom of the will been abolished by the torture? Obviously not.

Thus, the fact that a tortured person discloses the information does not show that the freedom of her will has been successfully "abolished" by the torture. Perhaps she could have endured much more torture, but she just *decided* not to take any more. If, however, one just insisted on taking the disclosure of the information as proof that the freedom of the will has been "abolished," then, of course, we would also have to take a serial rapist and killer's ceasing his violent attack in light of the armed woman's threat, "If you come any closer, I shoot," as proof of the abolishment of his free will—after all, we do not want any double standards, do we? The woman's threat, therefore, would be torture under Splett's and Beestermöller's definition, and both authors would have to say that this woman violated the poor, poor serial rapist and killer's human dignity. The same is true for legal sanctions, of course. If certain persons are only kept from murder, rape, and child abuse by the threat that they will go to prison if they commit those acts and are captured, then the laws against murder, rape, and child abuse abolish the freedom of the will of the would-be murderers, rapists, and child abusers and thus violate their human dignity. And who could possibly want that?

In other words, what I have said in this text against Bielefeldt's talk about "breaking the will" is also applicable to Splett's and Beestermöller's talk about the "abolition of the freedom of the will." One only has to replace the former phrase with the latter, as follows: without providing some phenomenological account of what "abolition of the freedom of the will" means and empirical evidence that it is caused by all forms of torture but not by coercive detention or death threats (or legal sanctions, for that matter), the whole talk that torture abolishes the freedom of the will while those other forms of coercion do not is nothing but empty rhetoric.

Beestermöller makes some other statements I find rather curious:

> In a conflict situation in which moral identity [*sittliche Identität*] stands against the preservation of non-moral goods, moral identity is always preferable.[106]

Note that the survival of a kidnapped child would count here as a "non-moral good," while the freedom of the will of the kidnapper (or, as I have pointed out, of would-be child abusers, rapists, and murderers whose freedom of the will is compromised by the threat of legal sanctions or by a threat of the form "Stop raping me, or I will shoot you") concerns moral identity. I have already criticized this position (obviously, I do not share Beestermöller's

priorities); here, however, I am more concerned with what Beestermöller says
a few sentences later:

> Inducement to sin does not exist merely by virtue of a person being
> exposed to incentives and pressure to deviate from a decision alleg-
> edly guided by his conscience [*vorgeblichen Gewissensentscheidung*].
> The intention that the tested person shall fail is also necessary.
> Only then would the act follow an inadequate value preference
> rule [*Wertvorzugsregel*], namely to give non-moral values priority
> over moral values.[107]

I must admit that I have severe difficulties following this. First, is it
really the intention that the tempted person deviate from a decision *allegedly*
guided by his conscience that is sinful, rather than the intention that the
tempted person deviate from a decision that is *actually* guided by his conscience? Beestermöller says the former, but doesn't the latter make more sense?
If Beestermöller really means the latter (and just expressed himself poorly),
then torturing a kidnapper whose conscience tells him to disclose the location
of the child while prudential incentives keep him from acting on the voice of
his conscience should be commendable; such torture seems to reinforce the
"moral identity" of the tortured person.

However that may be, note that according to Beestermöller, a father who
tries to save his child from a captured kidnapper who truthfully professes that
his conscience tells him to let the child slowly die and rot in a wooden box
would be acting sinfully if he offered the kidnapper money (or caviar) with
the intention that the kidnapper deviate from the decision to let the child
die, along with threatening him with a civil lawsuit in case he sticks to his
decision. And a district attorney who offers the kidnapper a deal (reduced
punishment) if the kidnapper discloses the location of the child but threatens
him with more severe punishment in case he does not, intending to thereby
bring the kidnapper to act against his conscience for the benefit of the child,
would also be acting sinfully. This, I submit, demonstrates just how absurd
Beestermöller's position is.

In his most recent article on the topic, however, he does address this
problem, suggesting the following escape route:

> If I pay a convinced terrorist money for [the information about]
> the hiding place of the bomb, do I then want him to sin? Not
> at all. I sincerely hope that the tempting situation will trigger a
> conversion experience. Perhaps in light of these entirely new living

possibilities he will realize the value of life as such and convert. In any case, the sin of this human being is not a necessary link in the chain of the pursuit of my goals. For this reason, the attempt to induce him with money to reveal the hiding place is not at all *eo ipso* connected with the intention to make him morally fail [*sittlich stürzen*].[108]

The sin would be to act against his conscience. However, it seems to be the case that acting on one's murderous conscience (see Adolf Hitler and Heinrich Himmler) is also a sin, and certainly the bigger one. Thus, with some money one could make the terrorist at least opt for the lesser sin and improve his moral standing—isn't that good?

Anyway, Beestermöller's argument here is an abuse of the doctrine of double effect, which follows the same (erroneous) logic as a famous argument of Jonathan Bennett. Bennett says that we normally reject terror bombing as morally wrong because the terror bomber intends to kill innocent human beings in order, for example, to put pressure upon a government or a civilian population. However, he notes that the death of innocents is not "a necessary link in the chain of the pursuit" (to use Beestermöller's words) of the terror bomber's goals; after all, he can "hope" that the innocent people will only *appear dead* long enough to reach his goals.[109]

My criticism is and was that if someone *knows* (and knowledge can be had without *certainty*) that killing people is the only realistic means of making them "appear dead" and tries to do exactly that, namely to kill them, one cannot honestly say that one does not intend to kill them.[110] Likewise, if one *knows* that the terrorist will *not* change his convictions but only act against them because of the money, and gives him the money with the intention that he act against his conviction, then one does intend "to make him morally fail." This will be how normal people, who have not the unrealistic hopes of the "I" in Beestermöller's example, will act and think, and in the case of the person trying to buy the information about the hiding place of the bomb, they will do so quite justifiably. On Beestermöller's account, however, only the sufficiently unrealistic and ridiculously optimistic would be allowed to offer the terrorist money. All others, after all, would do so unjustifiably and would have to be kept away. However, that reduces Beestermöller's position to absurdity again.

Besides, even if a person indeed hoped and implausibly deemed it possible that the convinced terrorist would convert if one offers him some money, one should still have a backup plan. Any at least *morally* sane "hoper" would therefore have a "plan B" hope when confronted with an unjustified terrorist: "I hope, a) that the terrorist will change his conviction because of the money and desist from blowing up many innocent people; and b) I also hope that if this does *not* happen, he will act against his conscience and reveal the location of the bomb." Beestermöller, however, must hope for this: "I hope, a) that the terrorist will change his conviction because of the money and desist from blowing up many innocent people; and b) I also hope that if this does *not* happen, he will resist my temptation, act on his conscience and accordingly keep pursuing his goal of blowing up many innocent people." This, I must bluntly say, following *my* conscience, is *not* a morally sane hope.

Finally, let me note that Beestermöller's "principle of hope" can be applied not just to temptation by money but also to "temptation" by torture, a fact that seems not to have occurred to Beestermöller. So let me modify the quote accordingly:

> If I torture a convinced terrorist in order to make him reveal the hiding place of the bomb, do I then want him to sin, or do I want to abolish his will? Not at all. I sincerely hope that the torture situation will trigger a conversion experience. Perhaps in light of the pain and suffering he will realize the value of the absence of pain and suffering (evils that he is about to inflict with his bomb) and convert. In any case, the sin of this human being is not a necessary link in the chain of the pursuit of my goals. For this reason the attempt to induce him with torture to reveal the hiding place is not at all *eo ipso* connected with the intention to make him morally fail.

What is good for the goose is good for the gander.

Let me finally say something about Beestermöller's talk about *Menschenwürde* (human dignity). That expression is not unequivocal. It can mean *Würde des Menschen* (the dignity of *humanity*), and it can mean *Würde der Menschen* (the dignity of *human beings*). In my view, the concept of the dignity of humanity is a totalitarian abstraction that is used to spurn individual rights and the dignity and autonomy of actual human beings.[111] In addition, "arguments" based on the dignity of humanity are never anything more than exercises in dogmatism. People like to appeal to the "dignity of humanity" when they run out of actual arguments.

Beestermöller's concern is precisely with the dignity of humanity, something that does not deserve any concern at all. Criticizing Reinhard Merkel's justification of self-defensive torture, he laments:

> In his argumentation for the legitimacy of self-defensive torture Merkel only considers particular [*partikulare*] goods of single individuals, not

the good of human dignity, which is shared by all. . . . But if the claim [*Anspruch*] that one may torture a kidnapper in self-defense violated the claim that human dignity itself has on our respect [*den Achtungsanspruch von Menschenwürde überhaupt*] and hence also the human dignity of the person who is supposed to be saved by torture, then one would also have done a grave injustice to the person saved; a graver injustice than even an omission of saving his life would be. Through the person of the perpetrator one would have denied all human beings that which makes them bearers of particular rights in the first place; rights that apart from humans nothing has.[112]

Beestermöller returns to this argument at the end of the paper again:

If what I have called proto-morality must, for the sake of human dignity, never be violated, then the victim of an unjust attack would, by torturing his desecrator, be done an injustice that would not be nullified by his preserved non-moral goods, including his life. For the precondition of injustice being done to him at all would be destroyed. This precondition is that the relation between victim and perpetrator is and remains a relation in the dimension of rights [*eine Rechtsbeziehung ist und bleibt*; the translation that suggests itself here is "legal relation," but it is clear that Beestermöller is also referring to morality, which influences the rest of this translation], which presupposes that the members of the community of right-holders possess an inalienable rights-subjectivity [*was unverwirkbare Rechts-subjektivität der Rechtsgenossen voraussetzt*, to have "rights-subjectivity" means to be a bearer of rights].[113]

What is to be said to this? To repeat some of what I have already pointed out, while adding a few new points:

1. Beestermöller has not given any *argument* why "proto-morality must, for the sake of human dignity, never be violated." He just *claims* that it must never be violated.

2. Beestermöller has not shown that protomorality is violated in all acts that are normally called torture while it is not violated in many acts we—and he—consider to be justifiable, for instance death threats, coercive detention, creating laws that are backed up with sanctions, or bribing a child kidnapper with money or caviar into not following his murderous consciousness.

3. Beestermöller simply *defines* torture as something that violates protomorality. Even if torture in this sense were always wrong, this still would not say anything about torture in the normal sense. Nor has Beestermöller shown that torture in his sense even exists.

4. Beestermöller has not given any epistemic criteria by which to decide whether, in a given situation, protomorality has been violated or not. Thus, his reasoning is entirely irrelevant and inconsequential for practice. In fact, he has not even explained what it *means* to violate protomorality. To simply state that it "abolishes the freedom of the will (while maintaining consciousness)" explains and clarifies nothing as long as one is not enlightened as to what *that* means. As in the case of Bielefeldt, we are faced with empty rhetoric.

These four points sum up some of the things I have said in the previous discussion. Let me now add some further remarks targeted specifically at the last two quotations:

5. Beestermöller's claim that by torturing someone in his sense— namely by "abolishing" (by physical or psychological means) his "freedom of the will" while maintaining his consciousness—one denies that which makes him a bearer of particular rights in the first place is wrong. By keeping self-defensive torture within the confines of justified self-defense, that is, by not using unnecessary or grossly disproportionate means, one does not deny that the tortured person still has certain rights, but rather clearly *accepts* it. And of course the tortured person still *does* have rights. If he had not, one might do *anything* to him. Does Beestermöller want to say that someone whose "freedom of the will" is "abolished" while his consciousness is not has no rights? Then I do not quite understand what his problem with torture is. Torture, in his sense, could *never* violate any rights.

6. Beestermöller's claim that a victim cannot suffer an injustice if the perpetrator is not a bearer of rights is also wrong. If the victim has a right not to be kidnapped, then this right can be violated and thus an injustice can be done to the victim by any responsible agent, whether that agent has rights or not.

However, Beestermöller might want to say that a victim cannot suffer an injustice from someone who is *not responsible* for his actions, for example from someone whose "freedom of the will" has been "abolished." But that is also wrong. While the child kidnapper is sleeping, his freedom of the will is in a rather straightforward sense abolished (which, as already mentioned, is not necessarily the case with all kinds of torture, in the normal sense of the word); yet he is still doing an injustice to the child. After all, he *is* responsible for not letting the child go before he went to sleep. Sleep does not absolve you from your past sins, nor does torture, even if it should "abolish" the "freedom of the will." The tortured child kidnapper should have disclosed the information before the torturers (allegedly) temporarily "abolished" his "freedom of the will."

7. Beestermöller talks a lot about rights and about an injustice allegedly (and mysteriously) done to the kidnapped person by torturing his kidnapper. Thus I assume that he thinks that the kidnapped person has a right that his kidnapper not be tortured. However, people can decide not to exercise their rights. In fact, they can even have a right that others assume that they would not *want* to exercise certain of their rights under certain circumstances. For example, a person normally has a right that others not open her chest cavity without her consent. However, if she is unconscious because of an accident and cannot be saved without a doctor opening her chest cavity, the doctors are not only entitled but in fact required to assume (without clear evidence to the contrary) that the accident victim would consent to have them open her chest cavity. The same is of course true of the kidnapped child. We are not only entitled, but required, to assume that under the circumstances the child would not insist upon his right that his kidnapper not be tortured in order to save his life.

And now it is time to return to my claim that the concept of the dignity of humanity is a totalitarian abstraction used to spurn individual rights. For, quite frankly, I suspect that Beestermöller does not really care what the child *wants* (which, of course, is not to say that he does not sympathize with the child's plight). *He* just knows that it is *unjust* toward the child to torture his kidnapper, *more* unjust indeed than to aid and abet the kidnapper in torturing the child by shielding him from self-defensive torture (how is that for a conflict with human dignity?). All he has to say about letting the child die is that it is "tragic"[114]—but of course necessary for "the dignity of humanity." Indeed, it is in the child's best interest.

What the innocent child would say, or any kidnapped innocent person for that matter, does not count. We can even imagine that the kidnapped person has a cell phone in his wooden box. It is not possible to locate the cell phone, nor does the kidnapper's victim have any idea where he is. But he is asked whether he wants to exercise his alleged right that his culpable kidnapper not be tortured, although torturing him could save the innocent victim's life. The victim says, no, he does not. "Go ahead, torture him."

But the theologian of human dignity says: "Sorry, but we will not. We will let you die. You know, it is in your own best interest, really, that he is not tortured. We really don't want to violate your human dignity."

"No, it isn't in my interest at all. I want you to save me."

"Yes it is in your interest. Really, you should leave these assessments to the expert. Good bye and die well." If *this* does not demonstrate an outrageous paternalistic arrogance of the theologian toward the kidnapped victim and indeed a gross violation of the latter's autonomy and dignity as a person, as an individual, as a single human being, that is, as something that is not simply a disposable part of an amorphous matter called "humanity," then I really do not know what does.

This is the problem with the "dignity of humanity." For all the talk about "freedom of the will" and "autonomy," the will and autonomy of the innocent victim of the kidnapper are sacrificed without much ado to the golden calf of the dignity of "humanity." Immanuel Kant, unfortunately, paved the way for this unpalatable totalitarian nonsense. For example, instead of leaving sexuality to the free will and autonomy and to the individual rights of consenting adults, he claimed that homosexuality violates human dignity, since he saw the end of humanity with regard to the sexual drive in procreation. However, with the typical double standard and illogic of those who appeal to the dignity of humanity in the first place, he failed to detect a violation of the dignity of humanity in his own (for all we know) lack of attempts to procreate or, for that matter, in the institution of celibacy. Kant's claim is of course a dogmatic one. He does not actually have the slightest idea of what the end of humanity is; he does not even know whether it has an end. And neither does he tell us why we should care in the least about the end or ends of humanity, nor does he show any concern for consistency when it comes to the "dignity of humanity."

Beestermöller's claim that the torture of the child kidnapper violates "the dignity of humanity" is also dogmatic. However, it is interesting in this context—and, incidentally, of considerable entertainment value—to note that the ideas about self-defense of none less than *Immanuel Kant himself* imply precisely the *contrary* claim: that *not* torturing the child kidnapper violates the dignity of humanity and thus also the child kidnapper's own dignity. Though I do not buy Kant's argument, I will describe it here to show that the whole appeal to the "dignity of humanity" is just a cheap legerdemain: you pull precisely that rabbit out of the hat you have put there in the first place; and you can put anything there. Moreover, this should also once more help to cure[115] certain absolutist antitorture opponents of their rather ridiculous illusions about Kant's philosophy, in particular about his stance toward self-defense and torture.

The fact is that according to Kant people not only have a right to self-defense; they also have a *duty to self-defense*. I follow here the excellent argumentation by Joachim Hruschka.[116] As we know, Kant does not think that people should merely be treated as a means. When are people treated as a means? This is what Kant says:

> This conflict with the principle about treating others as ends is even easier to see in examples of attacks on people's freedom and property; for in those cases it's obvious that someone who violates the rights of men intends to make use of the person of others merely as means, without considering that as rational beings they should always be valued at the same time as ends, i.e. as beings who can contain in themselves the end of the very same action.[117]

Of course, this refers to *unjust* attacks. For as Kant explains about the relationship between right and coercion:

> Resistance that counteracts the hindering of an effect promotes this effect and is consistent with it. Now whatever is wrong is a hindrance to freedom in accordance with universal laws. But coercion is a hindrance or resistance to freedom. Therefore, if a certain use of freedom is itself a hindrance to freedom in accordance with universal laws (i.e., wrong), coercion that is opposed to this (as a *hindering of a hindrance to freedom*) is consistent with freedom in accordance with universal laws, that is, it is right. Hence there is connected with right by the principle of contradiction an authorization to coerce someone who infringes upon it.[118]

Kant also subscribes to the following:

> *Be an honorable human being (honeste vive). Rightful honor (honestas iuridica)* consists in asserting one's worth as a human being in

relation to others, a duty expressed by the saying, "Do not make
you[r]self a mere means of others but be at the same time an end
for them." This duty will be explained later as obligation from the
right of humanity in our own person. (*Lex iusti*)[119]

Thus, according to Kant unjust attacks treat people as mere means. Since
people have a *duty* not to allow others to treat them as mere means, they have
a duty, owed to humanity in their own person, to defend themselves against
unjust attacks. In addition, Kant makes it very clear that the unjustly attacked
person owes his attacker *nothing*. He does *not* owe it to him not to use excessive means in his self-defense—for instance, he does not owe it to him not
to kill or to torture him if he could also save himself by simply knocking the
attacker out. Moderation—to do only what is necessary for self-defense, but no
more—might be owed to humanity or to himself, but not to the aggressor.[120]
In addition, Kant states that "[a]uthorities which prohibit self-defense involving
grave damages to the other [that is, the aggressor] must know that they deprive
the human being of his most holy right"[121] and adamantly opposes the "renun-
ciation of rigorous means (*rigorosa*) for preventing the recurrence of wrongs by
others; for then a human being would be throwing away his rights and letting
others trample on them, and so would violate his duty to himself."[122]
   On Kant's account of self-defense and of duties owed to humanity, then,
the kidnapper from our example definitely does not have a right not to be
tortured. However, if the kidnapped person were able to torture the kidnapper
from his wooden prison through some strange powers and to thereby effect
his own release, not only would he be justified in doing this in proportionate
and necessary self-defense, but he would have a *duty* to do it—he would have
a duty, owed to humanity in himself (and to that extent also to the kidnapper
as part of humanity), to torture the aggressor.
   It seems that Kant makes a poor patron saint for absolutist opponents
of torture. I therefore take the liberty to rightfully claim him for my side.
   We can conclude that the brandishing of all these (pseudo-) concepts
like "breaking the inner freedom of the will" (or simply "breaking the will"—
which is not a pseudoconcept, but also entirely justifiable), "abolishing the
will while maintaining consciousness," "denying an individual's subject status,"
"undermining the preconditions of self-legislative rulership," or on top of it
all, "human dignity" amounts to only so much hot air and certainly does not
show that breaking a person's will by torturing that person is unjustifiable.
With Kant we have to say that the limitation of self-defense, and thus the
prohibition of self-defensive torture, is a violation of the individual's right. In
fact, Kant would even say that it is a violation both of his most holy right
and of the dignity of humanity.

6.7 Torture and the Doctrine of Double Effect

Sometimes one hears the claim that torture violates the principle of double effect and is therefore impermissible. This is, indeed, Florian Lamprecht's main argument against torture. He did not invent it, but he develops it at length.

My criticism of his position, in contrast, will be rather short. First of all, an argument like his depends on the correctness of the doctrine of double effect. But, as Lamprecht himself notes, "this principle has lost some of its philosophical esteem in recent years."[123] Indeed it has. Therefore one would assume that Lamprecht, who realizes this problem, would first try to refute the devastating criticisms that have been leveled against this principle. But he does not; he just dogmatically assumes its validity. Sure enough, he refers to a book by Peter Knauer, in which this author has allegedly undertaken "the attempt to critically reconstruct this principle with the aim of overcoming 'the defects of the traditional interpretation.'"[124] Unfortunately, Knauer, too, completely ignores the most devastating criticisms of the principle of double effect; and I fail to detect any argument in his book (or elsewhere) that would in the slightest way undermine those criticisms.[125]

It is not necessary here to discuss the doctrine of double effect independently of Lamprecht's argument, for by discussing the latter we will easily enough see that the former is wrong too.

Lamprecht thinks that (interrogative) torture is wrong because (a) a bad effect of torture, namely, breaking a person's will, is not only accepted as a side-effect of torture but is actually *intended*; (b) this bad effect of torture is a *means* to achieve the goal (to get the information); and (c) because "through torture the will of the tortured person is always broken and therefore his human dignity violated."[126]

I do not have to say anything about (c) here. We have already seen in the last section that even interrogational torture does not always break the will (it is not always successful) and, what is more important, that breaking someone's will does not violate his human dignity and is certainly not unjustifiable. If Lamprecht thinks it is, he would have to criticize the woman in the cigarette lighter example for not allowing the serial killer to strangle her to death and for instead breaking his will by burning his hand with the lighter. He would also have to oppose coercive detention and a lot of other things that are quite clearly justifiable. Indeed, that the strangled woman breaks the will of the strangler is not only justifiable, but morally desirable.

There is also no need to talk about point (a), for it is actually implied by point (b). And I do not deny that Lamprecht is right about (b)—of course breaking the tortured person's will (in the entirely colloquial sense of "breaking someone's will") is the means by which one intends to get the required information. I definitely do deny, however, that using a bad effect, an evil, as means to achieve a good effect makes an act impermissible. (By the way, I *also* deny that breaking a child kidnapper's will not to give the information where the kidnapped child is *is* a bad thing in the first place. Lamprecht certainly does not show that it is. He just assumes it; and that assumption is certainly anything but evidently correct—quite the contrary. The following discussion, however, just grants Lamprecht that assumption for the sake of argument.)

If it did, by the way, it would also make certain things impermissible that Lamprecht actually considers to be perfectly permissible. For instance, he does not want to prohibit lethal self-defense, so he has to suppose that lethal self-defense is compatible with the doctrine of double effect. That supposition, however, is wrong. Let us see how he tries to construct the difference between torture and killing in self-defense:

> Since the breaking of the will that results from the violent assault on the physico-psychological integrity of a human being is an indispensable precondition for the achievement of the goal of the action, namely the saving of a life, and does not directly arise (as it does in the cases of killing in self-defense and the life-saving lethal shot) from the act of torture, "life-saving torture" remains a means to achieve an end, which according to the maxim "The good end does not justify the bad means" cannot be allowed.[127]

First of all, in the case of killing in self-defense the achievement of the goal (of ending the aggressor's life) does not result from an act of torture, for there is no act of torture. There is an act of killing. Thus, I suppose that the relevant difference is, according to Lamprecht, that the achievement of the goal of ending the aggressor's life directly arises from killing the aggressor, while the goal of breaking the aggressor's will does not directly arise from torturing the aggressor.

As I had to ask so often here when faced with absolutist antitorture arguments: so what? *Of course* acts of torture do not always (though they sometimes do) directly result in breaking the will of the tortured person. After all, the tortured person might be able to resist. But acts of shooting directed against an aggressor also do not always directly result in the death of the aggressor, for the defender can miss, can't he? A *lethal* shot at an aggressor, on the other hand, does directly result in the death of the aggressor. But a *will-breaking* act of torture against an aggressor *also* directly results in the broken will of the aggressor. In other words, what Lamprecht wants to sell us as an apple and a peach are in fact either two apples or two peaches. There is no difference.

Second, what does this whole talk about what "directly arises" from what have to do with the question whether something is a *means* to an end anyway? Obviously, if the ending of the aggressor's life is the direct result of the lethal shot directed against him, then ending the aggressor's life *is* the means by which the aim of stopping the aggression and thus saving an innocent life was achieved. Fiona Leverick nicely sums up the discussion (apparently one ignored by Lamprecht) of the doctrine of double effect in this context:

> The use of the doctrine of double effect to justify self-defensive killing has been extensively criticized, primarily on the basis of whether there really is a meaningful distinction between the intended effects and merely foreseeable effects of lethal self-defensive force. Uniacke uses the example of repelling an aggressor by blowing her up and questions whether the defender can truly maintain that she did not intend to kill, especially given that an effect is strictly intended *if it is a means of achieving the actor's aim* in the circumstances. I would agree. The moral distinction between intending to kill an aggressor in self-defence and using lethal force in self-defence but merely foreseeing (but not intending) that the death of the aggressor would result is too fine to be meaningful. Indeed, for this reason, Grisez, a supporter of the doctrine of double effect in other contexts, casts doubt on whether it can meaningfully be applied to self-defensive killing.[128]

In other words, if a defender or sniper intentionally puts a bullet into the brain of an aggressor, then ending the aggressor's life is the means by which the aggression is stopped and the life of an innocent person is saved. Dead aggressors cannot continue to be aggressive, and thus ending their life is an excellent means to stop the aggression. It would simply be disingenuous to claim: "I did not really intend to kill him; I only wanted to blow out his brain."

Besides, that, at least, the sniper did want. However, it seems that intentionally destroying someone's brain is a very severe "violent assault on the physico-psychological integrity of a human being." And of course it is "an indispensable precondition for the achievement of the goal of the action," since if the bullet does not immediately destroy the physico-psychological integrity of the aggressor, this aggressor can still pull the trigger of the gun that he holds to the head of his hostage. Thus, the police sniper *intends* to destroy the target's brain. He not only accepts this as a side-effect of something else (for example, of his pulling the trigger); for he knows that if he pulls the trigger *without* achieving the destruction of the target's brain, the whole purpose of pulling the trigger in the first place has not been accomplished. Destroying the target's brain is the *means* of incapacitating him and saving the hostage's life.

Thus, if it is permissible—and obviously it is—to intend the *destruction of an aggressor's brain* as a means of stopping his aggression, then the doctrine of double effect must be wrong. And of course it is. Furthermore, if it is permissible to intend the destruction of an aggressor's brain as a means of stopping his aggression, then temporarily breaking an aggressor's will as a means of stopping his aggression must be permissible as well. After all, having one's will temporally broken is definitely preferable to having one's brain permanently destroyed. It is rather difficult to exercise one's will if one's brain has left one's skull in pieces.

Thus, (intentional) torturing, killing, and injuring in self-defense are not compatible with the doctrine of double effect. However, since the doctrine of double effect is itself incompatible with reason and morality, this says nothing against such self-defensive measures. They are perfectly justifiable.

6.8 Is the Ticking-Bomb Example Unrealistic?

That the ticking-bomb argument is "unrealistic" is another claim repeated like a mantra by absolutist torture opponents.[129] One of the first to make this claim is certainly *Henry Shue*. In section 3, we focused on his complaint about the alleged "idealization" of the rare case and considered his concern about the alleged "abstraction" from the allegedly inevitable institutional context of (successful) torture. We saw that his argument does not hold water. However, it is worth coming back to him while also looking at certain complaints about the ticking-bomb argument made by others in order to get a fuller picture of the charge that the ticking bomb-argument is unrealistic.

Shue says:

> There is a standard philosopher's example which someone always invokes: suppose a fanatic, perfectly willing to die rather than collaborate in the thwarting of his own scheme, has set a hidden nuclear device to explode in the heart of Paris. There is no time to evacuate the innocent people or even the movable art treasures—the only hope of preventing tragedy is to torture the perpetrator, find the device, and deactivate it.

While Shue had once seen "no way to deny the permissibility of torture in a case *just like this*,"[130] he has increasingly stressed the unlikelihood of this situation over the years, coming to the conclusion "that one should absolutely never torture."[131] The "idealizations" Shue detects in this ticking-bomb case include the idea that the person to be tortured "is somehow known with certainty actually to be the person who planted the ticking bomb" and that the torture victim "quickly divulges the crucial information before the bomb has had time to explode."[132]

But *whose* idealizations are these? Shue claims that "someone" always invokes this ticking-bomb scenario, but note that in his description of the scenario those idealizations are missing. And in fact Shue *never actually* provides a reference revealing the identity of this mysterious someone engaging in the unrealistic idealizations that bother Shue so much. So who is it?

The fact is that it is Shue himself. *He* conjures up a ticking-bomb argument of his very own making in order to then conveniently detect idealizations in it he himself has personally put there in the first place.[133] If anyone is being unrealistic here, it is Shue himself.

No one who has ever used a ticking bomb scenario to argue for the permissibility of torture in the real world (instead of only to test the strength or scope of our presumably absolutist convictions) has ever used a scenario that involved the two idealizations just mentioned. And no one needs to, as we have already seen quite clearly above, in section 3.[134] The following analysis of the charges of unrealism from other authors will further confirm this result.

Shue is not the only critic of "the" ticking-bomb argument who attacks a straw man. Actually, pretty much all do (I have not encountered a single exception). *David Luban* is a particularly prominent example and therefore worth mentioning (he is frequently quoted, after all). He, too, complains about certain assumptions that "taken together are vanishingly unlikely."[135] However, he then admits: "Some of these assumptions can be dropped or modified, of course." Yet, he immediately adds: "But in its pure form, the TBS [ticking-bomb scenario] assumes them all."[136] As one might expect, he then criticizes the "pure" form of the TBS, that is, a straw man. Thus, while Luban claims "that ticking-bomb stories are built on a set of assumptions that amount to intellectual fraud,"[137] it is, I think, quite obvious who is *actually* committing intellectual fraud here.

Ironically, even in attacking the straw man—who, one might think, would not be such a difficult target—Luban relies, in my view, not so much on argument as on a completely overblown rhetoric. For example, he uses the expression "friends of torture" twice in "Unthinking the Ticking Bomb." To whom is this expression supposed to refer? Would I be a friend of torture, because I dare to defend the justifiability of torture in some narrow circumstances? If so, then this would make Luban, who has argued in several articles that war is justified under certain conditions, a friend of killing and mutilation, I suppose, for he must certainly know that people get killed and mutilated in war.

Another term Luban really likes is "liberal ideology of torture."[138] Well, I have nothing much to say to that, except that I prefer my liberal philosophy of self-defensive torture any day to Luban's illiberal ideology of aiding and abetting child kidnappers (and child torturers, for that matter).

Another expression of Luban's overblown rhetoric (incidentally, I do not object to his sharp tone and rhetoric; I object to his *replacing* argument with little more than rhetoric) is that in the examples of his "Unthinking" paper, by the end practically everybody gets tortured by deluded consequentialists, especially innocent children. Telling apocalyptic stories is not the same as providing an argument, however.

Yet in his defense it has to be said that at some point he realizes that there is "a coherent deontological response" to his question as to why we shouldn't torture innocent children (and pretty much everybody). This answer would come in the form of the self-defense argument or another rights-based argument.[139] (Incidentally, I have shown in section 2.3 that the necessity justification also goes some way toward giving this explanation, although it cannot rule out the deliberate torture of innocent and nonthreatening people under *all* circumstances—nor should it, as I have demonstrated with several examples.) Luban himself, without using the term "self-defense," refers to an article by Jeff McMahan. He claims, however: "Now the morality turns out to be consequentialism limited by a deontological restriction inexplicable on consequentialist grounds."[140]

But McMahan's argument and other rights-based arguments are not consequentialist at all, they are simply deontological. As the "pure TBS" is a figment of Luban's imagination, so is the tension between consequentialism and deontology he tries to detect here in order to be able to ask the following question:

> And, having allowed one restriction to consequentialist calculation . . . advocates of torture must explain why it is the only one. In particular, they must answer the question of whether it really is true that our wrongful actions can waive all rights, even the right against torture.[141]

I already answered this question. The ticking-bomb terrorist or child kidnapper does not forfeit *all* rights, but he does forfeit the right not to be tortured if torturing him is a necessary and proportionate means to save innocent people from his unjust attack. The reason for this lies in the right to self-defense itself. Thus, it is Luban who actually has to answer a question: why should the innocent victim of the ticking-bomb terrorist or child kidnapper forfeit the right to self-defense?

Luban thinks, of course, that torture "is worse than killing."[142] However, it simply is not, as we have seen,[143] and Luban's dogmatic insistence to the contrary changes nothing about this fact. Moreover, even if torturing one person were worse than killing one person, it would certainly not be worse than killing hundreds or thousands or millions of persons. Thus, Luban's critique of the ticking-bomb argument collapses.

Besides, his critique of the ticking-bomb argument poses as a critique of torture per se. But the ticking-bomb argument is not the only argument for torture. We have encountered many others here. One, of course, is the example of the child kidnapper. And in light of this example it has to be said: Even *if* torturing one person were worse than killing hundreds or thousands or millions of persons (and it certainly is not), torture would still not be worse than torture. That is logical, is it not? Thus, if the choice is between either having the innocent child be tortured until his death by the child kidnapper who put him into a wooden box or nonlethally torturing the culpable kidnapper, the latter option is certainly preferable.[144]

Probably the weirdest version of the charge that the ticking-bomb argument engages in unrealistic idealizations comes from *Richard Matthews*. He claims that "the ticking-bomb hypothesis uses nonsense terms just as this hypothetical case does."[145] The hypothetical case he is referring to (for reasons of his own) is one involving "little green men from Mars."[146] I am not a native English speaker, but even I know what the terms "little," "green," "men," and "Mars" mean. If Matthews does not, then this is very deplorable. To be sure, there might be a question whether little green men from Mars exist, but this question can only be asked if the terms involved are *not* nonsensical, but sensical, that is, endowed with meaning. Obviously, they are.

What are the relevant concepts in the ticking-bomb case? Matthews informs the reader that "the ticking-bomb hypotheses include some and often all of the following constituents. Often they do not do so overtly while tacitly presupposing dubious assumptions about each concept." The concepts he criticizes are imminence, threat, necessity, epistemic state of the interrogator, suspect/source.[147] Thus, these terms are, according to Matthews, nonsense. Unfortunately, this only shows that Matthews does not know what a nonsense term is. "Grblwrmpf," "blrwzsrha," "prime number with reduced pollutant emission," and "democratically elected interdisciplinary apple" are nonsense terms. The terms Matthews mentions are not. If he does not understand these terms, he can, for instance, easily look them up in a dictionary.

Besides, Matthews contradicts himself. The conclusion of his discussion of these terms is—in line with the conclusions drawn by Shue—"that there is no possible empirical correlate to the imagined situation."[148] However, this conclusion can only be drawn if one *understands* what the imagined situation is, and this obviously presupposes that the terms used to describe the situation are not non-sensical but *understandable*. Matthews should make up his mind.

Incidentally, in his chapter on the ticking bomb, Matthews advances *two* arguments (which, unfortunately, he does not clearly distinguish from one another): the usual slippery slope argument, that is, the social-ticking-bomb argument; and the no less popular idealization/abstraction argument. We have already dealt with both, but let us have a look at Matthews's version of the latter anyway.

The whole "argument" boils down to the rather trifling and, more importantly, irrelevant observation that some of the terms he criticizes are "vague," "have its grey zones," "admit of grey areas," the equally irrelevant claim that "the absence of alternatives is stipulated" or that "the claim that there are no alternatives must always be empirically dubious,"[149] and the confused claim that knowledge presupposes certainty.

Let us begin with the last claim. Matthews declares that one version of the ticking bomb argument "assumes knowledge on the part of the interrogator"[150] (he realizes that there is another version; I do not need to consider that other version here) and that "the strict case corresponds to no possible interrogation situation." Why not? Because, Matthews informs us: "If we know something to be the case, that thing cannot be false. . . . If I know something is the case, this is because it is the case."[151] But how is that supposed to show that an interrogator cannot know that there is a ticking bomb? If the interrogator believes that there is a ticking bomb and there *is* a ticking bomb, then it cannot be false that there is a ticking bomb (in a certain sense of "cannot be false"—Matthews does not realize that "it cannot be false" might have different meanings; and in the *epistemic* sense of "cannot be false" things one knows *can* be false,[152] contrary to what he claims). At this point, however, Matthews introduces a further assumption: "If they cannot locate the bomb in space and time at a given moment [which would make torture superfluous], they cannot be certain that it exists." The assumption, thus, is that knowledge presupposes *certainty*. That assumption, however, is simply false and does not correspond at all to our use of the term "knowledge"; and one would be hard pressed to find any modern-day epistemologist who would make that assumption.[153] Epistemologists usually define "knowledge" as "justified true belief,"[154] but obviously I can be *justified* in believing something without being *certain*. *Nothing* is certain. I *know* who my parents are if they really are who I think they are (in this sense knowledge cannot turn out to be wrong), but I cannot be certain (human beings are fallible—there is no *guarantee* that their beliefs are true). Thus, the knowledge requirement can be satisfied in the ticking bomb case, since interrogators obviously can have a justified true belief that a suspect has planted a bomb.

As regards the claim that "the absence of alternatives is stipulated"—why did I say that this claim is irrelevant? For a simple and rather obvious reason: suppose I want to prove a certain philosophical point about rabbits. Suppose further that I use an example that begins: "There is a rabbit on a desk . . ." Thus, with regard to this example I have stipulated that there is a rabbit on the desk. How is the fact that I have stipulated this supposed to show that it is empirically impossible for rabbits to be on desks? Obviously, it *is* possible. There have been rabbits on desks.

With respect to Matthews' assertion that "the claim that there are no alternatives must always be dubious,"[155] it suffices to point out that the fact (if it is a fact) that something is dubious does not mean that it is wrong. And when Matthews claims that "intelligence agents always have alternatives to torture,"[156] he is quite right (they can pray, or try a séance); but the question is whether the alternatives would work. It is entirely possible that they would not, while torture would. If Matthews denies even the empirical possibility of this, it is he who is engaging in unwarranted stipulations.

The fact that Matthews' concerns about "vagueness" are completely irrelevant for the question of whether there can be ticking-bomb cases also shows itself in the fact that the term "big dark forest" is entirely made up of vague terms (for example, is a group of 27 trees a forest?—it is not so clear). Yet, there *are* big dark forests.

One final observation: if reliance on the terms that Matthews mentions makes all examples or justifications relying on them "unrealistic" or even "impossible," then we would have to give up self-defense and self-defense laws altogether, for philosophical theories and the law of self-defense rely on the concepts of imminence, threat, necessity, reasonableness (which refers to the epistemic state of the interrogator), and aggressor or attacker (suspect/source) (criminal lawyers and judges will probably find Matthews' charge that they have been relying on nonsense terms the whole time preposterous—and rightly so). Thus on Matthews' account one would have to conclude that there is also "no possible empirical correlate to the imagined situation" of a person who reasonably believes or even knows that she is threatened by an aggressor with imminent harm for the prevention of which the use of lethal violence is necessary. Thus, killing in self-defense would be morally ruled out. That, I submit, is a *reductio ad absurdum* of Matthews' position.[157]

Bob Brecher also dedicates a whole chapter in his book *Torture and the Ticking Bomb* to "The Fantasy of the Ticking Bomb Scenario." It is he who is fantasizing and joining Shue and Matthews "in dreamland," to use Shue's term again. Some of the arguments he provides in the chapter are actually quite good; unfortunately, they only apply to Dershowitz' absurd torture warrant proposal. The ticking-bomb argument, however, can do quite well without that proposal. Beyond that, Brecher only offers the usual stereotypes. Thus, he claims that torture is not particularly effective and that the "institutionaliza-tion of the profession of the torturer is a necessary condition of the example's [that is, of the ticking-bomb scenario's] getting off the ground."[158] This is of course simply Shue's second argument, which has already been refuted above.[159] While Brecher reproaches others of "not taking into account such basic factual considerations,"[160] it is actually he who is ignoring the facts, not least because, as we have seen,[161] he sees fit to simply dismiss rights-based arguments for torture, and thus in particular the self-defense argument. Thus, he not only does not take into account the empirical facts; he also does not adequately account for the normative arguments that have been provided for the justifi-ability of torture in certain circumstances.

The other argument he provides—what else could we expect?—is the "no certainty" argument.[162] I have already dealt with this insipid argument extensively.[163] No more needs to be said.

Yet I cannot resist the temptation to say a *little* bit more. First, Brecher claims:

> The ticking bomb scenario, presented in a context of terrorism, is a fantasy. But that is not to say that there can be no genuine cases where torturing one person seems the only possible way left of saving the life of one or more others and where it really is known that they have the requisite information. Doris Schroeder's recent analysis of the Gäfgen case [I refer to it as the Daschner case] in Germany in 2002 offers one example. Having collected evidence from his flat and watched him collect the ransom, the police knew that Magnus Gäfgen had kidnapped Jakob von Metzler, the 11-year-old son of a banker.[164]

Indeed. However, Brecher never in his whole book gives any explanation as to why the police cannot also collect evidence in the ticking-bomb scenario, evidence enough to *know* that the captured person really is the ticking-bomb terrorist. Brecher flatly contradicts himself.

Besides, while Brecher says about the case of the kidnapped child: "Noth-ing is to be done. It is too late,"[165] we have already encountered a case, the Mook case, where the child was actually saved. Brecher notes that "reality is not something that should be made to serve the purposes of fantasy."[166] He is right, and he should try to live up to this insight.

The second point I cannot resist making refers to the following statement of Brecher:

> The "necessity" that gives the thought experiment its force is inevitably absent in the real case. In the real world, necessity is always retrospective.[167]

Is "retrospective necessity" supposed to be an ontological innovation, so that we have pseudo-necessities on the one hand and retrospective necessities on the other? If so, then Brecher's ontology is hopelessly confused. However, since he introduces retrospective necessity in a discussion where he talks a lot about the lack of certainty, all he means is probably that we can only *know* after the fact that something was necessary.

However, first, that is simply wrong. Knowledge does not require certainty. Second, it is logically and semantically clear (as Matthews confirms) that if you *know* after the fact that something was the case at a previous time, then it *really* was the case at that time. Thus, if someone will *know* in the future that the torture contemplated now was really necessary, then it *is* necessary—not only retrospectively, but *now*.

J. Jeremy Wisnewski and *R. D. Emerick* go so far as to claim, as Matthews does, that the ticking-bomb scenario is semantically and logically *impossible*.[168] Why? They see two essential elements in the scenario:

> (a) there is a finite amount of time before the bomb will detonate. The time in question makes alternative means of intelligence gathering unacceptable. Interrogation by torture is thus demanded given our time constraints. (b) A greater loss will occur as a result of a *failure* to engage in torture. We will argue that once we have fleshed out what is involved in information-gathering (or "interrogational") torture, we will be in a position to see that (b) is false in the ticking-bomb case. It is false because interrogational torture, to be effective, simply cannot be carried out in the amount of time postulated in the ticking-bomb argument. Once we give up (b), the ticking-bomb argument falls apart.[169]

"Simply cannot"? Not quite, as the two implicitly admit. For they say that the "ability to draw out torture indefinitely is crucial to its potential effectiveness in *virtually* every case."[170] However, since Wisnewski and Emerick talk about logic and semantics and claim that the ticking-bomb scenario is impossible, I will be allowed to point out that semantically and logically it is of course impossible that something is impossible if it is only ruled out in *virtually* all cases. It would have to be ruled out in *absolutely* all cases. Yet, what Emerick and Wisnewski would like to rule out is not ruled out at all, as they again concede, this time quite explicitly:

> We should emphasize, again, that the point here is not that torture
> will *never* result in accurate information. It might very well (at least
> in a few cases) result in accurate information. But we are not at
> leisure to simply postulate that torture *will* work in the case we
> are considering. If effective torture, by its very nature, requires the
> judicious use of time, then postulating that torture can work in
> the ticking-bomb case (where time is limited) might well be like
> postulating that one can jump without moving.[171]

Fascinatingly, in the second sentence after these confessions the two authors *again* repeat the claim that they have "shown that there is a semantic contradiction in the very idea of interrogational torture that can be effectively executed in a small amount of time." Yet it should be rather obvious for any competent speaker that there cannot be "a semantic contradiction in the very idea of interrogational torture that can be effectively executed in a small amount of time" if interrogational torture *can* indeed be effectively executed in a small amount of time. And both authors admit that it can.

As regards their claim that "we are not at leisure to simply postulate that torture *will* work in the case we are considering"—well, that actually depends. We are at leisure to simply postulate that torture will work in a *hypothetical* case. The ticking-bomb case as advanced by most philosophers is a *thought experiment* (Wisnewski and Emerick surely must have noticed that). Thus, we *are* at leisure to ask: "What if the explosion of a nuclear bomb actually *can* be averted in a certain case by torturing the culpable aggressor—would that be allowed?" This question would only be "nonsensical," or at least irrelevant for practice, if such a case really were *impossible*. It is not irrelevant when the case is only "virtually" impossible—and thus *possible*.

On the other hand, we are certainly not allowed to simply postulate in a *real* case that torture will work. Thus, if we have captured a terrorist who, according to two doctors, suffered brain damage during his capture that makes it impossible for him to communicate, we cannot simply stipulate: "Torturing him will work."

Conversely, since torture *can* work, we are not at leisure to simply *postulate* that it won't in a certain real case. We cannot be *certain* that it will, but certainty, again, is not required. In fact, as the self-defense argument shows, torture can even be permissible if the chances of success are *extremely low*.[172]

Naturally, since Wisnewski and Emerick, like so many other absolutist torture opponents, simply dismiss the self-defense argument,[173] this important fact escapes their attention.

There are countless other critics of the ticking-bomb argument. They all repeat the same themes over and over again, fiercely and relentlessly attacking a straw man. The result is little insight and much boredom. True, there might never have been a *real* ticking-bomb case, but that is not the issue. The issue is whether such a scenario, as actually advanced by its proponents, is possible. Obviously, it is.

In addition, there are countless other scenarios in which torture would be justified. The child-kidnapping case, the case of the ten prisoners (torture one for half an hour to save both his life and that of all the other prisoners), the case of the father and the son (waterboard the son for half an hour in order to prevent him from being executed or slowly being tortured to death), the case of the genocidal aliens (torture a human dictator and mass murderer for an hour to save humanity from slowly being tortured to death by aliens), and so on. To seriously claim that there can never be an occasion where torture would be justified betrays either a particularly mindless form of absolutism or a simple lack of imagination.

6.9 "Torture Knows No Limits"

A further strange argument one sometimes encounters is that torture is "inherently limitless." What is that supposed to mean? Carl von Clausewitz said that war is inherently limitless, that the logic of war is escalation. However, he admitted that in reality war can be restrained and often has been restrained successfully. The same holds for torture (whether justified or not). In the Middle Ages punitive torture was often used in a restricted way—that is, the amount of torture previously prescribed as punishment was administered, rather than limitless amounts of torture. Interrogative torture has also been limited in many cases by certain regulations (for example in Israel). But must interrogative torturers, if they want to be successful, not be ready to use any means necessary so that as long as the tortured person does not give up the information, they will use harsher and harsher means? Well, *if* the interrogator is ready to use any means, she will use any available means unless somebody stops her. So she might become an interrogator who uses very painful means. But the same logic applies to *any* course of action that aims at making another person do something. Thus, it applies not only to painful interrogation, but to *any* interrogation. *Any* interrogator who is ready to use any means necessary will transform into an interrogator using painful means, if need be, and very painful means, if need be, and so on. Thus, the argument "proves" too much. Besides, there actually *is* an inherent limit to interrogative torture: killing the painfully interrogated person is not an available means to get the information. Dead people do not speak. Thus, killing is not a possible means for interrogative torture (one can of course accept the death of the person as the side-effect of torture, but that still rules out killing as a *means*). Other forms of self-defense, however, do not acknowledge this limit. Killing *is* a means by which one can keep an aggressor from attacking with a knife. Thus, it seems that self-defensive interrogation is actually more limited than self-defensive noninterrogative beating, stabbing, or shooting. Besides, why should the fact that a certain course of action *could* escalate into something excessive make the course of action wrong even if it does not so escalate? After all, *any* self-defensive course of action, for example in the form of hitting an opponent or stabbing him, *could* escalate; however, that obviously does not make all self-defensive action wrong. In short, the argument that torture is "inherently limitless" and therefore unjustified is confused.

In that context, in would be good if authors like Ginbar and Luban (and quite a few others, for that matter), who seem to think that the assertion "If you allow torture, you cannot avoid allowing it in the form of rape" is a marvelously good argument[174]—or at least one that has the rhetorical advantage of embarrassing and silencing the opponent[175] (if not exactly proving him wrong)—would realize that it can be turned against them: if Ginbar and Luban do not oppose self-defense (and they don't), they cannot oppose self-defense in the form of rape.

After all, self-defense can take the form of rape: for example, if the child kidnapper could only be made to disclose the location of the kidnapped child by raping him, this would be a case of self-defensive rape. A variation of this example would be the case of a young man who has been abducted by a ring of rapists and enclosed in a dungeon that is secured by an electronic combination lock (unfortunately, this case is very realistic). If the young man can overwhelm one of the rapists and can only get the combination of the lock by raping the rapist himself, this too would be a case of justified self-defensive rape.[176]

And if someone here is still convinced that there is no self-defense against a defenseless person—an assumption we have already shown to be wrong[177]—one can easily come up with a hypothetical case in which the aggressor is not defenseless at all. Since many absolutist torture opponents seem to suffer from a lack of imagination, let me give just one example here (if you are squeamish, skip it, but one should bear in mind that this is a philosophical treatise, not a children's book):

Innocent Jenny, naked in her bedroom, is attacked by Serial Killer, who has broken in. He too is naked. Jenny, who is a doctor, is currently treating her vaginal infection with a potent new ointment, which has the side-effect of killing any man whose penis is exposed to it long and severely enough, something best achieved by sexual intercourse. While the killer is trying to strangle her, they are wrestling on the ground, she gets on top of him, and he gets his hands on her throat and squeezes. In her desperation, she shoves the aggressor's penis—while the aggressor explicitly says "No"—into her vagina and starts to move up and down while the man still strangles her. But suddenly the ointment works, the man goes into shock and dies. Jenny is safe.

This is a case of justified self-defensive rape; and I really do not think that one proves one's feminist inclinations by denying an innocent woman her only means to defend herself against a serial killer.

If Ginbar and Luban now make an ad hoc maneuver, saying that while they allow necessary and proportionate self-defense in nearly all cases, they do not allow it in those cases that take the form of rape, a defender of self-defensive torture can make exactly the same move. Thus, if the rape argument does not undermine the case for self-defense generally, it does not undermine the case for self-defensive torture either.

Ginbar makes some other points that could be subsumed under the general heading of the "torture-knows-no-limits" argument. In order to better appreciate them, it might be useful to have a further look at the issue of "absolutism."

First, antitorture absolutism is the position that torture can never be justified. Torture can be justified. Thus, anti-torture absolutism is wrong. Ginbar, however, argues for what he calls "minimal absolutism" in order to show that an absolute prohibition of torture is at least not already ruled out by the (alleged) erroneousness of minimal absolutism.

> Minimal absolutism is the moral view that certain acts must be prohibited absolutely, namely that they must never be performed, whatever the consequences.[178]

His prime example—and certainly the most convincing one—for the correctness of minimal absolutism is the prohibition of the act of torturing babies to death for fun.[179] If this means *just* for fun, I completely agree with him. Any act of torturing babies just for fun is wrong. Thus, I am a minimal absolutist.

The reason why minimal absolutism is correct is that acts are partly defined by their intention. And what people intend is morally very relevant.[180]

What Ginbar overlooks, however, is that arguing for "minimal absolutism" is not quite enough to show that antitorture absolutism is not already ruled out by the erroneousness of *absolutism*. I define absolutism as follows: absolutism is the moral view that certain acts must be prohibited absolutely; they must never be performed, whatever (i.e., irrespective of) the consequences *or intended consequences*.

I reject absolutism, and the example of torturing babies just for fun does certainly not stand in the way of such a rejection. After all, torturing little babies just for fun is not absolutely prohibited *whatever* the consequences or intended consequences, but it is absolutely prohibited precisely *because of* the intended consequences. The intended consequences *matter*.

If minimal absolutism is right, Ginbar's antitorture absolutism would still be wrong as long as absolutism is wrong. Absolutism indeed is wrong.

However, *even if* absolutism were right, this in itself would still not be an argument against torture. As we saw, the self-defense argument for torture is perfectly compatible with the view that it is absolutely prohibited, whatever the consequences or intended consequences, to keep someone from engaging in necessary and proportionate self-defensive torture of a culpable aggressor. Torture proponents can be absolutists.[181]

So let us now have a look at Ginbar's recapitulation of the three "minimal absolutist arguments generally."[182]

> *Justifying atrocities:* While anti-absolutist views may, in certain, immediate circumstances, enable the prevention of catastrophes which minimal absolutists would not, the former would actually *commit*, or justify the commission, of the worst atrocities, even on a large scale (such as mass-murder), provided this was the only way to prevent a horrendous catastrophe (such as murder on a larger scale).[183]

Two observations: First, as already pointed out, the self-defense justification of torture is perfectly compatible with absolutism, for example with an absolute prohibition of attacks on the innocent. Thus, Ginbar's first argument misses the self-defense argument for torture completely.

Second, it is true that a threshold deontologist and someone accepting the necessity argument is committed to what Ginbar points out here.[184] However, taking this in itself as an argument against threshold deontology or the necessity defense of torture is simply begging the question. Thus, the real question is: what is the morally more plausible, more humane view: that it is absolutely prohibited to kill 50 innocent people in order to save the whole of humanity (apart from those 50 people) or that it is justifiable to kill 50 people in order to prevent all of humanity, including those 50 people, from being killed? Most people will certainly opt for the latter. They prefer moral responsibility to "purity of heart." Ginbar will also have to think that the father who could save his son from being slowly tortured to death by waterboarding him himself for half an hour would act unjustifiably if he took the latter option, thus saving his son from an agonizing death. In my view, *pace* Ginbar, this absolutist stance borders on moral insanity.

Ginbar's second "argument" has nothing really to do with the "no limits" charge, but let me present it here anyway:

> *Moral enslavement:* In the face of a looming catastrophe, the anti-absolutist loses his or her freedom to make a moral choice. A terrorist . . . may, through the threat of a disaster . . . or the promise of averting one . . . actually dictate what the moral thing to do—or at least what the morally justifiable thing to do—must be.[185]

This is a somewhat funny reproach.[186] After all, the moral or morally justifiable action is *always* dependent on the circumstances, including the action of others, including others that happen to be villains. Even if someone is an absolutist, for example someone believing in an absolute prohibition on torture or in an absolute prohibition on eating bananas, a villain's torturing a baby for fun makes it obviously justifiable to kill that villain in necessary and proportionate self-defense (all else being equal). And a villain's credibly threatening to torture a little baby for fun unless you step on an innocent person's toes makes it justifiable to step on that person's toes. If that is "moral enslavement," it is inescapable, for both absolutists and antiabsolutists.

And finally:

> *Moral corruption:* A principled anti-absolutist must admit every single act, including the worst atrocities imaginable, into moral consideration. Most of us may want to steer away from a person who weighs the pros and cons of torturing children, murdering our parents, raping our partners and the like, as we may find their thought process revolting, if not threatening, and may find their insistence that they would only resort to such actions in extremely rare situations a less than satisfactory reassurance.[187]

Ginbar further states that

> such moral corruption may affect a person's life, or at least inner
> life, not only in extreme situations but in everyday ones as well.
> Visiting friends and seeing their child, one would often say some-
> thing like: "that's a really cute little child you've got there." Under
> the anti-absolutist view, it would be *morally legitimate* for a moral
> agent to have the following thought, or calculation (apologies for
> what follows): "Under what circumstances would I (or worse—the
> friends) be *justified* in torturing this child? I wonder what method
> would be best?"[188]

Ginbar is confusing quite a few things here. First of all, one can very well
be an absolutist and find such thought processes morally legitimate. A consistent liberal, after all, would have to say that thoughts are free, while actions
have to be restrained by morality. To subject thoughts to moral demands is in
my view the expression of a somewhat totalitarian attitude.

Second, and conversely, many illiberal antiabsolutists can find such
thoughts morally illegitimate under nearly all circumstances. That they are
antiabsolutists only means that they admit of *some* circumstances where such
thoughts are legitimate.

Third, does Ginbar really think that they are *never* legitimate? If he does,
then it might be that his friends should steer clear of him. After all, I cannot
conceive of a friend or parent being highly appreciative of a "No" to the following question: "If some villain who is known for being able to read minds
credibly threatens to *actually* slowly torture my child to death unless you *think*
about circumstances under which it might be justified to torture my child
for half an hour, would you engage in such thoughts to save my poor child
from a terrible fate?" Who would be the better friend here? The person who
thinks about circumstances under which torture would be justified in order
to avoid, with such thoughts, the actual torture of an innocent child; or the
person who prefers the alleged purity of his own thoughts to his friend's child
being saved from torture?

Fourth, as already said, self-defense knows no limits *beyond* necessity
and proportionality. Thus, if one's antiabsolutist posture implied that it would
be morally legitimate to consider under what circumstances one would be
justified in torturing the child of a friend, then of course the endorsement of
self-defense would imply that it would be morally legitimate to consider under
what circumstances one would be justified in killing, mutilating, or burning
the child of a friend (and, as law and morality acknowledge, there are such

circumstances). If this does not count against self-defense—and it obviously does not—then it cannot count against torture, either.

Thus, Ginbar's "minimal absolutist arguments" fail.

Of course, we could also look at the slippery-slope arguments that include, or are based upon, the uncertainty and the abuse arguments as so many additional unsuccessful variants of the torture-knows-no-limits argument. However, since we have already dealt with and refuted those arguments,[189] there is no need to go into them again.

So I rest my case for the justifiability of torture under certain extremely narrowly circumscribed circumstances. Torture can be justified.

Is Justifying Torture Bad Even If
Torture Is Sometimes Justified?

Some people claim that our talk about torture should be accompanied by a certain "shyness." What that means is that rational argumentation should only be allowed to go so far. Bielefeldt, for example, claims:

> The uncircumventability [*Unhintergehbarkeit*] of human dignity also has an emotional side. It manifests itself, for instance, in a kind of *intuitive shyness* about argumentatively engaging with fictional scenarios that are aimed at undermining the unconditional respect of human dignity.[1]

He experiences this shyness with regard to one of my examples, namely the one in which a dictator confronts a prisoner with the choice to either kill 1 of 10 prisoners or to torture 1 of them for 2 hours (all these prisoners are innocent and have no special relation to the first prisoner). If the prisoner refuses to choose and to act on his choice, all 10 prisoners will be killed. He is not permitted to ask them (if he did, all 10 prisoners would be killed). Of course, I argue that the prisoner is justified under these conditions in torturing one of the other prisoners.[2] Bielefeldt declares:

> The intuitive shyness about argumentatively engaging with such a constructed scenario has nothing to do with ingenuousness or intellectual incompetence. One might even admit that the macabre situation constructed by Steinhoff could become reality. However, to positively develop, in light of such a mere eventuality, a normative criteriology that is supposed to make it possible to weigh violations of dignity against one another is a monstrous undertaking; it leads us legally and ethically astray.[3]

First of all, this scenario is not one of self-defensive torture. However, most of my examples are, and they are precisely supposed to show that torture does *not* always violate human dignity (after all, self-defensive killing does not violate human dignity either). To not even rationally consider such examples and to simply *stipulate* instead that all torture violates human dignity might not attest to shyness so much as arrogance.

Second, this talk about the "normative criteriology" that "leads us legally and ethically astray" is sheer phrase mongering. As already said, the case of the 10 prisoners is not a case of self-defense. It is a case of what the German law calls justifying emergency (*rechtfertigender Notstand*) and what other jurisdictions call *necessity*. The laws of necessity *were made precisely to cover extreme situations like this one*. In fact, since the international torture conventions are arguably not applicable to private torture, torturing a prisoner in my scenario probably *is* legal under German, British, and American law. But whether legal or not, necessity clauses *require and allow* the weighing of health against health, injuries against injuries, lives against lives,[4] life against health, injuries against lives, pain against lives, and so on; why should the weighing become more difficult or even "monstrous" when torture is involved? I assume Bielefeldt is too "shy" to ask this question, let alone to answer it.

Besides, examples like the Daschner case, my Jeanette/Paolo/Bill case, and the case of the prisoners not only show that torture is justified in such circumstances, but they *also* show that the shyness Bielefeldt and others recommend is quite inappropriate. If the police officers in the Daschner case said, "Oh, no, no, we are too shy to even consider the possibility of torture, when in doubt it's just better if the child suffocates"; if the prisoner who could save the life of one other prisoner said, "Oh, no, no, I am too shy to even consider the possibility of torture, when in doubt it's better if one of you dies, whether you agree with me or not"; when Paolo says, "Oh, no, no, I am too shy to even consider the possibility of torture, when in doubt it's better if we just blow somebody up," then this is not only irrational but also *immoral*. I think the 10 prisoners, Bill, and the suffocating child would agree. They would have little sympathy for Bielefeldt's "shyness."

It happens on occasion that some absolutist opponents of torture cannot resist the temptation of morally blaming a proponent of a limited permission of torture for somehow contributing to the spread of illegitimate torture. Of course, they think that all torture is illegitimate. I don't. If I somehow contribute to the spread of self-defensive torture that helps to save innocent children from culpable kidnappers, then that would be a good thing. If absolutist torture opponents with their arguments or pseudoarguments contribute to more children suffocating in the hands of kidnappers, then that would be a bad thing.

However, I completely agree that *nearly all* torture currently being under-taken on our planet is *immoral*. There are very few cases of defensive torture or torture justified in light of a justifying emergency. (There are also very few cases of killing that are justified by self-defense or in light of a justifying emergency.) Thus, one criticism I have heard (and several times) is this: "Even if you were right about self-defensive torture, by publicly justifying torture in some cases you contribute to a slippery slope, you contribute to there being more cases of illegitimate torture too." Can this criticism stick?

First of all, let us remember that absolutist torture opponents argue against torture by appealing to the notion of rights. When, for example, they argue against a nuclear ticking-bomb case, they say: "Even if millions of lives are at stake, the terrorist has a *right* not to be tortured. This right cannot be overridden by utilitarian considerations." Well, perhaps my right to speak my opinion also cannot be overridden by utilitarian considerations. In other words, even if by speaking my opinion I contributed somehow to the spread of torture, I would still have the right to do so. To be sure, one might object that liberty of speech is not absolute (the right not to be tortured isn't, either). So it could perhaps be overridden. But, of course, if it were to be overridden, this would have to happen on grounds of *credible and substantial evidence* that my speaking my opinion indeed does cause harm on a scale large enough to override my right to free expression.

Maybe, however, the criticism does not so much aim to suggest that one does not have the *right* to present arguments that justify torture under certain circumstances, but rather that one *ought not* to present such arguments. After all, one can have a right to do immoral things. Having a right only means that others are not at liberty to forcibly keep you from doing what you have a right to. For example, people have a right to claim that the Holocaust never happened; however, making such a claim is still immoral. Thus, if the claim is only that I ought not to justify some forms of torture, the opponents would perhaps bear weaker burdens of proof.

They do still bear a burden of proof, though. And in fact there is not a shred of evidence for the claim that by justifying self-defensive torture one also contributes to the spread of torture that is not self-defensive. Indeed, the claim is rather silly. *How* is this contribution supposed to work? Is some spokesperson of the U.S. State Department supposed to quote me in support of torturing in Guantanamo? That would be counterproductive, for antitorture groups could immediately point out that I have argued that the torture in Guantanamo is not self-defensive nor an instance of a justifying emergency, and therefore not justified, and that I have argued that the *institutionalization* of torture is wrong.[5] They could thus blame the spokesperson for manipulating and distorting things. That would hardly help his case.

I suspect that there is nothing more behind the charge that by justifying torture in some circumstances one also contributes to the spread of illegitimate torture than the vague suspicion that one contributes to some kind of "general atmosphere" in which torture can "thrive."[6] This charge is more or less as intelligent and substantiated, though, as the claim—and such claims *have* been made—that by arguing for the right to sexual self-determination one contributes to a general atmosphere of sexual permissiveness in which rape will thrive. The claim is also comparable to the one—which, interestingly, is hardly ever made—that by arguing for the right to self-defensive killing one contributes to an atmosphere in which murder thrives. There is no way of either proving or disproving such claims. Making them anyway simply amounts to the manipulative and defamatory attempt to shut people up whose arguments one doesn't like and probably cannot refute.

Finally, there *is* some evidence that morality and moral behavior profit more from rational discussion than from censorship, prejudice, and thought restraint.

Conclusions

Discussing specific topics in applied ethics often necessitates the exploration of themes that are of significance beyond the specific topics discussed. Thus, it is worth mentioning that the preceding investigations of self-defense, of the difference between legalization and institutionalization, of coercion and "breaking the will," of Kantian philosophy and "using as a means," of the concept of "dignity," and of the principle of double effect, among other issues—whose main results I have already anticipated in the introduction, so I will not repeat them here—are of considerable relevance in themselves and can be fruitfully applied to other problems.

Here, however, these examinations were applied to the subject of torture. Against absolutist torture opponents, I have argued here that torture can be morally justified under certain circumstances by an appeal to the self-defense argument, to the argument from the culpability for a forced choice situation, and to the necessity justification. Thus, I have argued that torture is justified in *very rare and extreme circumstances*, since the cases in which these justifications can be validly applied are extremely rare. Torturing so-called terrorists to find out more about their networks, that is, torturing in the course of "fishing expeditions," is not a case where those justifications can be validly applied. The Daschner case, that is, the child-kidnapping case, however, is a case in which self-defensive torture could have been applied; and the case of the sadistic but honest sergeant who gives the father of a twelve-year-old boy the option to either waterboard his son for 30 minutes or to have him executed by the sergeant is a case where the necessity justification can be correctly applied. We have seen that all attempts to show the contrary fail.

I have also argued that while it is not in itself contradictory to legally prohibit torture while admitting that it can in certain circumstances be morally justified, there is nevertheless no reason to think that all torture *should* be legally prohibited. However, there is as little need to introduce a special paragraph allowing self-defensive torture into the penal codes as there is a need to introduce a special paragraph allowing self-defensive throat cutting. Both forms of self-defense and "emergency action" can be easily covered by the normal self-defense or necessity regulations, provided that whatever absolute prohibition of torture might exist is abolished.

Finally, I am adamantly against the institutionalization of torture—and thus against training torturers or introducing the infamous torture warrants. Doing so is completely unnecessary and likely to have disastrous consequences once a certain scale has been reached. As history has shown, the state is not to be trusted to use torture only in self-defense cases once it becomes *institutionalized* (at least beyond a very rudimentary form). However, this in no way undermines the argument that the legalization of self-defensive torture is morally permissible, let alone that self-defensive torture itself is morally permissible.

Notes

Introduction

1. Sussman (2005), p. 4.

Chapter 1

1. Note that on this definition strategic bombing can amount to torture. Some will regard this as counterintuitive and as speaking against this definition. (However, let me point out that quite a few definitions found in the literature also have this implication—without many people noticing it—notably including the one provided by the United Nations Convention against Torture and Other Cruel, Inhuman, or Degrading Treatment or Punishment). I don't; in fact, I think it reflects reality very well. That war and torture might have more intimate connections than many think has also been pointed out by Scarry (1987).

2. Wisnewski (2010), p. 73, confidently claims that "[a]ll forms of torture (be it punitive, interrogational, terroristic, or judicial)—has [sic] one aim: the breaking of the agent. This conception of torture as destructive of agency, and as aiming at the 'breaking' of the subject of torture, has achieved near-universal recognition in the literature surrounding treatment of torture victims, and a growing recognition in other disciplines that aim to understand torture." He then selectively quotes a couple of these authors, not mentioning the fact that "the literature surrounding treatment of torture victims" deals nearly exclusively with victims of torture in dictatorships and therefore might not be conclusive for torture as such—a methodological problem that many of the authors of this literature are quite aware of (see the quote pertaining to n. 32 of ch. 2), in contrast to Wisnewski. Besides, the example of *Sophie's Choice*-situations, for instance the example of a father torturing his son because a war criminal credibly threatened to slowly torture the son to death unless the father himself tortures the son by waterboarding him for 20 minutes (in that case the war criminal will let both of them go) is clearly an example where the act of the father is torture (waterboarding *is* torture) but where the father will not aim at breaking his son; rather he aims at sparing him a fate far worse than 20 minutes of waterboarding. Miller (2005), p.

191, n. 2, accepts, though, "that, notionally at least, there might be some cases in which extreme physical suffering is inflicted but in which the torturer does not have as a purpose the breaking of the victim's will. However, I do not regard these as the central cases when it comes to torturing human beings, as opposed to other sentient beings that lack a will in anything other than an attenuated sense." As I say in the main text, punitive torture was widespread in the Middle Ages and is still practiced today. There is no reason to exclude it from a definition of torture, which after all as a definition should include the "notional" cases—the more so if those cases are also very real. Miller (2011) still admits that torture only "in general" aims at breaking the will; and this time he finally relaxes his definition accordingly, having condition (c) of his definition claim that torture is "*in general*, undertaken for the purpose of breaking the victim's will." However, definitions are supposed to give necessary and sufficient criteria for what they define; therefore, putting a term like "in general" into a definition is simply confused. For instance, if one accepted Miller's definition, then, to answer the question whether the father in the above example tortures his son, one would have to answer the further question whether the father aims with *this* act of waterboarding *in general* at breaking his son's will—obviously, however, such a question does not even make sense, and hence nor does Miller's definition. Moreover, it is also confused to put empirical contingencies into *definitions*. Whether torture aims "in general" at breaking the will of the persons subjected to it is an empirical question, not one that can be decided by definitional *fiat*. However, if one accepted Miller's definition, and if empirical and historical research showed that all those gruesome practices described in books on torture have rarely ever aimed at breaking the wills of the persons subjected to them (and thus do not satisfy condition (c)), one would have to say *that there is no such thing as torture in the real world*. That, however, would be absurd. The correct conclusion, one allowed by an *acceptable* definition of torture, would obviously be that those gruesome practices *are* torture but that one was mistaken in assuming that torture in general aims at breaking a person's will. Thus Miller's definition must be rejected.

3. Ibid.; Miller (2005), p. 179; Davis (2005), p. 164.

4. I have been confronted here by an anonymous critic with the objection that I "confuse being defenceless (not being able to prevent an attack) with not having the ability to attack." Actually, it is the critic who confuses things, namely, as the brackets show, being defenseless *against the person by whom one is being attacked* with not being able to prevent or block an attack *by that very same person*. When Klitschko and Lewis were boxing against each other, they were also not able to prevent the other's attack. Yet we would certainly not say that they were defenseless. They were not defenseless precisely because they could fight back. My example of the paraplegic child murderer below, however, is an example of a person who can and does attack a child while simultaneously being *defenseless against a third person*, namely, against the person defending the child.

5. Wisnewski (2010) thinks that what I have just done—namely, provide a definition of torture—"is not possible . . . : torture is too diverse, too multifaceted for any easy definition to capture its range and barbarity," and he offers a "preliminary account of the range of types of torture" in order "to better illustrate the difficulty of any single

definition" (ibid., p. 8). His "preliminary account" points out that there are at least the following types of torture: judicial, punitive, interrogational, dehumanizing, terroristic/deterrent, and sadistic (ibid., pp. 7–8). But, so what? There are also judicial, punitive, interrogational, dehumanizing, terroristic/deterrent, and sadistic kinds of *imprisonment*. Yet it seems to be fairly easy to provide a definition of imprisonment: to imprison a person means to lock her up in a prison or an equivalent to a prison and to desist from letting her out when she wants to get out. Or consider still another complex and diverse phenomenon, namely that of bachelorhood: there are communist, National Socialist, liberal, white, Chinese, black, short, tall, stupid, intelligent, German, and Somalian bachelors, with one leg, two legs, one ear, two ears, blind, deaf, not blind, not deaf, who are musicians, electricians, philosophers, child abusers, rapists, philanthropists, Samaritans, and so on. Yet all this diversity certainly does not "illustrate the difficulty of any single definition," for bachelors, diverse or not, are unmarried men—that's it. Thus, Wisnewski's "illustration" of the "difficulty of any single definition" of torture is confused and certainly not an excuse for his inability and lack of effort to provide such a definition. Incidentally, I doubt that my definition solves all problems, but it is a useful starting point and certainly preferable to Wisnewski's definitional defeatism.

Chapter 2

1. I am following the standard, encyclopedic (and philosophically sophisticated) German commentaries on self-defense law: Laufhütte (2006); Joecks and Miebach (2003); and Rudolphi (2010). These commentaries, incidentally, take the legal right to self-defense as the codification of a preexisting *moral* right. Kindhäuser (2008) provides a succinct overview of German self-defense law. Fascinatingly, in his criticism of Steinhoff (2009), Christian Volk (2010), p. 558, claims—without any argument—that I dissolve "the legal conception of self-defense to the point of unrecognizability." That he does not recognize the legal conception of self-defense in my writings might be due to his obvious ignorance of self-defense law. Incidentally, this author also quotes me in a completely misleading way (whether on purpose or out of negligence I cannot say). By the way, Volker Erb, the author of the entry on self-defense in Joecks and Miebach (2003), did recognize self-defense law in my exposition. He just corrected one minor point (which was thankfully not relevant for my argument). This correction is incorporated in the present text. Obviously, if any mistakes remain, they are mine.

2. Baskind (2008).

3. For overviews of this debate, from opposing viewpoints, see Lührmann (1999) and van Rienen (2009).

4. To be sure, from a moral standpoint it is actually not evident that defending an innocent person's property against a culpable aggressor by using deadly force if necessary really *is* disproportionate. But this is not a question we have to go into here.

5. This was actually also the case in the movie *Dirty Harry*. In Steinhoff (2006a) I had remembered this movie incorrectly.

6. Erb (2006), p. 19.

7. See Nourse (2001).

8. Erb (2006), pp. 28–33. In an earlier article (Steinhoff 2006, p. 346), I mistakenly took the legal prohibition of torture for granted.

9. Thus, self-defense law paints a quite adequate picture of the *conditions* under which self-defense is morally permissible. This is also confirmed by a philosophical look at the *foundations* of permissible self-defense. See Steinhoff (2007), pp. 71–94 (also for further references), and (2012), section 2.1.

10. Brecher (2008), p. 75.

11. Ibid., p. 77. I will deal with the mistaken charge that torture breaks a person's will and is therefore always unjustifiable in section 6.6.

12. Wisnewski (2010), p. 64, admits that coercion "*requires* the autonomy of the agent being coerced. . . . [T]he victim of coercion is being asked to *choose* to engage in some kind of action, decision, etc." He claims, however, that "torture *destroys* the person." That this would, to repeat, be somewhat counterproductive in the case of interrogational torture seems to escape his attention. In fact, interrogational torture *is* a form of coercion.

13. Brecher (2008), p. 80.

14. Ibid., pp. 81–82.

15. Ibid., p. 85.

16. Wisnewski and Emerick (2009), p. 57.

17. Ibid.

18. Brecher (2008), p. 77.

19. Wisnewski and Emerick (2009), p. 60.

20. Ibid., pp. 61–62.

21. Ibid., p. 61; see also p. 56.

22. Ibid., p. 62. The quote is from Conroy (2007), pp. 179–80.

23. Wisnewski sticks to this view also in his new book, but he now leaves room for rare exceptions. See Wisnewksi (2010), pp. 64–66 and 121–23.

24. Wisnewski and Emerick (2009), p. 63.

25. Ibid.

26. Ibid., p. 61; see also p. 56.

27. Matthews (2008), for example pp. 6, 34, 39.

28. Brecher (2008), p. 77.

29. Ibid., p. 79.

30. Wisnewski and Emerick (2009), pp. 60–61.

31. See the text pertaining to n. 11 of ch. 5.

32. Somnier et al. (2007), p. 58.

33. Başoğlu (2007), p. 6.

34. Wisnewski (2010), p. 122.

35. Ibid., p. 88.

36. Ibid., p. 121.

37. However, his double standards are noteworthy. He claims that one "conclusion to be drawn" from the fact that some victims of torture long to die "is that death is to be preferred to the harm that results of torture." However, one page later he

informs us that the "fact that many torture victims do not commit suicide should not be regarded as evidence for the view that death is regarded as worse than a continued life." Oh yes, it should be so regarded, and one should also get the numbers right: not many, but *hardly any* torture victims commit suicide. Let me also add and repeat that the claim that death is preferable to 20 minutes of waterboarding is downright preposterous. Thus, it is simply and obviously wrong that all forms of torture are worse than death.

38. Wisnewski (2010), p. 122.

39. Ibid., p. 123.

40. See n. 5 of ch. 1.

41. Wisnewski (2010), p. 66.

42. He might think, however, that one does not need arguments where one can also rely on insults and moral hubris. Thus, at the end of his book (p. 231), he states: "The arguments for torture are *rational*, to some extent, but this is the kind of rationality one finds in arguments employed to justify eugenics, degradation, and oppression—it is the rationality of the market and the slave-owner, only protecting what is 'rightfully' his; it is the rationality of efficient execution, where carefully thought-out humaneness is deployed in an arena of inhumanity." He is wrong on that, but his own "rationality" is the "rationality" of those who justify aiding and abetting child kidnappers and child torturers by shielding them from self-defensive torture on behalf of the child.

43. BBC (2010).

44. Wikipedia (2010), formatting slightly changed.

45. Wisnewski and Emerick (2009), p. 63.

46. One comic at the Hull torture conference shouted in his talk: "Dr. Steinhoff likes to torture; Dr. Steinhoff likes to torture." What I do is defend torture in certain extreme circumstances. To do that I do not have to like torture any more than one has to like killing in order to argue for the right of self-defense. I am aware, though, that the subtle art of differentiation is well beyond the intellectual capabilities of some people.

47. See section 2.1.1.

48. Montague (1989), pp. 81–82. Ryan (1984), pp. 515ff., advocates a similar position to Montague's.

49. I borrow this expression from Jeff McMahan (1994), p. 258. However, I use this expression in a narrower sense than McMahan, for it seems that he might consider the ticking-bomb terrorist only as a culpable cause, not, like me, as an aggressor.

50. As quoted in Ginbar (2009), p. 176, n. 37. The present-day provisions in the Israeli Penal Law are different.

51. As quoted in Ginbar (2009), pp. 308–09.

52. Gur-Arye (2004). Here she quotes Moore (1989), p. 292. It should be pointed out, however, that Moore has since come to allow the torture of innocents: "I confess it: I am only a threshold deontologist. This means that over some threshold of truly awful consequences, I will potentially do virtually anything to avert such consequences. If I can locate and defuse a nuclear device at 42nd street only by torturing the innocent child of the terrorist who planted it there, I torture." See Moore (2007),

p. 44. German law, however, also allows for a form of necessity that, while not being self-defense, is also not necessarily directed against an innocent. This is called *defensive necessity (defensiver Notstand)*. Going into this form of justification would lead too far for present purposes.

53. Gur-Arye (2004), p. 192.

54. Penal Code of the Federal Republic of Germany (1987). Any deviation from the original translation is the responsibility of the Buffalo Criminal Law Center.

55. Ginbar (2009) p. 340.

56. Ibid., pp. 320–21.

57. Herdegen (2005).

58. See pp. 107–08.

59. Kershnar (2001), p. 189.

60. See section 2.1.2.

61. Ginbar (2009), p. 68.

62. See p. 14.

63. See Dworkin (1978), esp. ch. 7.

64. Alexander and Moore (2010).

65. For example Bielefeldt (2007), p. 22.

66. Of course, we already saw this in the Jeanette/Paolo/Bill example above. Let me also remind the reader of the unpalatable implications of the absolutist anti-torture position for third-party action. See section 2.1.2.

67. I will say more about what absolutism is and is not in section 6.9.

68. Sinnott-Armstrong (2006).

69. Trapp (2006b), pp. 87ff.

70. Matthews (2008), p. 102–03.

71. Jeremy Bentham (1973), pp. 313 and 308. Matthews (2008) quotes Bentham on p. 106.

72. Sinnott-Armstrong (2010).

73. See below, pp. 49–50.

74. Matthews (2008), p. 104–05.

75. See section 6.8.

76. Matthews (2008), p. 137.

77. For the Gachelin case see http://cases.justia.com/us-court-of-appeals/ F2/734/770/365150/, accessed on 12 May 2010.

78. This is overlooked by quite a few authors. Paradigmatic examples are Arrigo (2004) and Bufacchi and Arrigo (2006). For an excellent critique of their argument (actually by an absolutist torture opponent), see Wisnewski (2009).

79. Matthews (2008), pp. 100–01.

80. Ibid., p. 38.

81. Ibid., p. 47.

82. Kant (1996), p. 130.

83. Matthews (2008), p. 60. He quotes Shue (1978), p. 132. The abridged version in Levinson (2004) omits parts of the text here.

84. Shue (1978), p. 133.

85. Matthews (2008), p. 61. One may add that Bustos, writing in 1990 or the end of the 1980s, talks about "contemporary torture," referring to dictatorships. See Bustos (1990), p. 143. Matthews seems unable to stand any qualifications when he is writing about torture, and thus obviously prefers (in order not to unnecessarily confuse his readers, I bet) to leave out the word "contemporary" when referring to Bustos. It all has to be "inevitable" and "100%."

86. Matthews (2008), p. 100.

Chapter 3

1. See section 2.1.2.

2. Shue (1978). I will refer here to the reprinted version in Levinson (2004), that is, to Shue (2004).

3. See section 6.2. I originally discussed it in Steinhoff (2006a), pp. 337–38.

4. Shue (2006), p. 231.

5. Ibid., n. 2.

6. Sussman (2006), p. 230.

7. For a criticism of Sussman, see section 6.4.

8. Sussman (2005), p. 4.

9. Ibid.

10. Shue (2009), p. 310.

11. Shue (2006), p. 233.

12. Ibid., p. 234 (see also p. 238). Shue adds in a footnote: "If anyone knows a case, I would appreciate an e-mail giving its name." May I add here that I would appreciate an e-mail from Shue giving me the name of a ticking-bomb theorist making the certainty assumption while arguing that such an idealized ticking-bomb scenario demonstrates the justifiability of torture in the real world?

13. Ibid., p. 235.

14. Shue (2009), p. 310.

15. See BBC (2008) and Hanson (2009).

16. Shue (2006), p. 237.

17. Wolfendale's (2006) argument seems to have a similar structure.

18. In my view, many absolutist opponents of torture, in particular those obsessed with the ticking-bomb argument, overlook this distinction between legalization and institutionalization. Some even overlook the distinction between legalization and moral justification.

19. See http://www.sueddeutsche.de/politik/983/394772/text/; http://www.faz.net/s/Rub77CAECAE94D7431F9EACD163751D4CFD/Doc-E5BEDC3E9486349B2B18DAB56D584C1BB-ATpl-Ecommon-Scontent.html; http://www.bild.de/BTO/news/aktuell/2006/09/26/denis-entfuehrung-kiste/denis-entfuehrung-kiste.html, all accessed on 4 December 2009.

20. Shue (2006), p. 233.

21. See p. 14, which also offers a second example.

22. Shue (2004), p. 57, and (2006), p. 233.

23. This also true for the treatment of exceptions from moral rules. Not allowing exceptions to the moral prohibition of torture but allowing them to the moral right to self-defense is simply arbitrary.

24. Erb (2006), pp. 30–32.

Chapter 4

1. Dershowitz (2004), p. 257. He emphasizes that *that* was his question and not the "old, abstract" one "over whether torture can ever be justified," and he complains about "misleading" descriptions of his proposals (ibid., p. 266). Maybe the next time he addresses the former question instead of the latter he could help to avoid "misleading" descriptions of his intentions by not using titles like "Should the Ticking Bomb Terrorist Be Tortured?" See Dershowitz (2002), p. 131.

2. Dershowitz (2004), pp. 270–71.

3. Ibid., p. 266–67.

4. Ibid., p. 267. " 'Testilying' is a term coined by New York City police to describe systematic perjury regarding the circumstances that led to a search, seizure, or interrogation." Ibid., p. 278, n. 13.

5. Compare Scarry (2004), p. 288.

6. Dershowitz (2002), p. 158.

7. Langbein (1977).

8. Dershowitz (2002), p. 158.

9. On Dershowitz's misreading of Langbein, see also Waldron (2005), p. 1739, n. 250.

10. Langbein (2004), p. 100.

11. Incidentally, Dershowitz seems to be actually mistaken in thinking that wiretapping without judicial warrant was legal in the early 1960s; the Communications Act of 1934 would seem to have prohibited such wiretapping. (I offer thanks to an anonymous referee for pointing this out to me.) This would be a still further embarrassment for Dershowitz's argument.

12. Dershowitz (2004), p. 257.

13. Ibid., p. 276.

14. Langbein (2004), p. 101.

15. Dershowitz (2002), p. 145.

16. Ibid., p. 147.

17. Ibid.

18. See Hillyard (1994) and Gross (2001), esp. pp. 47ff.

19. See also Arrigo (2004), Wolfendale (2006), Bufacchi and Arrigo (2006). However, contrary to what these authors seem to think, the fact that the *institutionalization* of torture is not justifiable does not show that *torture* is not justifiable. See on this also section 3.

20. Trapp (2006a), p. 132. All translations from German sources are mine.

Chapter 5

1. See for example Shue (1978); Machan (1990); Miller (2005); McMahan (2008).

2. Trapp (2006b), ch. 4.

3. Ibid., p. 62.

4. Ibid., p. 55.

5. Ibid., p. 64.

6. Ibid.

7. Ibid., n. 79.

8. Brecher (2008), p. 61.

9. Biletzki (2001).

10. Brecher (2008), p. 61.

11. Ibid., p. 19. The Shue quote is from Shue (1978), p. 141. In Shue (2004) it is on p. 57.

12. Ginbar (2009), p. 182. This little difficulty is also overlooked by Lamprecht (2009), p. 229. His confident claim that thanks to the Israeli example "the postulated consecutive connection between allowing preventive acts of torture in exceptional cases and their abusive extension can thus be considered as empirically confirmed" is therefore amusing at best. I would also like to point out that the concept of "empirical confirmation" in science normally requires more than just one case study. Generalizing over one example is like seeing a black rabbit and immediately concluding that all rabbits must be black.

13. Ginbar (2009), p. 182.

14. Ibid., p. 176.

15. McMahan (2008), p. 125.

16. However, McMahan seems to think that the ratio of justified torture to unjustified torture is worse than that of justified killing to unjustified killing. He states (personal communication): "In just wars, extensive killing can be morally justified. Yet [Steinhoff] presumably agrees that there have been no occasions when it has been justifiable to engage in mass torture." First, even if I agreed, this statement of McMahan's still would not provide any evidence, for how many wars are justified is clearly open to debate, and I am simply far less "optimistic" about the justifiability of certain real wars than McMahan is. So what *are* the numbers for computing the respective ratios, and where exactly does he take them from? Second, no, I do not agree. The UN Convention against Torture defines torture as follows: "[T]orture means any act by which severe pain or suffering, whether physical or mental, is intentionally inflicted on a person for such purposes as obtaining from him or a third person information or a confession, punishing him for an act he or a third person has committed or is suspected of having committed, or intimidating or coercing him or a third person, or for any reason based on discrimination of any kind, when such pain or suffering is inflicted by or at the instigation of or with the consent or acquiescence of a public official or other person acting in an official capacity. It does not include pain or suffering arising only from, inherent in or incidental to lawful sanctions." It is, however,

justified in some wars to intentionally inflict severe suffering on soldiers (for example by bombing them) for the purposes of intimidating or coercing them or others. If one is to complain here that bombing cannot be a form of torture (and why not? because that makes it more difficult to talk about "just wars"?), one would have to complain to the UN. Incidentally, McMahan himself does not provide any definition of torture at all. Third, I am talking about the domestic case, not about wars. Domestic self-defense law does not apply to the killing that soldiers do in war; therefore McMahan's example is beside the point anyway. Thus, if any ratio were relevant here, it would be the one between justified killing and unjustified killing in the domestic case and justified and unjustified torture in the domestic case. In many states, this ratio is much better for torture.

17. McMahan (2008), p. 125, claims: "Any legal permission to use torture, however restricted, would make it easier for governments to use torture, and would therefore have terrible effects overall, including more extensive violations of fundamental human rights. The legal prohibition of torture must therefore be absolute." He provides no evidence that the results in the case of torture must be terrible, although the results in the case of killing, injuring, and imprisoning people are not. Of course, there is no such evidence. Besides, the leap from "make it *easier*" to "would therefore have *terrible* effects" is a rather big one.

18. Miller (2011) seems to think that any training of police snipers is already an institutionalization of self-defensive *killing*. But that appears to be a gross overstatement. After all, police snipers also exist where the "live-saving final shot" has not been legalized.

19. Waldron (2005), pp. 1726–27.

20. Ibid., p. 1723.

21. Ibid., p. 1735.

22. Ibid., pp. 1728–39.

23. As an aside to Waldron, let me note that in a debate on torture among him, David Rodin, and me at the Oxford Jurisprudence Discussion Group, Waldron took issue with my argument from self-defensive killing. He claimed that the analogy I would really have to consider is not killing in self-defense as such, but killing someone in self-defense who is in police custody. That, however, is, first, wrong, since I do also argue for the permissibility of private self-defensive torture, and second, it is also irrelevant since police are clearly justified under self-defense law in self-defensively killing somebody in custody if this is a necessary and proportionate means to thwart his unjust attack. Waldron also stated that torture might be wrong in ways that killing is not. Well, yes, it might, but so might shoplifting. In that context, Waldron also invoked the arguments provided by Shue and Sussman. I had, however, already criticized Shue's and Sussman's arguments in Steinhoff (2006a) and (2010). Waldron ignores this criticism. Incidentally, in his new book (Waldron 2010) he also simply reprints his article "The Uses of Terror" without dealing with the criticism I have subjected his views to in Steinhoff (2007), pp. 112–15.

24. Luban (2005), p. 1430. A comparable argument is put forward by Kreimer (2003–2004).

25. See pp. 53 and 60.

26. If the state does aid and abet those aggressors, it might well undermine the basis of his own legitimacy in the eyes of a large part of the population (and in fact), as Winfried Brugger correctly points out. See Brugger (2003), p. 85. This, incidentally, is a slippery slope never considered by absolutist opponents of torture. Hecker (2003), p. 216, n. 30, thinks that Brugger's point has "unmistakable relations to populist patterns of thought." That is a revealing complaint: if you cannot show that an argument is wrong, just try to defame it by association. Be that as it may, Hecker's own argumentation against torture is wrong—or should I more insinuatingly say: "it has unmistakable relations to illogical and erroneous patterns of thought"?

27. Erb (2006), pp. 19–38.

28. I thank Heikki Pihlajamäki for pressing me on this point.

29. McMahan (personal communication) says that my "examples of the Weimar republic and interwar Sweden and Finland seem . . . irrelevant. It's irrelevant if torture isn't used even when it's legal during a time and in a place in which there's no perceived need for it. . . . But when peasant groups and the Catholic church threatened the power of the wealthy elites in El Salvador, and when advocates of democracy threatened the regime of the generals in Argentina . . ." I find these statements very odd. If somebody claims that all swans are white, then showing a black swan disproves the claim. If somebody claims that the legalization of torture in a state will automatically lead to "metastatic" effects, then showing states where it did not disproves the claim. However, McMahan's example of Argentina *is* irrelevant: torture *was* illegal there (it was probably also illegal in El Salvador, but I have not yet been able to verify that) and done anyway. So what is the example supposed to prove: that prohibiting torture does not even make a difference? It seems that this would provide support for my position rather than McMahan's.

29 Incidentally, all it takes to legalize self-defensive torture is to not prohibit it. Thus, there is as little need to introduce a special paragraph allowing self-defensive torture into the penal codes as there is a need to introduce a special paragraph allowing self-defensive throat cutting. Both forms of self-defense can easily be covered by the normal self-defense regulations and should be dealt with accordingly in case law.

Chapter 6

1. Bybee (2002).
2. Kershnar (2005).
3. Tindale (2005), p. 212.
4. Ibid.
5. See ch. 5.
6. See ch. 3.
7. See Leverick (2006), p. 5; Baskind (2009).
8. Tindale (2005), p. 212.
9. Ginbar (2009), pp. 73–74.

10. See section 2.1.1.

11. See also Miller (2006), p. 184, and Sussman (2005), p. 16.

12. Ginbar (2009), p. 74.

13. Bagaric and Clarke (2007). Ginbar also mentions Barrie Paskins. Paskins, however, is an absolutist opponent of torture.

14. Ginbar (2009), p. 305.

15. Massimo La Torre (2009), p. 27, claims: "Bybee concedes that this case does not make a fit with the traditional understanding of self-defence, which becomes available to us only when confronted with an immediate frontal threat that is certain to materialize," and then quotes as alleged proof for this assessment the same passage that Ginbar quotes. But, as in Ginbar's case (see the main text), this passage does not at all concede what La Torre claims it concedes. Besides, La Torre's claim that self-defense only becomes available to us when we are confronted with an immediate *frontal* threat that is *certain* to materialize is flatly wrong, both in law and in morality.

16. Bybee (2002), p. 44. The memorandum quotes Moore (1989), pp. 280, 323.

17. Ginbar (2009), p. 305. The quote is from Gur-Arye (2004), p. 194.

18. See ibid.

19. Ginbar (2009), p. 305. The quote is, again, from Gur-Arye (2004), p. 194.

20. Ginbar (2009), p. 306.

21. Gur-Arye (2003), p. 33.

22. Ginbar (2009), p. 306–07.

23. See for example Brugger (2003), Kershnar (2005), Erb (2006), Steinhoff (2006a).

24. See Gur-Arye (2004), pp. 194–95.

25. See Allhoff (2012), section 8.3.

26. Miller (2011).

27. I have explained that in Steinhoff (2009a). Miller ignores this article of mine.

28. Richard Louis Trammel, "A Criterion for Determining Negativity and Positivity," *Tulane Studies in Philosophy* 33 (1985), pp. 75–81, esp. pp. 76–7. See also section 6.3 in this work.

29. Miller (2011).

30. Matthews (2008), p. 189.

31. See sections 2.1.1 and 6.9.

32. Matthews (2008), p. 9.

33. Ibid., p. 204.

34. Ibid., pp. 204–05.

35. See Allhoff (2005).

36. See Kershnar (2005).

37. Brecher (2008), p. 12.

38. Ibid., pp. 10–11.

39. Waldron (1981), p. 29.

40. Applbaum (1998); Steinhoff (2007), pp. 57–58.

41. Shue (2004), p. 49.

42. Ibid.

43. Ibid., pp. 50–51.

44. Ibid., p. 51.

45. In the meantime Henry Shue has somewhat distanced himself in conversation from drawing a parallel between the prohibition of torture and *jus in bello* requirements. He also no longer mentions this older argument in his more recent publications on torture.

46. David Rodin claims that, unlike torture victims, soldiers in trenches are not entirely defenseless, for they could surrender, retreat, or dig into deeper trenches; and, had they been better prepared, they would have found more protective shelter or been equipped with longer-range guns (personal communication). However, had the torture victim been better prepared, she might have escaped or killed herself in order not to become a torture victim in the first place. But if she indeed has become a torture victim, she is defenseless under the torture, as are the soldiers in the trenches who are not lucky (or good) enough to have suitable weapons. As to the first point, the torture victim can surrender too and disclose the information. Such surrender might not always be accepted, but likewise the surrender of soldiers in trenches is not always seen by artillerists miles away or hidden behind a cloud of smoke. Finally, to suggest that trench soldiers subjected to heavy artillery fire should in that situation be able to dig into deeper trenches seems to be as unrealistic as to suggest that a torture victim should protect herself by yoga or meditation techniques.

47. Jeff McMahan thinks that the relevant principle here is not proportionality but minimal force (personal communication). I disagree, but the disagreement may simply be a semantic one, namely, one about what "proportionality" *means* within the context of *jus in bello*. Within that context, in my view, proportionality *includes* what in the domestic self-defense case would be called "necessity." Be that as it may, the important point for the purposes of the present discussion is that an alleged principle of the immunity of the defenseless plays no role here.

48. Münkler (2003), p. 234.

49. Sussman (2005), p. 16. For a similar assessment, see Miller (2006), p. 184.

50. Shue (2006), p. 231.

51. I think this is true for Henry Shue, Jessica Wolfendale, J. Jeremy Wisnewski, R. D. Emerick, Yuval Ginbar, and David Luban, to name a few. Only on the last three pages of his book on the ticking bomb does Bob Brecher (2008) finally mention the child-kidnapping case—and says that nothing can be done for the child. Denis Mook is lucky that the police in Bremen did not share this view.

52. McMahan makes the same distinction in other words, though: "Attacker" and "Culpable Cause." See McMahan (1994), pp. 255 and 258.

53. Kaufman (2008), p. 98.

54. Ibid.

55. Ibid., p. 115, n. 71.

56. See also section 6.2.

57. Kaufman (2008), pp. 109–10.

58. For a critique in particular of Kaufman's objections against what he calls the "distributive justice theory of self-defence"—on which my criticism of Kaufman does not rely in the least—see Segev (2008).

59. Uniacke (1996), p. 187.

60. Ibid., p. 187, n. 38, and the text this note refers to.

61. Hill (2007), p. 397.

62. Ibid., pp. 397–98. Hill notes that this latter case "was suggested by Dr James Heather. Dr Heather intended this example as a *reductio ad absurdum* of the view in this paper, however. The reader may judge for him- or herself whether he was right." I am a reader, and my judgment is that Heather is right.

63. Ibid., p. 398. As mentioned above, Gur-Arye (2004) also thinks that the distinction between acts and omissions is very important and that cases like Withholding might not be *genuine self-defense* cases. However, unlike Hill, she does *not* think that the pain infliction in Withholding is *impermissible*. I argue here, of course, that the terrorist *is performing* an act *by omitting* to pull up the detonator: if the bomb does explode, his omission will have been an integral part of his act of blowing up innocent people. See the discussion below.

64. See note 62 of this chapter.

65. Kaufman (2008), p. 97.

66. Hill (2007), pp. 399–400.

67. Ibid., p. 400.

68. Ibid., p. 401.

69. Trammel (1985), pp. 76–77.

70. Sussman, (2005), p. 4.

71. Ibid., n. 10.

72. Ibid., p. 4.

73. Ibid., p. 21.

74. Ibid., p. 30.

75. The example is a variant of Bernard Williams' famous example of Jim and the twenty Indians.

76. Kant (2008), p. 24.

77. However, for a detailed and devastating critique of the attempt to use the Kantian Formula of the Universal Law of Nature as an argument against self-defensive torture, see Trapp (2006b), pp. 109–21.

78. This also refutes another rather bad argument I came upon: a Kantian maxim allowing torture in certain cases would be too complicated. I offer two replies: (1) complicated ≠ wrong. (2) A Kantian maxim allowing self-defensive torture is not more complicated than a Kantian maxim allowing self-defensive killing. Kant did allow self-defensive killing and injuring. So where is the problem?

79. Kant (2008), p. 29, translation corrected ("*brauchest*" means "use," not "treat"), format changed.

80. See also Trapp (2006b), p. 122, n. 126.

81. For convincing criticisms of some of them, see Kershnar (2001), pp. 186–90.

82. Trapp (2006b), p. 123.

83. Ibid., pp. 51, 123–45.

84. See the last paragraphs of section 6.6.

85. Kant (2008), p. 36.

86. Kant (1996), p. 130.

87. See section 6.6.

88. Bielefeldt (2007), p. 13. Sussman argues similarly. For a critique of Sussman, see section 6.4.

89. Bielefeldt (2007), pp. 12–13.

90. To be sure, if Bielefeldt understood "unbearable" in such a way that pain would only be unbearable if people preferred death to this pain, my argument of this paragraph would not work. His argument against torture as such, however, would not work either, for not all torture is unbearable in this sense.

91. Bielefeldt (2007), p. 13. Bielefeld quotes Splett from an unpublished manuscript. The text is meanwhile available as Splett (2006), p. 108.

92. La Torre (2009), p. 31.

93. Brunkhorst (2009), p. 81.

94. Ibid., p. 80.

95. In an email conversation I had with him, Brunkhorst claimed that the idea that "everybody who is affected by a legally binding decision has to have sufficient and equal access to the discussion, creation and implementation of legal norms" is entirely compatible with not allowing foreigners to participate in democratic domestic decision-making processes that will also affect them. However, for obvious logical reasons it simply is not. It is, however, apparently and unfortunately the case that the lofty *rhetoric* of "participation" is only too compatible with a less noble *practice* of exclusion and of the philosophical "justification" of such a practice. On this see also Steinhoff (2009b), section 3.3.3., esp. pp. 222–26.

96. Brunkhorst (2006), pp. 99–100.

97. Brunkhorst (2005), p. 76.

98. This is made very clear by Hruschka (2003), esp. pp. 221–23.

99. Splett (2006), p. 108. Beestermöller (2009) quotes this definition of Splett on p. 468.

100. Beestermöller (2009), p. 466.

101. Ibid., pp. 470–71.

102. Ibid., p. 471, n. 43.

103. Ibid.

104. Beestermöller, ibid., p. 474, n. 47, notes that "in any case Splett's strict definition does not say that any infliction of pain or the threat with pain with the aim of bringing a human being to an act he would otherwise omit already has to count as torture." That is entirely correct. The problem is, however, that Splett's "strict definition" does not offer *any* actually applicable criteria of what torture is and what it is not, for he does not give any hint of when the freedom of the will is "abolished" and when it is not. See on this the following remarks in the main text.

105. He made this point in an email exchange I had with him.

106. Beestermöller (2009), p. 473.

107. Ibid., p. 474.

108. Beestermöller (2010), p. 144.

109. Bennett (1981), pp. 100–01.

110. Steinhoff (2007), pp. 37–41.

111. See Steinhoff (2006b), p. 174; for the same point, see also Erb (2006), p. 34.

112. Beestermöller (2009), p. 460–61.

113. Ibid., p. 475.

114. Ibid.

115. The first therapy session is, of course, to be found in section 6.5.

116. Hruschka (2003).

117. Kant (2008), pp. 29–30.

118. Kant (1996), p. 25 (Introduction to the Doctrine of Right, §D).

119. Ibid., p. 29.

120. As Hruschka (2003), p. 213, points out with regard to Kant's position on the necessity or (in Kant's words) moderation requirement in self-defense situations: "This is the reason why, as the 'Metaphysics of Morals' states, 'a recommendation to show moderation (*moderamen*) belongs not to right but only to ethics." See Kant (1996), p. 28.

121. Kant (2010), AA XIX, Refl. 7195.

122. Kant (1996), p. 208.

123. Lamprecht (2009), p. 231.

124. Ibid. Lamprecht quotes Knauer (2008), p. 33.

125. For my own criticism of this principle, and references to further literature, see Steinhoff (2007), pp. 33–52.

126. Lamprecht (2009), pp. 238–40; the actual quote is from p. 240.

127. Ibid., p. 242.

128. Leverick (2006), p. 54.

129. The most recent example (at the time of writing, April 2010) is McDonald (2010). She attacks an argument provided by Bagaric and Clarke as "ludicrous," but actually it is her argument that is ludicrous. It is also entirely unoriginal and therefore succumbs to criticisms advanced against other authors in this section and elsewhere in this book.

130. Shue (2004), p. 57.

131. Shue (2009), p. 308.

132. Shue (2006), p. 233.

133. This is also the way David Luban proceeds. See Luban (2005), esp. pp. 1440–45, and (2008), esp. pp. 7–8.

134. See in particular there the criticisms of premises 1 and 3.

135. Luban (2008), p. 7.

136. Ibid., p. 8.

137. Luban (2005), p. 1427.

138. Ibid., pp. 1427 (five times), 1439, 1441, 1453, 1461.

139. See sections 2.1 and 2.2.

140. Luban (2008).
141. Ibid., p. 17.
142. Ibid.
143. See section 2.1.2.
144. See ibid., pp. 32–33.
145. Matthews (2008), p. 71.
146. Ibid.
147. Ibid., p. 73.
148. Ibid., p. 98.
149. Matthews (2008), pp. 74, 75, 78, 80, 83.
150. Ibid., p. 83.
151. Ibid., p. 84.
152. See Reed (2008).
153. See ibid.
154. They often add "plus X" in order to deal with the so-called "Gettier problems." Gettier problems are a puzzle that need not concern us here. Suffice it to say that "X" is not certainty. For a very useful discussion of attempts to explicate the concept of knowledge, see Steup (2006).
155. Matthews (2008), p. 83.
156. Ibid., p. 81.
157. In fact, he would have to answer the question why he only opposes torture and not self-defense generally.
158. Brecher (2008), p. 24.
159. See ch. 3.
160. Brecher (2008), p. 24.
161. See section 6.1.
162. Brecher (2008), pp. 35–38.
163. See pp. 17–18, 87, 138–39, 142–43.
164. Brecher (2008), p. 86.
165. Ibid., p. 87.
166. Ibid., p. 86.
167. Ibid., p. 37.
168. Wisnewski and Emerick (2009), p. 25. Wisnewski repeats all the mistakes he makes together with Emerick in their discussion of the ticking-bomb argument in Wisnewski (2010), pp. 128–48.
169. Wisnewski and Emerick (2009), p. 24.
170. Ibid., p. 29; italics changed.
171. Ibid., p. 32.
172. See pp. 12, 14–15, 59.
173. They claim that it is "clear" that the self-defense argument *relies* "on the presumed moral permissibility of torture. The arguments themselves are meaningless without this presupposition." Wisnewski and Emerick (2009), p. 15. However, that is not "clear" at all, but rather nonsense. The self-defense argument does not presuppose the justifiability of torture; it attempts (quite successfully) to *demonstrate* it. Wisnewski

(2010), pp. 109–14, finally says a little bit more about the self-defense argument, dedicating five and a half pages in a book of 273 pages to it. However, he completely misinterprets the necessity condition, missing the fact that a defender has only to choose the milder means if this is *equally* promising (this is the case in German law; it is also the case in many other jurisdictions; and there is no Western jurisdiction I am aware of where the defender would have to choose a milder means if this unreasonably reduces the chances of success); he ignores the fact that the child kidnapper and the ticking-bomb terrorist are *continuing* aggressors; and he mistakenly assumes that self-defense against the defenseless cannot be justified. (Incidentally, he relies on Shue to support this latter assumption, ignoring my criticism of Shue in Steinhoff (2006), pp. 337–38, although he must be perfectly aware of it, having quoted my article in other contexts.) I have already dealt with all of these points in sections 2.1.1 and 6.1–3.

174. Luban (2008), 34–35; Ginbar (2009), pp. 60–61.

175. I am happy to report that such strategies do not work on me.

176. The influential German law professor Reinhard Merkel came up with this example. See Beestermöller (2009), p. 469, n. 41.

177. See section 6.2.

178. Ginbar (2009), p. 30.

179. Ibid., p. 42. He takes the example from Judith Jarvis Thomson, who, if I am not mistaken, took it from Gertrude Elizabeth Margaret Anscombe.

180. This does not mean that it is more relevant than what people foresee.

181. See section 2.4.

182. Ginbar (2009), p. 59.

183. Ibid., p. 60.

184. Ginbar (2009), pp. 61–63, also points out that the necessity argument can justify terrorism. That is a good ad hominem argument against those people who think that torturing innocent people can be justified while terrorism cannot, but it is not a good ad hominem argument against those authors who think that, assuming the stakes are high enough, both can be justified. For a defense of certain forms of terrorism in this light, see Steinhoff (2007), ch. 5.

185. Ginbar (2009), p. 60.

186. But one also made by Luban (2008), p. 29. Luban also complains there that "consequentialists" have easy answers to a couple of difficult questions. However, the fact is that absolutist deontologists like Luban have the easy answers to the difficult questions he asks there: "No" in each case. "Unthinking" indeed.

187. Ginbar (2009), p. 60.

188. Ibid., p. 44.

189. See sections 2.1.1, 3, 4, 6.1, 6.8.

Chapter 7

1. Bielefeldt (2007), p. 22.

2. Steinhoff (2006a), p. 339.

3. Bielefeldt (2007), p. 22.

4. Weighing of life against life is, according to majority opinion, not allowed under the German justifying emergency paragraph. It is allowed under the necessity statutes of some U.S. states. See Heberling (1975), n. 33.

5. See ch. 4.

6. In this context, I offer one observation: if thought experiments like the ticking-bomb case are so dangerous and might be "abused," then one probably should not give them a platform. However, in most pamphlets and articles of torture opponents, these and other examples are always described (if not always discussed) and presented to people who probably have never heard of them before. Those torture opponents who really think that these thought experiments are dangerous can then hardly exclude the possibility that they themselves are contributing to the spread of torture by acquainting their audience with these arguments. In other words: why, then, aren't *they* quiet?

References

Alexander, Larry and Michael S. Moore (2010). "Deontological Ethics." http://plato.stanford.edu/entries/ethics-deontological/, accessed on 17 February 2010.

Allhoff, Fritz (2005). "A Defense of Torture: Separation of Cases, Ticking Time-bombs, and Moral Justification." *International Journal of Applied Philosophy* 19(2), pp. 243–64.

———. (2012). *Terrorism, Ticking Time-Bombs, and Torture*. Chicago and London: University of Chicago Press.

Applbaum, Arthur Isak (1998). "Are Violations of Rights Ever Right?" *Ethics* 108, pp. 340–66.

Jean Maria Arrigo (2004). "A Utilitarian Argument against Torture Interrogation of Terrorists." *Science and Engineering Ethics* 10, pp. 543–72.

Bagaric, Mirko and Julie Clarke (2007). *Torture: When the Unthinkable Is Morally Permissible*. Albany: State University of New York Press.

Baskind, Eric (2008). "The Law Relating to Self Defence." http://www.bsdgb.co.uk/index.php?Information:The_Law_Relating_to_Self_Defence, accessed on 25 March 2008.

Başoğlu, Metin (2007). *Torture and Its Consequences: Current Treatment Approaches*. Cambridge: Cambridge University Press.

BBC (2008). "Can an Alcoholic Have an Occasional Drink?" http://www.addiction-info.org/articles/3077/1/Can-an-alcoholic-have-an-occasional-drink/Page1.html, accessed on 2 December 2009.

———. (2010). "The Processes of Death and Decomposition." http://www.bbc.co.uk/dna/h2g2/A2451683, accessed on 18 April 2010.

Beestermöller, Gerhard (2009). "Erlaubnis zur Rettungsfolter—Imperativ der Gerechtigkeit? Erwiderung auf ein persuasives Argument." *Freiburger Zeitschrift für Theologie und Philosophie* 56, pp. 451–76.

———. (2010). "Gibt es die Folter? Ein Plädoyer für ein absolutes Folterverbot jenseits der Frontstellung von Deontologie und Teleologie." In Paul Chummar Chittilappilly CMI, (ed.). *Ethik der Lebensfelder: Festschrift für Philipp Schmitz SJ*. Herder, Freiburg, pp. 120–154.

Bennett, Jonathan (1981). "Morality and Consequences." In Sterling M. McMurrin (ed.). *The Tanner Lectures on Human Values*. Vol. II. Salt Lake City: University of Utah Press, pp. 45–116.

Bentham, Jeremy (1973). "Of Torture." In W. L Twining and P. E. Twining, "Bentham on Torture." *Northern Ireland Legal Quarterly* 24, pp. 305–56.

Bielefeldt, Heiner (2007). "Menschenwürde und Folterverbot: Eine Auseinandersetzung mit den jüngsten Vorstößen zur Aufweichung des Folterverbotes." Deutsches Institut für Menschenrechte. Berlin. http://files.institut-fuer-menschenrechte.de/437/IUS-028_E_Folter_RZ_WWW_ES.pdf, accessed on 25 March 2008.

Biletzki, Anat (2001). "The Judicial Rhetoric of Morality: Israel's High Court of Justice on the Legality of Torture." http://www.sss.ias.edu/publications/occasional, accessed on 2 March 2010.

Brecher, Bob (2008). *Torture and the Ticking Bomb*. Oxford: Blackwell.

Bufacchi, Vittorio and Jean Maria Arrigo (2006). "Torture, Terrorism and the State: a Refutation of the Ticking Bomb Argument." *Journal of Applied Philosophy* 23, pp. 355–373.

Brugger, Winfried (2003). "Darf der Staat ausnahmsweise foltern?" *Der Staat* 35, pp. 67–97.

Brunkhorst, Hauke (2005). "Folter vor Recht: Das Elend des repressiven Liberalismus." *Blätter für deutsche und internationale Politik* 1, pp. 75–82.

———. (2006). "Folter, Würde und repressiver Liberalismus." In Gerhard Beestermöller, Hauke Brunkhorst (eds.), *Rückkehr der Folter: Der Rechtsstaat im Zwielicht?* München: C. H. Beck, pp. 88–100.

———. (2009). "Torture and Democracy." In Clucas, Johnstone, Ward (eds.), pp. 73–82.

Bustos, Enrique (1990). "Dealing with the Unbearable: Reactions of Therapists and Therapeutic Institutions to Survivors of Torture." In Peter Suedfeld (ed.), *Psychology and Torture*. New York and London: Hemisphere Publishing Corporation, pp. 143–63.

Bybee, Jay S. (2002). "Memorandum for Alberto R. Gonzales (August 1, 2002)." http://news.findlaw.com/nytimes/docs/doj/bybee80102mem.pdf, accessed on 1 February 2010.

Clucas, Bev, Gerry Johnstone, Tony Ward (eds., 2009). *Torture: Moral Absolutes and Ambiguities*. Baden-Baden, Nomos.

Conroy, John (2007). *Unspeakable Acts, Ordinary People: The Dynamics of Torture*. Berkeley: University of California Press.

Davis, Michael (2005). "The Moral Justification of Torture and Other Cruel, Inhuman, or Degrading Treatment." *International Journal of Applied Philosophy* 19(2), pp. 161–178.

Dershowitz, Alan (2002). *Why Terrorism Works: Understanding the Threats, Responding to the Challenge*. New Haven, CT: Yale University Press.

———. (2004). "Tortured Reasoning." In Levinson (ed.), pp. 257–280.

Dworkin, Ronald (1978). *Taking Rights Seriously*. Cambridge, MA: Harvard University Press.

Erb, Volker (2006). "Folterverbot und Notwehrrecht." In Lenzen (ed.), pp. 19–38.

Ginbar, Yuval (2009). *Why Not Torture Terrorists? Moral, Practical, and Legal Aspects of the 'Ticking Bomb' Justification of Torture*. Oxford: Oxford University Press.

Gross, Oren (2001). "Cutting Down Trees: Law-Making under the Shadow of Great Calamities." In R. J. Daniels, P. Macklem, and K. Roach (eds.) *The Security of Freedom: Essays on Canada's Anti-Terrorism Bill.* Toronto: Toronto University Press, pp. 39–61.

Gur-Arye, Miriam (2003). "Legitimating Official Brutality: Can the War against Terror Justify Torture?" UC Berkeley: Center for the Study of Law and Society Jurisprudence and Social Policy Program. http://escholarship.org/uc/item/5pg6r1dm, accessed on 1 February 2010.

———. (2004). "Can the War against Terror Justify the Use of Force in Interrogations? Reflections in Light of the Israeli Experience." In Sanford (ed.), pp. 183–198.

Hanson, David J. (2009). "Alcoholics Can Recover from Alcoholism and Drink in Moderation." http://www2.potsdam.edu/hansondj/controversies/1109212610.html, accessed on 2 December 2009.

Heberling, Peter D. W. (1975). "Justification: The Impact of the Model Penal Code on Statutory Reform." *Columbia Law Review* 75(5), pp. 914–962.

Hecker, Wolfgang (2003). "Relativierung des Folterverbots in der BRD?" *Kritische Justiz* 36(2), pp. 210–218.

Herdegen, Matthias (August 2005). "Artikel 1 GG." In Theodor Maunz and Günter Dürig (eds.), *Grundgesetz, Kommentar.* München: C. H. Beck.

Hill, Daniel (2007). "Ticking Bombs, Torture, and the Analogy with Self-Defense." *American Philosophical Quarterly* 44, pp. 395–404.

Hillyard, Paddy (1994). "The Normalization of Special Powers from Northern Ireland to Britain." In Nicola Lacey (ed.), *A Reader on Criminal Justice.* Oxford: Oxford University Press.

Hruschka, Joachim (2003). "Die Notwehr im Zusammenhang von Kants Rechtslehre." *Zeitschrift für die Gesamte Strafrechtswissenschaft* 115(2), pp. 201–23.

Joecks, Wolfgang and Klaus Miebach (2003, eds.). *Münchener Kommentar zum Strafgesetzbuch, Vol. 1.* München: C. H. Beck.

Kant, Immanuel (1996). *The Metaphysics of Morals* (transl. and ed. by Mary Gregor). Cambridge: Cambridge University Press.

———. (2008). *Groundwork for the Metaphysic of Morals,* transl. by Jonathan F. Bennett. http://www.earlymoderntexts.com/pdf/kantgw.pdf, accessed on 5 April 2010.

———. (2010). "Erläuterungen Kants zu A. G. Baumgartens Initia philosphiae practicae primae" (ed. by Korpora.org). http://www.korpora.org/Kant/aa19/269.html, accessed on 20 April 2010.

Kaufman, Whitley (2008). "Torture and the 'Distributive Justice' Theory of Self-Defense: An Assessment." *Ethics and International Affairs* 22(1), pp. 93–115.

Kershnar, Stephen (2001). *Desert, Retribution, and Torture.* Lanham, MD: University Press of America.

———. (2005). "For Interrogational Torture." *International Journal of Applied Philosophy* 19(2), pp. 223–241.

Kindhäuser, Urs (2008). "Skript zur Vorlesung Strafrecht AT, § 16: Notwehr." http://www.jura.uni-bonn.de/fileadmin/Fachbereich_Rechtswissenschaft/Einrichtungen/Lehrstuehle/Strafrecht3/Strafrecht_AT/s-at-16.pdf, accessed on 25 March 2008.

Knauer, Peter (2008). *Handlungsnetze: Über das Grundprinzip der Ethik*. Knauer (BoD), Frankfurt am Main.

Kreimer, Seth F. (2003–04). "Too Close to the Rack and the Screw: Constitutional Constraints on Torture in the War on Terror." *University of Pennsylvania Journal of Constitutional Law* 6, pp. 278–325.

Lamprecht, Florian (2009). *Darf der Staat foltern, um Leben zu retten? Folter im Rechtsstaat zwischen Recht und Moral*. Paderborn: Mentis.

Langbein, John H. (1977). *Torture and the Law of Proof: Europe and England in the Ancien Régime*. Chicago: University of Chicago Press.

———. (2004). "The Legal History of Torture." In Levinson (ed.), pp. 93–103.

La Torre, Massimo (2009). " 'Jurists, Bad Christians': Torture and the Rule of Law." In Clucas et. al. (ed.), pp. 10–38.

Laufhütte, Heinrich Wilhelm, Ruth Rissing-van Saan, and Klaus Tiedemann (2006, eds.). *Strafgesetzbuch: Leipziger Kommentar, Großkommentar*, Vol. 2: §§ 32 bis 55. Berlin: De Gruyter Recht.

Lenzen, Wolfgang (ed., 2006). *Ist Folter erlaubt? Juristische und philosophische Aspekte*. Paderborn: Mentis.

Leverick, Fiona (2006). *Killing in Self-Defence*. Oxford University Press, Oxford.

Levinson, Sanford (ed., 2004). *Torture: A Collection*. Oxford: Oxford University Press.

Luban, David (2005). "Liberalism, Torture, and the Ticking Bomb." *Virginia Law Review* 91(6), pp. 1425–61.

———. (2008). "Unthinking the Ticking Bomb." http://lsr.nellco.org/cgi/viewcontent.cgi?article=1070&context=georgetown/fwps, accessed on 28 October 2008.

Lührmann, Olivia (1999). *Tötungsrecht zur Eigentumsverteidigung?* Frankfurt am Main: Peter Lang.

McDonald, Catherine (2010). "Deconstructing Ticking-Bomb Arguments." *Global Dialogue* 12(1–2), http://www.worlddialogue.org/content.php?id=456, accessed on 22 April 2010.

Machan, Tibor R. (1990). "Exploring Extreme Violence (Torture)." *Journal of Social Philosophy* 21, pp. 92–97.

McMahan, Jeff (1994). "Self-Defense and the Problem of the Innocent Attacker." *Ethics* 104(2), pp. 252–290.

———. (2008). "Torture in Principle and in Practice." *Public Affairs Quarterly* 22(2), pp. 111–128.

Matthews, Richard (2008). *The Absolute Violation: Why Torture Must Be Prohibited*. Montreal and Kingston: McGill-Queen's University Press; London: Ithaca.

Miller, Seumas (2005). "Is Torture Ever Morally Justified?" *International Journal of Applied Philosophy* 19(2), pp. 179–192.

———. (2011). "Torture." http://plato.stanford.edu/entries/torture/, accessed on 21 February 2011.

Montague, Phillip (1989). "The Morality of Self-Defense: A Reply to Wasserman." *Philosophy and Public Affairs* 18, pp. 81–89

Moore, Michael S. (1989). "Torture and the Balance of Evils." *Israel Law Review* 23, pp. 280–344.

————. (2007). "Patrolling the Borders of Consequentialist Justifications: The Scope of Agent-Relative Restrictions." *Law and Philosophy* 27, pp. 35–96.

Münkler, Herfried (2003). *Die neuen Kriege.* Reinbek bei Hamburg: Rowholt.

Nourse, V. F. (2001). "Self-Defense and Subjectivity." *The University of Chicago Law Review* 68(4), pp. 1235–1308.

Penal Code of the Federal Republic of Germany (1987), transl. by Joseph J. Darby. In Edward M. Wise (ed.), *The American Series of Foreign Penal Codes*, Vol. 28, http://wings.buffalo.edu/law/bclc/germind.htm, accessed on 16 February 2010.

Reed, Baron (2008). "Certainty." http://plato.stanford.edu/entries/certainty/, accessed on 3 March 2010.

Rudolphi, Hans-Joachim, Eckhard Horn, Erich Samson et. al. (2010, eds.). *Systematischer Kommentar. zum Strafgesetzbuch.* Köln: Luchterhand.

Ryan, Cheyney C. (1984). "Self-Defense, Pacifism, and the Possibility of Killing." *Ethics* 93, pp. 508–524.

Scarry, Elaine (1987). *The Body in Pain: The Making and Unmaking of the World.* Oxford: Oxford University Press.

————. (2004). "Five Errors in the Reasoning of Alan Dershowitz." In Levinson (ed.), pp. 281–90.

Segev, Re'em (2008). "Response to Whitley Kaufman: The Distributive Justice Theory of Self-Defense." *Ethics & International Affairs* (Online Exclusive Issue) 22(1). http://www.ciaonet.org/journals/cceia/v22i1/12.html, accessed on 11 December 2008.

Shue, Henry (1978). "Torture." *Philosophy and Public Affairs* 7, pp. 124–143.

————. (2004). "Torture." In Levinson (ed.), pp. 49–60. (This is a slightly abridged version of the original 1978 article.)

————. (2006). "Torture in Dreamland: Disposing of the Ticking Bomb." *Case Western Reserve Journal of International Law* 37, p. 231.

————. (2009). "Making Exceptions." *Journal of Applied Philosophy* 26, p. 310.

Sinnott-Armstrong, Walter (2006). "Consequentialism." http://plato.stanford.edu/entries/consequentialism/, accessed on 17 February 2010.

Somnier, Finn and Inge Kemp Genefke (1986). "Psychotherapy for Victims of Torture." *British Journal of Psychiatry* 149, pp. 329–329.

Somnier, Finn, Peter Vesti, Marianne Kastrup, Inge Kemp Genefke (2007). "Psycho-Social Consequences of Torture: Current Knowledge and Evidence." In Başoğlu (ed.), pp. 56–71.

Splett, Jörg (2006). "Theo-Anthropologie: Ein Antwortversuch." In Hans-Ludwig Ollig (ed.), *Theo-Anthropologie: Jörg Splett zu Ehren.* Würzburg: Echter, pp. 105–111.

Steinhoff, Uwe (2006a). "Torture—The Case for Dirty Harry and against Alan Dershowitz." *Journal of Applied Philosophy* 23(3), pp. 337–353. Reprinted in David Rodin (ed., 2007), *War, Torture and Terrorism: Ethics and War in the 21ˢᵗ Century*, Oxford: Blackwell, pp. 97–113.

————. (2006b). *Effiziente Ethik: Über Rationalität, Selbstformung, Politik und Postmoderne.* Paderborn: Mentis.

————. (2007). *On the Ethics of War and Terrorism.* Oxford: Oxford University Press.

————. (2009a). "Justifying Defensive Torture." In Clucas et. al. (eds.), pp. 39–60.

————. (2009b). *The Philosophy of Jürgen Habermas: A Critical Introduction.* Oxford: Oxford University Press.

————. (2010). "Defusing the Ticking Social Bomb Argument: The Right to Self-Defensive Torture." *Global Dialogue* 12(1), http://ftp4.dns-systems.net/~worlddiag/index.php.

————. (2012). "Rights, Liability, and the Moral Equality of Combatants." *Journal of Ethics*, 16, pp. 339–366.

Steup, Matthias (2006). "The Analysis of Knowledge." http://plato.stanford.edu/entries/knowledge-analysis/, accessed on 3 March 2010.

Sussman, David (2005). "What's Wrong with Torture?" *Philosophy and Public Affairs* 33, pp. 1–33.

————. (2006). "Defining Torture." *Case Western Reserve Journal of International Law* 37, pp. 225–30.

Trammel, Richard Louis (1985). "A Criterion for Determining Negativity and Positivity." *Tulane Studies in Philosophy* 33, pp. 75–81.

Trapp, Rainer (2006a). "Wirklich 'Folter' oder nicht vielmehr selbstverschuldete Rettungsbefragung?" In Lenzen (ed.), pp. 95–134.

————. (2006b). *Folter oder selbstverschuldete Rettungsbefragung?* Paderborn: Mentis.

Tindale, Christopher W. (2005). "Tragic Choices: Reaffirming Absolutes in the Torture Debate." *International Journal of Applied Philosophy* 19(2), pp. 209–22.

Uniacke, Suzanne (1996). *Permissible Killing: The Self-Defence Justification of Homicide.* Cambridge: Cambridge University Press.

van Rienen, Rafael (2009). *Die "sozialethischen" Einschränkungen des Notwehrrechts: Die Grenzen privater Rechtsverteidigung und das staatliche Gewaltmonopol.* Baden-Baden: Nomos.

Volk, Christian (2010). (Review of Bev Clucas, Gerry Johnstone and Tony Ward (eds.). *Torture: Moral Absolutes and Ambiguities*). *Politische Vierteljahresschrift* 51, pp. 557–558.

Waldron, Jeremy (1981). "A Right to Do Wrong." *Ethics* 92(1), pp. 21–39.

————. (2005). "Torture and Positive Law: Jurisprudence for the White House." *Columbia Law Review* 105, pp. 1681–1750.

————. (2010). *Torture, Terror and Trade-Offs: Philosophy for the White House.* Oxford: Oxford University Press.

Wikipedia (2010). "Decomposition." http://en.wikipedia.org/wiki/Decomposition#Human_decomposition, accessed on 18 April 2010.

Wisnewski, J. Jeremy (2009). "Hearing a Still-Ticking Bomb Argument: A Reply to Bufacchi and Arrigo." *Journal of Applied Philosophy* 26, pp. 205–209.

————. (2010). *Understanding Torture.* Edinburgh: Edinburgh University Press.

Wisnewski, J. Jeremy and R. D. Emerick (2009). *The Ethics of Torture.* London and New York: Continuum.

Wolfendale, Jessica (2006). "Training Torturers: A Critique of the 'Ticking Bomb' Argument." *Social Theory and Practice* 32(2), pp. 269–287.

Index

absolutism, *defined* 150. *See also*
	antitorture absolutism; minimal
	absolutism; rights absolutism
abstraction in the ticking-bomb scenario,
	56, 57–59, 138, 142
Abu Ghraib, 64
Afghanistan, 64
agency, 20, 22, 23–24, 27–30, 105,
	107, 161n2
aggressor, 12–16, 19, 20, 33, 35, 42–43,
	44, 45, 53, 59, 60, 75–76, 80,
	81, 87, 88–89, 91, 96, 105, 109,
	120–21, 122, 134, 171n26
aiding and abetting aggressors, 53, 60,
	75–76, 131–32, 140, 165n42
alcoholism metaphor, 56, 74
Allhof, Fritz, 55, 85, 87–89, 91
Améry, Jean, 22, 24–25, 26
antitorture absolutism, 17, 20, 26, 27,
	30, 33, 35, 36, 41, 42, 44–45,
	46, 54–55, 64, 65–66, 70, 76, 77,
	79, 83, 87, 89, 95, 96, 108–109,
	111, 112, 121, 133–34, 136, 138,
	147, 148, 149, 156, 157, 158,
	167n18, 171n26. *See also* minimal
	absolutism
Argentina, 171n29
Arrigo, Jean Maria, 166n78, 168n19
attack, 11, 14, 35–36, 37, 38, 81,
	82–84, 85–86, 95–96
	defined, 13
	See also self-defense
Auschwitz, 25

Bargaric, Mirko, 55, 82
Başoğlu, Metin, 26
Beestermöller, Gerhard, 121–34
Bentham, Jeremy, 46–47
Bielefeldt, Heiner, 112–15, 121, 124,
	125, 130, 155–56
Biletzki, Anat, 71
bombing, 127, 161n1
breaking
	the inner freedom of the will, 110,
	112–15, 124, 134
	the tortured person, 20, 23, 161n2.
	See also agency; breaking the will
	the will, 7, 112–34, 135–36, 138,
	158, 161n2
Brecher, Bob, 20–22, 24–25, 26,
	27, 30, 70, 72, 90–92, 143–45,
	173n51
Brugger, Winfried, 55, 171n26
Brunkhorst, Hauke, 116–21
Bufacchi, Vittorio, 166n78, 168n19
Bustos, Enrique, 51
Bybee memorandum, 79, 82–83

categorical imperative, 108–112
	kingdom of ends formula, 108–109
	means/humanitarian formula, 109–11
	universal law formula, 111–12
certainty, 17–18, 87, 127, 139, 142–43,
	144, 145, 146, 153
child-kidnapping case, 13–14, 15–16,
	17, 18, 26, 32–33, 35, 36, 37, 38,
	45, 46, 50, 51, 58, 60, 77, 81,

child-kidnapping case *(continued)*
    83, 84, 85–86, 88, 96, 97, 99,
    100, 105, 112, 120, 122, 125–26,
    131–32, 141, 144, 147, 156, 158
Clarke, Julie, 55, 82, 176n129
coercion, 10, 49–50, 114, 125, 133,
    158, 164n12. *See also* coercive
    detention
coercive detention, 65, 112, 114, 116,
    121, 124, 125, 129, 135
collusion. *See* self-betrayal
combatant, 83, 93
confession, 66, 169
Conroy, John, 22, 23, 25
conscience. *See* tempting to sin
consent, 49–50, 116, 118, 121, 131,
    169
consequentialism, 35, 36, 40, 53, 60,
    70, 82, 85, 87–88, 89, 140. *See
    also* rule-utilitarianism; utilitarian
    justification
culpability for a forced choice
    justification, 11, 35–38, 158
Culpable Cause, 37, 165n49
custody, 85, 97, 99, 170n23

Daschner case, 13–14, 18, 41, 58, 59,
    69, 113, 144, 156, 158
death, 16
    as compared with torture, 18–35,
    54, 64, 92–93, 107–108, 117,
    119–20
death threats, 49, 50, 107, 114, 125,
    129
defenselessness, 7–8, 35, 51, 81, 82–84,
    92–96, 148
defining torture, 7–10, 16, 24, 28–29,
    114–16, 121, 124–25, 130
    definition, 7
democracy, 116–21
deontology, 11, 45, 54–55, 87, 140. *See
    also* threshold-deontology; rights-
    based arguments
Dershowitz, Alan, 61–66, 144

dignity, 17, 23, 35, 41, 49–50, 54, 60,
    74, 75, 76, 110, 112–15, 121–34,
    135, 155–56, 158
doctrine of double effect, 127–28,
    135–38, 158
dreamland, 55, 56, 143
duty
    enforcing, 113
    negative, 86, 104–105
    positive. *See* duties, negative
    to retreat, 12
    to self-defense, 133–34

effectiveness, 12, 14–15, 42, 47, 48–49,
    57–59, 144, 145–46
El Salvador, 171n29
emergency laws, 66
Emerick, R. D., 21–27, 30, 32, 145–47,
    173n51
emotion, 41, 106, 107–108, 155
Erb, Volker, 17, 60, 76, 163n1

fair fight, 93
fraud, intellectual, 139

Gachelin case, 49
Gäfgen case. *See* Daschner case
Gina cases (hypotheticals), 16, 95, 96,
    102
Ginbar, Yuval, 40–41, 71–72, 81–84,
    92, 148–52
Guantanamo, 56, 64, 157
guilt, 90–92. *See also* aggressor
Gur-Arye, Miriam, 40, 84–85

hard cases, 59–60
Hecker, Wolfgang, 171n26
Hill, Daniel, 84, 96, 101–105
history, 56, 62, 63, 70–74
human rights, 35, 54, 64, 65, 114. *See
    also* rights
hypocrisy, 69

idealizations in the ticking-bomb
    scenario, 56, 59, 138–39, 141–47

identity, 49, 50, 125–26
ignoring differences between cases, 26,
    71–72
imminence, 15–16, 17, 35–36, 79,
    85–86, 88, 141, 143
imprisonment, 32, 50, 64–65, 73, 75,
    81, 162–63n5
innocents, 12, 13
    protection of, 75–76, 88–89
    torture of, 39–45, 79, 82, 84–85,
        86–87, 140
    See also aggressor; guilt
Inquisition, 72
institutionalization of torture, 47–49,
    53, 57–59, 61–67, 72–74, 144,
    157, 158, 159. See also legalization
    of torture
interrogational torture, 7, 10, 19, 20,
    24, 25, 49, 51, 57, 59, 80, 83,
    84, 90, 101–105, 114, 116, 119,
    121, 123, 135, 147–48. See also
    child-kidnapping case; ticking-bomb
    scenario
Israel, 39, 70–72, 147

Jeanette cases (hypotheticals), 33, 35,
    94–95, 115, 156
justification of torture, moral, 155–58.
    See also necessity justification;
    culpability for a forced choice
    justification; self-defense
    justification; utilitarian justification
justifying emergency. See necessity
justifying atrocities, 150–51

Kant, Immanuel, 47, 49–50, 51,
    108–12, 114, 120, 132–34, 158
Kaufman, Whitley, 96–101, 103–105
Kershnar, Stephen, 41–42, 44, 55, 79,
    87–89
kidnapping. See child-kidnapping case
killing. See death
Knauer, Peter, 135
knowledge. See certainty

Lamprecht, Florian, 135–38
Landau Commission, 39, 70–72
Langbein, John, 62, 63–64
last resort 23, 25, 28–29, 30, 52
La Torre, Massimo, 115–16, 119,
    172n15
legalization of torture 59–60, 61, 69–77,
    80, 116–21, 159
    as opposed to institutionalization, 48,
        66, 158
lesser evil, 33, 41, 43, 81–82
Leverick, Fiona, 137
liberalism, 75–76
limits, 147–53
literature on torture, 22, 24, 27, 36,
    85, 90
Luban, David, 75–76, 139–41, 148–49,
    173n51, 176n133, 178n186

McDonald, Catherine, 176n129
McMahan, Jeff, 55, 72–73, 96, 140,
    165n49, 169n16, 170n17, 171n29
Matthews, Richard, 24, 26, 27, 46–52,
    86–89, 91, 141–43, 145
Merkel, Reinhard, 128–29, 178n176
methodological problems of studying
    torture, 25–27
Metzler, Jakob von, 144
Miller, Seamus, 21, 55, 85–86, 90–92,
    161–62n2, 170n18
minimal absolutism, 149–53
Model Penal Code, 16, 39, 43
Montague, Phillip, 36–37
Moore, Michael S., 165n52
Mook case, 49, 58, 59, 60, 144
moral corruption, 151–53
moral enslavement, 151
moral justification of torture. See
    justification of torture, moral

Nazi Germany, 72
necessity condition (of justified self-
    defense), 11–13, 14–15, 16, 17, 18,
    20, 35, 48, 53, 60, 70, 77, 79, 80,

necessity condition (of justified self-defense) *(continued)*
81, 82, 89, 109, 110, 118, 120, 130, 134, 140, 141, 143, 145, 149, 150, 152–53
necessity justification, 11, 36, 39–45, 79, 81, 82, 83, 84, 85, 140, 150–52, 156, 158–59
Nozick, Robert, 37

pain compliance hold, 114
Paolo case (hypothetical), 33–34, 115, 156
Paskins, Barrie, 172n13
personhood, 25. *See also* identity
phenomenology, 114, 125
physical torture, 7–9
political torture, 49–50
private torture, 47–48, 156
proportionality, 12–13, 15, 17, 18–35, 42, 80, 91, 92, 94, 152
proto-morality, 121–22, 123, 129
psychological torture, 9
punitive torture, 7, 49, 114–15, 119, 147

Radovan cases (hypotheticals), 37–38, 102–103, 110
rape, 15, 106, 148–49, 158
reasonable belief. *See* certainty
recovery from torture, 26–27
reliability of information. *See* certainty
repugnance, 40–42, 45
right(s), 11, 35, 40, 43, 44, 45, 50, 53–54, 59–60, 75–76, 109, 120, 128–29, 130–34, 140, 157–58
    justified violation of, 70, 91. *See also* necessity justification
    to do wrong, 91–92
    See also rights-based arguments
rights absolutism, 11, 45. *See also* absolutism
rights-based arguments, 35, 79–92, 140, 144. *See also* culpability for a forced

choice justification; self-defense justification
Rodin, David, 173n46
rule-utilitarianism, 49, 65–67, 101, 103–104, 134

sadistic torture, 49, 119
Schulz, William, 62
self-defense. *See* necessity condition (of justified self-defense); proportionality; self-defense justification; rights
self-defense justification, 11–38, 40, 42–43, 44, 59, 75, 79–87, 92–105, 109, 120–21, 130, 132–34, 136–38, 140, 143, 146–47, 148–49, 150, 158, 159
self-legislative rulership, 116–21, 134
Shue, Henry, 51, 54–60, 71, 92–96, 138–39, 141, 143–44
slippery slope, 64–66, 77, 142, 153, 157
Somnier, Finn, and Genefke, Inge, 22, 25, 26
Sophie's Choice cases, 41–42, 44, 106, 147, 155, 161n2
specific intent, 8–9
Splett, Jörg, 114, 121, 124–25
state torture, 47–49, 87–89
subject status, 112–15, 134
successful torture requires institutionalization argument, 57–59, 144
Sussman, David, 23–24, 55, 95–96, 105–108

tempting to sin (by acting against one's conscience), 126–28
terrorism, 144, 178n184. *See also* ticking-bomb scenario
terrostic torture, 49, 50–51
threshold deontology, 44–45, 70, 150–51
ticking-bomb scenario, 15–16, 17, 19, 26, 35, 36, 37, 38, 40–41, 42, 44,

45, 52, 64, 65, 67, 69, 71–72,
81, 83, 90, 91, 96, 96–105,
138–47, 157. *See also* abstraction
in the ticking-bomb scenario;
idealizations in the ticking-bomb
scenario
ticking-social-bomb, 53–60, 70, 73
time constraints, 145
Tindale, Christopher, 79–81
torture warrants, 48, 58, 61–66, 144,
159
torturers, training of, 48, 58, 159
Trammel, Richard Louis, 105
Trapp, Rainer, 66, 69–70, 101–11, 113

uncertainty. *See* certainty
Uniacke, Suzanne, 97, 98–99, 137
United Nations Convention Against
Torture, 161n1
utilitarian justification, 11, 35, 43–44,
45–52, 79, 80, 90, 157

vagueness, 48, 50, 142, 143
Volk, Christian, 163n1

Waldron, Jeremy, 74–76, 91, 170n23
Wisnewski, J. Jeremy, 21–30, 32,
145–47, 161n2, 162n5, 173n51
Wolfendale, Jessica, 167n17, 173n51